D1033489

WINGED WONDERS
The Story of the Flying Wings

E. T. Wooldridge

Published for the
NATIONAL AIR AND SPACE MUSEUM
By the
SMITHSONIAN INSTITUTION PRESS
Washington, D.C.

Library of Congress Cataloging in Publication Data

Wooldridge, E. T.
  Winged wonders.

  Bibliography: p.
  Includes index.
  l. Airplanes, Tailless—History. 2. Northrop
aircraft—History. I. National Air and Space Museum.
II. Title
TL670.3.W66   1983   629.133'34   83-600296
ISBN 0-87474-966-2
ISBN 0-87474-967-0 (pbk.)

Second printing, 1985

Frontispiece: John K. Northrop and the first piston—
engined XB—35 at Muroc Army Air Base in July 1946.

Contents

Foreword

Almost since the beginning of flight, both designers and pilots have been fascinated with the concept of the flying wing. There are a number of reasons for this, many grounded in engineering concepts of stability, drag reduction and so on, but I think that there are also emotional, aesthetic reasons that are equally compelling. The flying wing somehow captures the imagination as being an aircraft of the purest sort, unencumbered by fuselage, tail or other structures, one in which man could truly soar as freely as the birds.

There is an interesting parallel between the development of the flying wings and the development of this book. Flying wings have been the object of what amounts to an obsessive fascination with a number of the engineers you will read about herein; they seemed to exercise an almost mystical control over the minds and careers of the men who developed them. In a similar way, Tim Wooldridge found himself increasingly preoccupied with a book that had started off intending to be only the story of the Northrop N-1M and its restoration. As he gathered material, he realized that as important as the Northrop wings were, they were but a part of the larger picture of the flying wing story. Even more important, the innovations and achievments of John Northrop and his company with the American flying wing are more understandable, and even more meaningful, when considered in the light of the efforts of others.

In a similar way, the restoration itself paralleled the development of the book. The original manhour estimates were found to be far too conservative, for the aircraft presented entirely new problems in restoration. Originally intended to be a test bed, with little expectation of a long service life, the N-1M had not neen given the traditional protective internal coatings that would have been found in a production aircraft. As a result, the restoration process was very complex. The entire interior of the craft was a profusion of complex glue joints, all of which had to be separated, sanded, and then reglued. In addition the wing surfaces were extremely complex, and the reskinning of the aircraft took far more time and effort than is ordinarily the case. I believe that you will find that both the completed restoration and the completed book are well worth the effort and the care.

As Tim became more and more engrossed in the book, as more and more questions arose, so did there arise helpful informed people to assist him with the answers. He has noted this in his acknowledgments, but it seemed to me that there was rather more interest in this project than others of a similar nature. The men and women who were associated with the flying wings, of whatever country, seem to have a genuine desire to have the full story told. As is often the case, each new bit of information led to both new questions and additional sources. Author Tim Wooldridge has done an excellent job of distilling the vast amount of information he compiled into this compelling account.

The wide ranging review of the men and planes of the flying wing era has a new and rather unexpected meaning today. Historic aircraft and their restoration have always shown interesting bits of the past. In the case of the flying wing there may very well be an interesting association with the future. There are currently several design studies for large freighter type aircraft of the flying wing configuration, and it may be that the next generation bomber, the stealth bomber, may also be a flying wing. Thus both the restoration and the book are timely.

I believe that when you have read this account you will agree with me that Tim Wooldridge has done an admirable job in pulling together not just the facts, but also the soul of the flying wing story. The story began with the human spirit, in a quest for new and better means of flying; it concludes in the same way, at another level of technology but at the same soaring level of human endeavor.

Walter J. Boyne
Director
National Air and Space Museum

Introduction

Since the late nineteenth century, well-qualified aerodynamicists, engineers, and inventors have sought ways to reduce the drag contributed by various airplane parts such as engines, fuselage, tail surfaces, and landing gear. For many reasons designers experimented with the tailless configuration, which frequently had no tail section at all, or retained only the vertical fin and rudder for directional stability.[1] Some innovators took the clean lines of the tailless design one step further and attempted to eliminate all vertical surfaces and protuberances such as canopies, propeller shafts, and gun turrets. Few attained this ideal all-wing airplane or flying wing, in which all functions of the aircraft were combined in one large airfoil.

A wide variety of factors motivated both serious aerodynamicists and eccentrics, many of whom found the solution to their problems in tailless or flying wing aircraft. The goal of some inventors was the development of inherently stable aircraft, while other inventors dreamed of the roadable airplane that could be driven to the local airport and changed to a flying configuration. Designing a truly safe airplane was a lifelong challenge for some; short takeoff and landing characteristics motivated others; and carrying larger payloads for greater distances more efficiently was a realistic goal for a few of the more practical designers. Whatever the goals and design considerations, a seemingly infinite variety of designs for tailless airplanes emerged over the years, some of which were given the popular appellation of "flying wing." Very few designers, however, developed machines that even approached the ideal flying wing.

No one person or nation can claim a monopoly on the development of the tailless or flying wing aircraft. Among the distinguished European designers who built successful tailless aircraft were Dunne and Hill of Great Britain and Lippisch and the Horten brothers of Germany. In the United States, the recognized leader in developing the flying wing was John K. Northrop.

Although Jack Northrop's name has been synonymous with the flying wing for 40 years, his record as a designer of conventional aircraft is equally distinguished. Northrop's aeronautical career has been associated with many breakthroughs in aircraft design, ranging from the famous Lockheed Vega of the 1920s to the giant Northrop flying wings of the 1940s. The 1920s provided the ideal setting for Northrop to display his unusual talent for aircraft design. The Vega, flown by such prominent aviators as Wiley Post, Amelia Earhart, Frank Hawks, and Roscoe Turner, became the aircraft of its day for speed and distance records. Northrop's revolutionary all-metal, multicellular, stressed-skin wing structure was tested in 1929 in his first attempt at a flying wing design. Later, these concepts were applied with notable success to the Alpha and the Gamma, which set new performance standards for aircraft of the 1930s, and to Donald Douglas's early DC series of commercial transports, which revolutionized the airline industry.

By 1939, Jack Northrop was one of the most renowned aircraft designers in the United States. He was known and respected internationally, and aircraft designed by Northrop had been flown over all the continents and oceans of the world. At that time, he chose to renew his lifelong quest for the ultimate in simple, clean airplane design. He founded Northrop Aircraft, Inc. and in 1940, produced the N-1M, the first of the true Northrop flying wings.

The N-1M was an experimental craft designed to test Jack Northrop's theories on flying wing design. Success with this prototype encouraged Northrop to apply his ideas to various types of war planes, and finally, to the family of huge flying wing bombers, the B-35 and B-49.

The first part of this book provides the reader with an insight into the development of tailless aircraft throughout the world through World War II and the years immediately following. The second part is devoted entirely to the story of Jack Northrop's flying wings. An account of the National Air and Space Museum's restoration of Northrop's N-1M is contained in Appendix A.

The bibliography is divided into sections for ease of reference. The outline of the bibliography is as follows:

General
United States Tailless Aircraft
    John K. Northrop Designs
    Non-Northrop Designs
Non-United States Tailless Aircraft
    Canada
    Denmark
    France
    Germany
    Japan
    Switzerland
    Turkey
    United Kingdom
    USSR

Each section is alphabetized separately. The footnotes include parenthetical annotations that point to the applicable section of the bibliography. They are: General (begins on p. 209); U.S., Northrop (p. 211); U.S., Non-Northrop

NOTE

1. Two configurations which are frequently called "tailless" are the canard and the tandem-wing, neither of which will be addressed in detail in this book. The canard is a tail-first airplane, normally with the horizontal stabilizer in front of the main wing, and a rudder in the normal position at the rear of the fuselage. The tandem-wing has two or more sets of wings of substantially the same area placed one in front of the other, sometimes on about the same level, sometimes with the aft wing lower than the top wing. A conventional empennage may be included, or the functions of the rudder and elevator may be incorporated in the aft wing.

Acknowledgments

I extend my sincere thanks to those members of the Northrop "family," present and past, who provided me with written material, photographs, personal recollections, and encouragement. The historians Ira Chart, Jim Donahue, and Gerry Balzer shared their knowledge and perceptions of Northrop aircraft and Northrop, the man. Test pilots John Myers, Max Stanley, and Moye Stephens recalled their experiences in the flying wings, from the N-1M to the giant bombers. Jack Mannion, Vice President for Administration and Public Affairs, Northrop Corporation Aircraft Group, provided guidance and invaluable assistance.

Appreciation goes to Anthony Stadlman, former associate of Jack Northrop, who at age 96 told of his own early dreams of flying wings. Robert J. Smith, Chief, Office of History, Air Force Logistics Command, kindly provided the case histories of the XB-35 and YB-49 airplanes. Charles G. Worman, Chief, Research Division, U.S. Air Force Museum, Ted Bear, past historian at the Air Force Flight Test Center, and Dick Hallion, present historian for the center, provided valuable material to document the flight-test programs of the Northrop flying wings. Another Northrop associate and a renowned engineer in his own right, Edward H. Heinemann, recalled his early days with Jack Northrop and discussed the pros and cons of tailless designs.

The following people generously contributed expert opinions and historical material on Northrop and other tailless aircraft: Richard S. Allen, aviation historian; Donovan R. Berlin, engineer; David L. Crippins, vice-president of KCET-TV, Los Angeles; David E. Dunlap, aviation enthusiast; Thomas J. Gregory, NASA engineer; Randy Hughes, Lockheed photographer; Dr. Hidemasa Kimura, engineer and historian; Harvey Lippincott, United Technologies archivist; Bernard L. Rice, aviation writer; Jan Scott, pilot and writer; Donald B. Smith, engineer; and Robert Storck, glider enthusiast.

Many members of the National Air and Space Museum staff and library provided advice, encouragement, and assistance during the project; special thanks go to Walter Boyne, Tom Crouch, Phil Edwards, Dale Hrabak, Donald Lopez, Helen McMahon, Robert Mikesh, Claudia Oakes, Pete Suthard, Frank

Winter, and members of NASM's Aeronautics Department who, by necessity, developed an interest in flying wings. Credit goes to summer interns Royce Ann Martin, John Gaertner, and Chris Ross for doing an excellent job of preparing a bibliography on tailless aircraft.

Garry Cline, John Cusack, Reid Ferguson, Karl Heinzel, Richard Horigan, and Harvey Napier of the Paul E. Garber Facility deserve major credit for the restoration of the Northrop N-1M; the author wishes to express his special thanks for their technical insight and information on the N-1M.

To Valerie Banks, Susan Owen, Vicki Rosenberg, Gladys Waters, and Claudia Oakes go thanks and appreciation for a superb job of typing a seemingly endless series of manuscript drafts.

PART I

A HISTORY OF TAILLESS AIRCRAFT

Chapter 1

The First Fifty Years of Tailless Aircraft: 1870-1920

For more than a century, there have been countless patents, projects, and concepts relating to tailless airplanes. Many models and prototypes were constructed; most enjoyed only a brief period of development and public interest, and then quickly disappeared. From an engineering viewpoint, a high percentage of these short-lived projects were possibly well founded and deserving of serious consideration and further development. The lack of adequate financial backing, lack of government or public interest, and politics often contributed to the premature end of a worthwhile project. For the most part, these projects were pursued by independent promoters who made little attempt to coordinate their investigations. Gradually, however, a large body of technical data on tailless aircraft was accumulated. Although no organized data-exchange program appeared to have existed during the 1920s and 1930s, articles on tailless projects could be read frequently in aviation journals, both in the United States and abroad. Whether these articles inspired or assisted the competition is conjectural.

Engineers and enthusiasts who developed versions of the tailless airplane had very different conceptions of what it should be. Some found their inspiration in the flight of birds. Surely the earliest example of tailless flight would be the *Quetzalcoatlus northropi*, a giant flying reptile that roamed the skies over North America some 70 million years ago. The winged seeds of the maple and the *Zanonia* plant served as the basis for designs of experimental models and gliders for others.

Whatever the source of inspiration, most designers persevered with their experiments and research despite the lack of experimental facilities and financial backing. The critical period was when experiments passed from the model and glider stages to powered flight. For the reasons previously cited, projects were often terminated altogether at this stage. In other cases, the problems of stability and control associated with the absence of the tail and addition of an engine proved insurmountable, so a conventional tail was added.

The history of tailless aircraft is replete with frustrated, brilliant men to

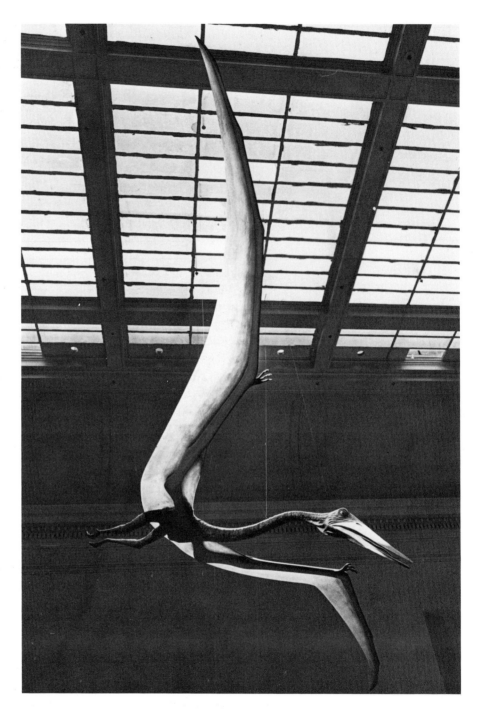

The prehistoric flying reptile Quetzalcoatlus northropi *was named after the winged serpent god of the Aztecs and the Northrop Flying Wings. This awesome tailless creature, with its 40-foot wingspan, existed between 65 and 100 million years ago. The reconstruction in this photograph soars above the Dinosaur Hall in the National Museum of Natural History. Like its namesakes, it looks as though it would fly with grace and beauty.*

whom the description "neglected genius" could have applied. Perhaps none would better qualify than Alphonse Penaud, an imaginative young Frenchman who, for one brief decade, astounded his contemporaries with concepts too advanced for his time.

Penaud was born in Paris in 1850, the son of a French admiral and seemingly bound for a Navy career himself. When a childhood illness precluded that option, Penaud turned to a brief but brilliant career in aeronautics, developing many theories concerning airfoils and the problems of stability and control in flight. He applied his theories to a succession of creative models of helicopters, ornithopters, and airplanes powered by rubber-band motors. In 1871, Penaud demonstrated the possibility of sustained flight by an airplane by flying a rubber-band powered monoplane a distance of 131 feet. His *Planophore* had lateral and longitudinal stability; the tail assembly, located some distance behind the wings, became known as the "Penaud tail."

In 1876, assisted by mechanic Paul Gauchot, Penaud synthesized several years of intensive research and experimentation with aerodynamics, materials, and engines in the design of a revolutionary airplane. By strict definition, the machine was not tailless, though at first glance it appeared to be almost a flying wing. But it incorporated many advanced concepts that were used by engineers and enthusiasts in flying wing designs for the next 100 years.

The drawings that accompanied Penaud's Patent No. 111574 show a high-wing, twin-tractor, monoplane amphibian with a retractable four-wheel undercarriage. The rudder and elevators were moved by means of a single control column in a cockpit with a glass canopy. The engine was buried in elliptical wings covered with varnished silk. The wings had dihedral, high aspect ratio, reverse camber at the trailing edge, washout, taper, and bent-up wing tips. Although the wings were braced by upper and lower stays, the inventor planned to eliminate these wires eventually, which would result in a cantilever construction. Elevators were balanced by counterweights or springs.

Since the airplane was an amphibian, the nacelle was watertight, with portholes in the cabin for passengers. Propellers were entirely metal and had variable pitch; they were connected by crankshafts to the engine in the wings, where the flight crew could have direct access for repairs. The list of innovations even extended to aircraft instruments, including angle-of-attack indicators, airspeed indicators, and aneroid altimeters.

Whether the airplane was capable of flight or not, given the fact that contemporary power plants were inadequate, is obviously pure conjecture. Penaud was unable to raise the necessary funds to continue his research, and his radical concepts were met with skepticism and ridicule by officials and fellow aeronautical enthusiasts. Discouraged and depressed, Alphonse Penaud committed suicide in October 1880, at the age of 30, leaving many of his ideas to be "rediscovered" years later.

Ten years after Penaud's tragic death, another Frenchman, Clément Ader, established his niche in aviation history. Ader succeeded in taking off in an aircraft of his own design under its own power on October 9, 1890, at Armainvilliers, France. The aircraft, named *Eole*, was once described as "a chaos of mechanisms."[1] Penaud's practical genius, combined with just a small amount of Ader's imagination, probably would have produced a practical contribution to aeronautical science. Unfortunately, in the *Eole*, and his only other completed machine, the *Avion III*, Ader allowed his imagination to run rampant.

5

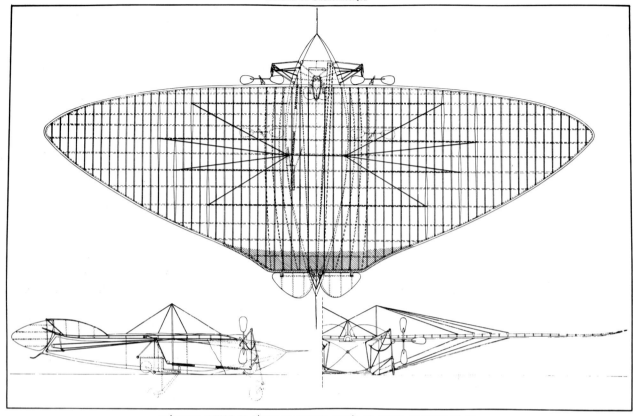

L'AÉROPLANE AMPHIBIE DE PÉNAUD ET GAUCHOT, D'APRÈS LES DESSINS DU BREVET DE 1876
Vues en plan, en élévation et de profil.

Some of the unusual features of the radical 1876 design of Alphonse Penaud and Paul Gauchot (above) are apparent in this 1940s model (right) by Paul K. Guillow. The two castoring nose wheels and two main wheels were fully retractable, folding backward and upward. The Penaud wing was equipped with horizontal brake rudders at the wing tips. (SI Negative 74-9238)

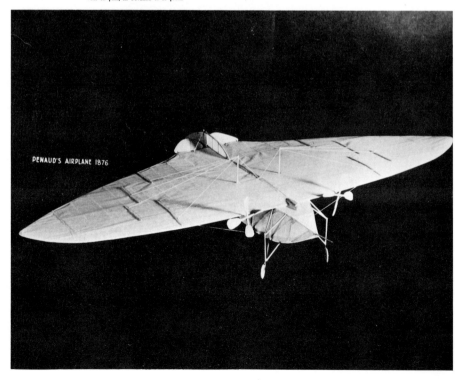

PENAUD'S AIRPLANE 1876

The *Eole* was described as a single engine (steam) tractor monoplane, with a four-bladed bamboo propeller made in the form of bird feathers. The wings were bat-like, with extreme canopied curvature. There were no elevator, no rudder, and no conventional flight controls. Each wing could be swung forward and aft separately by a hand-operated crank, thus changing the position of the center of pressure and consequently the pitch of the airplane. Wings could be flexed up and down by foot pedal; wing area and camber could also be changed by crank action. In all, six hand-operated cranks, two foot pedals, and engine controls had to be operated by the pilot in flight!

Despite the herculean efforts that must have been required to become airborne and remain in that state for any period of time, Ader did accomplish his takeoff; the subsequent flight of about 165 feet was not considered controlled or sustained, however. Encouraged by his craft's performance, and subsidized by the French government, Ader started but never completed a second machine.

A third aircraft was completed in 1897, the *Avion III*. It was generally similar in concept and appearance to *Eole*, but significant changes had been effected. The airplane now had two engines; wing structure had been simplified, as had the swing-wing arrangement, although the latter remained a dangerous and virtually unworkable system. Ader would have been well advised to study the Penaud tail, details of which had been published in contemporary aeronautical journals. The only additional flight control was a small rudder connected to the tail wheel, and operated by pedals. A mechanism was also provided to effect differential speed of the two propellers, giving some additional control in yaw.

Two tests of the *Avion III* were conducted on a circular track. These trials were witnessed by the proper officials, who prepared a written report stating that the *Avion III* did not fly. The report was kept secret until 1910, at which time it was made public. In the interim, however, in the absence of official statements to the contrary, Ader claimed to have flown a distance of 300 meters at the 1897 trials. The publication of the official report in 1910 did little to settle a controversy that has persisted to the present day.

Avion III marked the end of Ader's practical work in aeronautics, although he did considerable research on the principle of the air-cushion hydrofoil, applying for a British patent on such a machine in 1904.[2]

The credit for designing and flying the first tailless aircraft in Europe goes to the distinguished Danish inventor, Jacob Christian Ellehammer. Born in 1871, Ellehammer experimented during his youth with large kites capable of lifting heavy loads. As a young man, he developed an interest in electricity during his early days as an apprentice, journeyman, and later employee in an electro-mechanical shop. He became a tinkerer, experimenter, and soon, a serious inventor with an extraordinary understanding of mechanical devices.

It was quite logical that Ellehammer's attention would eventually turn to the design and construction of a practical reciprocating engine. At the turn of the century he produced a successful motor scooter and built his first airplane engine in 1904. It was a three-cylinder, air-cooled radial engine of 9 hp, the

Clément Ader's controversial 1897
Avion III is still preserved in the
Musée du Conservatoire des Arts et
Métiers in Paris. Two steam engines,
generating 20 hp each, drove two,
four-bladed, bamboo propellers re-
sembling eight gigantic quill pens.

Perched precariously in the pendu-
lum-like seat of his homebuilt flying
machine, Jacob Christian
Ellehammer became the first flying
Dane. This photograph was taken by
Ellehammer's cousin, Lars, as the
aircraft skimmed over a circular,
concrete runway a distance of 140 feet
on September 12, 1906.

forerunner of the same type of engine that was to become so popular in the 1930s and beyond.

In 1906, after unsuccessful attempts to fly with his own underpowered monoplane, Ellehammer paired an 18 hp engine with a tailless biplane, both of his own design. The craft appeared as two enormous kites, one mounted above the other, with pilot, engine, and a reverse tricycle landing gear suspended underneath. The lower wing was fixed, with a movable elevator attached to the trailing edge center section. The upper wing was a smaller, non-rigid wing, much like a sail to be held in shape by the slipstream of the tractor propeller. The elevator was connected by wire to the pilot's seat at the forward part of the airplane. The seat was hinged, so that the pendulum action resulting from the pilot's movement forward and aft caused a corresponding vertical movement of the elevator. There was no vertical fin and no rudder, but some directional stability and control may have been afforded by the large steerable tail wheel.

Assisted by his brother Vilhelm and cousin Lars, Christian set up facilities on the small, barren Danish island of Lindholm in 1905 to test the monoplane and then the biplane. After many changes in configuration, and tethered, unmanned flights around a circular track, Ellehammer confounded the skeptics on September 12, 1906, when he personally flew the airplane a distance of 140 feet at an altitude of about one and a half feet.

Many people gave Ellehammer credit for the first flight ever made in Europe, discounting the officially recognized flight of the Brazilian Alberto Santos-Dumont, near Paris, France, on November 12 of that same year. The latter flight, however, was officially sanctioned by the *Fédération Aéronautique Internationale*; a diary entry by Lars Ellehammer duly noting the particulars of Christian's flight was not considered sufficient evidence of the historic event. Detractors of Ellehammer's accomplishment also criticized his use of a circular runway with a pole at its center, to which the aircraft was tethered by a fine wire. The eminent aviation historian, Charles H. Gibbs-Smith, commented:

> Tentative as Santos' flights were, Ellehammer—in his second machine—did not even achieve the free flight which his admirers have so often claimed for him . . . the pilot was only a passive passenger, the machine having a fixed rudder and automatic (pendulum) longitudinal control, to say nothing of the advantage of centrifugal control. If Ellehammer had concentrated on his excellent engines, he might have played a major role in history.[3]

Notwithstanding Gibbs-Smith's rather brusque dismissal of Ellehammer's flight, the importance of the event should be recognized. The marvel is not that Ellehammer flew before or after anyone else of that era; it is that he and others like him ever flew at all.

Ellehammer continued his aeronautical experiments for a number of years, developing an improved biplane, which became the first heavier-than-air craft to fly in Germany, in 1908. He later experimented with a flying boat, a wheeled monoplane that flew repeatedly in 1909, and a successful helicopter that was completed in 1912—the last of his aeronautical developments. He eventually took out more than 400 patents on a variety of electromechanical devices.

Early aviation pioneers studied the flight characteristics of every conceivable type of flying animal—birds, insects, bats, flying fish, even flying foxes. Elsewhere in nature, flying seeds also provided the inspiration for serious investigations into the theory of flight; one of these was the *Zanonia macrocarpa* seed. This kidney-shaped seed came from a vine native to Java, and was a member of the family that included such familiar plants as ground watermelon, cucumber, and cantaloupe. The *Zanonia* seed could perform amazingly long glides, during which it demonstrated basic inherent stability. The seed was flat and about six inches long, with a central seed kernel surrounded by light, tough tissue stiffened by fibers. A number of the early experimenters with tailless aircraft were inspired by the *Zanonia's* flying qualities. Igo Etrich adapted the principles he gleaned from his observation of the *Zanonia* seed to the hard realities of powered, sustained flight in heavier-than-air machines.

Igo and his father, Ignaz Etrich, became aware of the qualities of this seed through the theoretical papers of German naturalist Dr. Frederick Ahlborn, published at the turn of the century. The Etriches were amateur flyers and industrialists from Bohemia (now Czechoslovakia). The younger Etrich had begun his practical investigations of unpowered flight with the purchase of a Lilienthal glider in 1898. Igo Etrich soon became a serious student of aeronautics, and, with the advice and assistance of Dr. Ahlborn and in collaboration with Austrian aviation enthusiast Franz Wels, built a tailless glider in the shape of the *Zanonia* seed in 1904. An unwieldy contraption of bamboo, canvas, and wire, the craft still had a graceful quality about it that eventually justified Igo Etrich's faith in the *Zanonia* concept.

By 1906, practice glides with sandbags for passengers had been successfully conducted, and the first Etrich-Wels manned glider was ready for test flights. Several sandbag flights were conducted with the glider being launched from a trolley after a run down an inclined track. After the successful unmanned flights, one of which continued for over 900 feet, pilot Franz Wels flew the glider on its first manned flight in October 1906. Because of the craft's unique *Zanonia* design, this was perhaps the first successful flight of an inherently stable, manned aircraft.

Impressed with his glider's performance, Igo Etrich decided to add power. In 1907, a small 24-hp engine with pusher propeller was added to the 1906 Etrich-Wels glider, now heavily modified with a rectangular stabilizing surface in front, cutaway wing to provide visibility for a seated pilot, and provisions for wing warping for roll control. The airplane would not fly because it was underpowered.

A tractor version followed in 1908, using the same 24-hp engine without the horizontal stabilizer. Called Etrich I, this machine too was a failure, due to directional instability. After dissolution of the Etrich-Wels partnership because of differences of opinion on aircraft design, Etrich further modified the

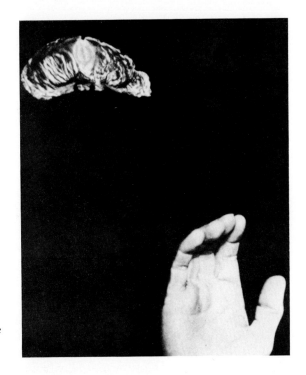

The Zanonia macrocarpa *seed of Java demonstrated extraordinary soaring characteristics and served as the basis for tailless gliders designed by Igo Etrich in the early 1900s.*

The shadow of the Zanonia *seed is cast by the Etrich I of 1908, one of the earliest aircraft designed with inherent stability.*

1907 Etrich I, installing a 40-hp engine. Finally, on November 29, 1909, Etrich flew his first sustained powered flight.

At this juncture in his early career as an aircraft designer, Igo Etrich made a radical departure from the design path that he had pursued thus far. It became obvious to Etrich that simply adding a power plant to the *Zanonia* wing was not the solution to his problems. In fact, the problems that resulted from this mismatch necessitated severe modifications to his basic design. Again, Etrich turned to nature for the solution. To the wing of the *Zanonia* seed he added the tail of a bird. The aircraft that evolved was the *Taube* (dove), a class of aircraft that was produced in a bewildering number of versions for both civil and military use. Between 1910 and 1914, 54 manufacturers produced over 500 of these aircraft, including 137 different configurations. All were easily recognized by their distinctive *Zanonia*-shaped wings and dove-like tail, and all possessed the inherent stability that had originally attracted Etrich to the *Zanonia* design. The *Taube* was so stable that it could literally fly itself.[4]

The *Taube* marked the end of Igo Etrich's experimentations with tailless aircraft. Etrich's aviation activities continued in the post-World War I years, although he eventually turned his considerable talents as an inventor to other industrial fields, particularly textiles. Although Etrich's involvement with tailless craft was relatively short, he proved the effectiveness of the stable characteristics of the *Zanonia* seed, and he must rank with his contemporaries, José Weiss and J.W. Dunne of England, as a serious investigator of stability problems.

These problems were also being investigated on the other side of the English Channel; for José Weiss, however, the soaring flight of birds provided the inspiration. A Frenchman by birth, but a long-time resident of Great Britain, Weiss was a keen student of birds since childhood, and for years had speculated on their remarkable ability to soar on seemingly motionless wings. Weiss devoted much of his time to studies of the theory of flight. Between 1902 and 1907 he designed, constructed, and flew hundreds of models, gradually developing his own theory of inherent stability based on bird forms.

Finally satisfied that his theories were fundamentally sound, Weiss constructed his first full-sized, man-carrying glider in 1909. Weiss's answer to the problem of inherent stability was in the curvature of the wings, which were thick at the roots but tapered outward until the tips were flexible. Positive incidence at the fuselage decreased gradually along the span until negative incidence, or washout, was produced at the tips, and the trailing edge was turned upward. Hinged elevators extended along part of the trailing edge. Christened *Olive* after one of Weiss's five daughters,[5] the tailless craft was flown quite successfully by test pilot Gordon England. Subsequent attempts to fly the aircraft with power, however, were unsuccessful.

Later in the same year, Weiss built a powered, single-seat tailless monoplane (*Madge*) on the same general lines as his 1909 glider. Powered only by a 12-hp Cenzana engine driving two pusher propellers through chains, the frail cloth-covered bamboo craft was incapable of flight.

Elsie, Weiss's first tractor monoplane, still tailless, appeared in 1910, but apparently enjoyed little success. A second monoplane, *Sylvia*, was also tested in 1910, but by now Weiss had abandoned the tailless configuration. The airplane was fitted with a Penaud tail, but still retained the distinctive curved, twisted wings designed by Weiss. The craft had a few successful flights, but a structural failure in flight resulted in a crash in late 1910.

Although Weiss's attempts at powered flight did not meet with notable success, his theories on wing design for inherent stability were recognized and respected in aviation circles of the day. In describing José Weiss's contribu-

One of the hundreds of models and gliders designed and constructed by José Weiss between 1902 and 1907. Although this model had some semblance of a tail, many of Weiss's successful flights were made with tailless gliders.

Frederick Handley Page poses with his first experimental glider in 1909. Handley Page, who eventually became one of the giants in the aviation industry in England, used Weiss-style wings in several of his early aircraft designs. (SI Negative 52747)

tions to aeronautical lore, one aviation historian compared his universal genius to that of Leonardo da Vinci.

> In this type the mind and the eye of the artist are conjoined with the scientific mind. They think with the eye and the soul as well as with the brain. Such men have the joy of great vision, of peering into the mysteries; but often others, inspired by them, accomplish the practical work.[6]

John William Dunne was a soldier, author, pilot, and designer. This thoughtful Englishman was totally dedicated to the principle of inherent stability. Inspired by a Jules Verne story at the age of 13, Dunne dreamed of a flying machine that needed no steering, that would right itself regardless of wind or weather. Like Igo Etrich of France, Dunne had studied the *Zanonia* seed, and was well aware of its amazing flying qualities. Like his countryman José Weiss, he had closely observed birds in flight. But both of those early pioneers had encountered problems when they attempted to add an engine to their successful tailless gliders. Dunne persisted, and produced a design which, though controversial, was the first successful tailless aircraft with swept back wings.

Dunne became seriously involved in the problems of flight in 1901, as an army lieutenant home on sick-leave from the Boer War. He began to plan, sketch, and make models, and he was encouraged in these endeavors by the science fiction writer H.G. Wells, who urged Dunne to concentrate on the problems of control and balance. Dunne's model-building efforts were temporarily interrupted by another tour to South Africa, from which he returned in 1903, now suffering from heart disease that would force his early retirement from aeronautical activities 10 years later.

Despite poor health, however, John Dunne resumed his aeronautical investigations, and by 1904 was ready to progress from the model phase to experiments with gliders and later, powered aircraft. Dunne sought an experienced engineer to assist him in the difficult job of putting theory into practice. His problem was solved when he was assigned in 1905 to the Army Balloon Factory at South Farnborough, England, then under the able leadership of Colonel John Capper. With Capper's guidance and support, Dunne began the design and construction of the the first British military airplane.

Months of tests with model gliders were followed in the spring of 1907 by the first passenger-carrying glider. It was the first of many craft with the distinctive V-shaped wing designed by Dunne, frequently described as an arrowhead minus a shaft.

Construction and flight testing of the first Dunne aircraft, the D.1-A, were conducted under great secrecy. The flimsy craft was shipped by rail in July 1907, to the village of Blair Atholl in the Scottish Highlands. In the hills north of the village, the D.1-A flew one successful eight-second flight, with Colonel Capper along for the ride. Although Colonel Capper was slightly injured in the crash that terminated the flight, the experimental glider had demonstrated the stability Dunne considered so essential.

Dunne's design experiments during 1907 and 1908 can be summarized as follows: the D.1-A glider, built in 1907, had limited success in its one flight; the D.1-B powered airplane (modified D.1-A), also of 1907, crashed in its first flight; the D.2 training glider, designed in 1907, was not constructed; the Dunne-Huntington powered triplane, designed in 1907–1908, was flown successfully in 1911; the D.3 man-carrying glider was flown successfully in 1908; the D.4 powered airplane, flown in 1908, had partial success (in Dunne's words, "more a hopper than a flyer"[7]).

By 1908, the British Army Council could no longer tolerate the limited potential demonstrated by Dunne's machines. Dunne left the Balloon Factory, and friends formed a small company, the Blair Atholl Aeroplane Syndicate, to finance his experiments. By 1910, a new aircraft was ready to be tested. The Dunne D.5 was a vast improvement over previous designs and one that would bring international acclaim to its designer.

Like previous models, the D.5 was a tailless biplane, with sharply swept back wings. A boat-like nacelle housed the pilot, with additional room for a passenger. An engine located at the rear of the nacelle drove two pusher propellers. The keys to the inherent stability demonstrated by the D.5, and the rest of Dunne's designs, were the twist and the camber designed into his swept wings. The angle of incidence changed gradually from root to tip so that the angle at the tip was less than that at the root. The camber (curvature of the top surface of the wing) also varied, so that near the wing root there was little curvature, while at the tips the wings were curved for the greater part of the chord. The British aviation historian Percy B. Walker, in his accounts of early aviation at the Royal Aircraft Establishment, Farnborough, explained Dunne's unusual swept wing design.

> For stability in pitch, which is the primary consideration, the same basic principles apply to the Dunne design as for the more usual tailplane at the rear end of a fuselage. Although the Dunne aeroplane is rightly regarded as tailless in the ordinary sense, there are in effect two tails, corresponding to the wing tips on either side. The essential characteristic of the wings in these tip regions is the presence of washout or reduction in the angle of incidence relative to the main portions inboard. Thus when an aeroplane of this design is flying steadily on a level course there is only a small vertical force acting on the outer portion of each wing, and this small force is usually, and preferably, acting downwards. The combination of reduced or slightly negative incidence at the tips, and the backward inclination of the wings as a whole, ensures stability in pitch and acts as a substitute for the tailplane of the more conventional types.[8]

On December 20, 1910, John Dunne, in the role of test pilot, demonstrated the extraordinary stability of the D.5 to an amazed audience that included Orville Wright. Taking off from Eastchurch, the site of many previous successful flights in the D.5, Dunne proved that an airplane could be flown for an extended period of time without handling any controls. Using both hands, Dunne scribbled a note on a flimsy piece of paper as he motored over the countryside, narrowly missing a windmill, and, despite a momentary failure to recognize the ground below, executing a successful landing for the appreciative audience. Dunne's historic thumbnail description of his flight:

Engine revs 1400
Levers normal
strong wind in face
turning now[9]

Dunne continued his design efforts for another three years, until ill health finally forced his retirement from a life of total devotion to his stability experiments. Beginning with the 1911 D.6 monoplane, Dunne's designs progressed in sequence through the D.10. He reverted to the biplane format for the D.8 and D.10, and probably enjoyed the most publicity and some limited commercial success with the D.8. Following a successful D.8 cross-Channel flight and demonstration tour in France, the Nieuport Company ordered a biplane, and W. Starling Burgess of the United States was given the manufacturing rights in that country. Burgess produced a number of successful land and seaplane variations of the Dunne machines, continuing to demonstrate the remarkable stability of the original aircraft.

Although two aircraft were ordered by the Royal Flying Corps, it was becoming increasingly obvious to those concerned with designing, building, and testing military aircraft that the inherent stability so coveted by Dunne was incompatible with the handling characteristics desired by military pilots. Maneuverability, ease of handling, and superior performance determined an airplane's acceptability by the military. Dunne's craft were relatively inefficient compared to conventional aircraft of equal horsepower; excessive stability did not result in ease of control and maneuverability. A reasonable compromise between control and stability was required.

Assessing John Dunne's impact on aeronautical history is difficult. Many of his theories on stability are valid and many designers have benefited from his far-sighted experiments. England's G.T.R. Hill and America's John K. Northrop, two of the more renowned investigators of tailless aircraft, often referred to Dunne when discussing the basic problems of stability and control. He was a true pioneer—the first to create a practical tailless airplane.

Dunne's tailless aircraft were successful because of his brilliant use of aerodynamic innovation in wing design. A totally different approach was taken in France by René Arnoux, who produced a series of tailless designs from 1909 to 1923 that included monoplanes, biplanes, pushers, tractors, low-wing, and mid-wing arrangements. A typical Arnoux wing resembled a straight board with no sweepback, dihedral, wing tip droop, or the like—a wing so simple it was called the Arnoux "flying plank."

Arnoux first applied his "no frills" approach to a tailless biplane in 1909, a design about which little has been written. Two monoplanes followed in 1912, one of which, named *Le Stablavion*, was placed on display at the Paris Aero Salon in October 1912. This two-seater pusher model attracted the attention of visiting technical experts, and at least one aviation writer, Alexander Dumas, gave the airplane extensive coverage in the well-known aviation journal *L'Aérophile*.[10] The aircraft had not been flown before the exposition but was scheduled to begin tests in the near future.

Arnoux's experiments were interrupted by World War I. He resumed his

The 1910 Dunne D.6 monoplane was quite different from his well-known tailless biplanes. The monoplane's wing was set high in parasol fashion. The wing tips had pronounced wash-out, and the final few feet curved sharply downward outboard of the center of the ailerons to provide side area in the absence of fins or rudders. (Courtesy Royal Aircraft Establishment)

The Dunne D.8 of 1911–1912 was representative of the tailless pusher biplanes that Lieutenant J.W. Dunne designed as inherently stable aircraft. The vertical fins joining the wing tips were fixed. Movable control surfaces at the trailing edge of the wing could be operated independently of each other as rudders for turning, or they could be operated together in unison for movement "up" or "down." Two control levers were provided for the pilot. For pitch control, the pilot moved both levers backward or forward together; for roll control, he moved them in opposite directions. The levers were automatically locked in position when released by the pilot. (Courtesy Royal Aircraft Establishment)

investigations after the war, however, and his attempts to adapt the "flying plank" to racing aircraft in the 1920s will be discussed later (see page 26).

Professor Hugo Junkers of Germany was frequently mentioned in aeronautical journals in connection with the evolution of the so-called all-wing airplane. Much of the publicity stems from a famous 1910 Junkers patent for an airplane with a thick, hollow wing in which non-lift-producing components such as engines, crew, and passengers could be housed. Junkers's preoccupation with this "thick wing" concept was evident in many of his aircraft designs that evolved over the next 30 years. The idea was even applied to a World War II design for a large military transport glider, the Ju 322 *Mammut* (mammoth). This huge wooden aircraft, with a wingspan of 203 feet, carried most of its payload inside the wing. Although it flew successfully, it was not produced in quantity. Other than in some conceptual designs, such as his 1924 J 1000 giant airplane, or occasional wooden tailless models, there is little physical

The Stablavion *monoplane of René Arnoux is shown on display at the Paris Aéro Salon in October 1912. The secret of the success of the Arnoux "flying plank" aircraft was the up-turned trailing edge of the wing, called reflex camber, which prevented instability caused by excessive aft travel of the center of pressure.*

evidence that Junkers's ideas extended to the elimination of the tail section. Junkers applied his "all-wing" concepts only to the extent that they were economically feasible.

Although Junkers never received the necessary support to develop his ideal airplane, he did provide the aeronautical community with the perception that parasite drag could be substantially reduced by placing most components and loads inside a thick cantilever wing.

Before World War I the majority of design work on tailless aircraft took place in Europe. There were, however, two series of designs by Americans during those early years that deserve mention—one a modest commercial success based on John Dunne's developments in England, the other a "home-grown" product developed by three brothers from New Jersey with nothing to build on but intuition, common sense, and natural ability.

Operating his own boat yard at Marblehead, Massachusetts, prepared W. Starling Burgess for an equally successful career as aircraft builder. In an age when aircraft construction techniques and materials were rudimentary at best, Burgess found the high standards of workmanship and construction that helped him build fast racing yachts were in high demand by sportsmen and military aviators alike. By the time he acquired the license to build and continue to develop Dunne-style aircraft in 1913, he had become involved in the design and construction of aircraft for four years, primarily in partnership with his close friend Greely S. Curtis (not related to Glenn H. Curtiss). They built Wright airplanes under license for sport and for the U.S. Army Signal Corps. Flying schools were operated by the Burgess Company and Curtis, as the organization was named, and Burgess himself gradually became a pilot of considerable skill. By 1913, Burgess and Curtis had had considerable success developing seaplanes for both civil and military use. They also had become disenchanted with their arrangement with the Wright brothers, and consequently dissolved their firm and reorganized as the Burgess Company in early 1914.

Burgess had also acquired the exclusive American manufacturing rights for the Dunne aircraft in 1913. He refined the Dunne design, simplifying construction, cutting weight, and increasing engine horsepower. Not surprisingly for a yachtsman turned flyer, Burgess immediately undertook the task of modifying the Dunne design for operations hardly envisioned by the English designer. During 1914, Burgess and Curtis produced the first Burgess-Dunne Hydro, equipped with a single float underneath the center nacelle and a small pontoon under each wing tip. Test pilot Clifford L. Webster flew a successful first flight from Marblehead Harbor, Massachusetts, in March 1914. Subsequent flight tests and demonstrations elicited ecstatic reviews in the press and considerable interest by the U.S. Army and Navy, and later, by several wealthy sportsmen.

Despite favorable publicity accorded the Burgess-Dunne types, the fact of the matter is that virtually only a handful of the models were ever bought. The Army's only Burgess-Dunne, S.C. No. 36, was accepted in December 1914. Capable of operation from land or, with minor modification, from water, the airplane was used mostly for experimental work with the Coast Artillery rather than in its intended role as tactical reconnaissance scout. It was condemned on October 18, 1916, ending a rather brief and unglamorous service life.

The Navy acquired two Burgess-Dunnes, the AH-7 and AH-10. Both were hydroplanes. The AH-7 was an open, side-by-side cockpit craft that was dis-

In 1910, Professor Hugo Junkers, founder of the Junkers factories in Germany, submitted the All-Wing Airplane Patent DRP. No. 253,788 for an airplane consisting of one wing that would house all components: engines, crew, passengers, fuel, and framework. The design was crude, and neither material nor engines then existed to make it a practical proposition. The design eventually led to the Junkers G 38 aircraft of 1929 that featured an exceptionally large wing mated to a substantial fuselage.

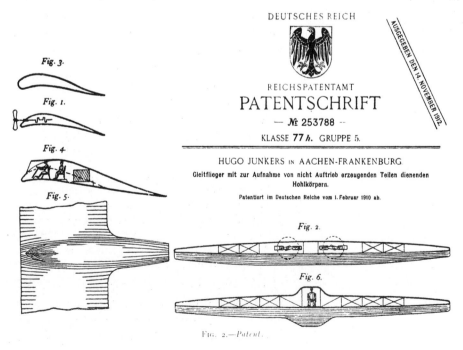

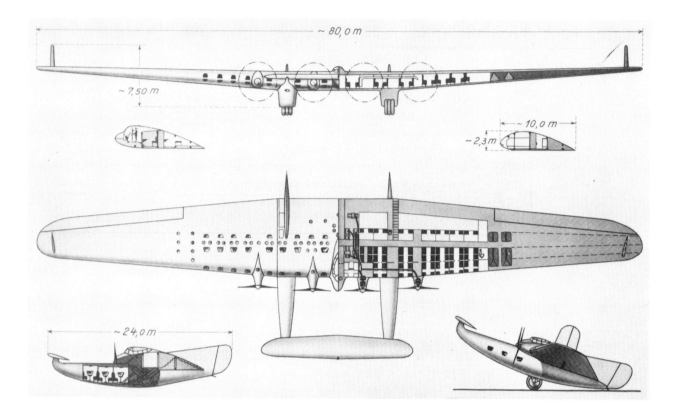

~ 80,0 m

~ 7,50 m

~ 10,0 m

~ 2,3 m

~ 24,0 m

Hugo Junkers's 1924 design for a giant airplane closely approximated a true flying wing in concept. The wing was to accommodate 26 cabins for 100 passengers, carry a crew of 10, and have enough fuel for 10 hours of flight.

tinguished not only by its unusual Dunne design but by a beautiful camouflage of lavender and green. In its sister ship, the AH-10, which had a 100-hp Curtiss engine, Lieutenant Patrick Bellinger established a new American altitude record for seaplanes by flying to 10,000 feet on April 23, 1915. Three similar aircraft were ordered by the Navy, and designated A-54, A-55, and A-56, but these aircraft never went into active service.

Burgess enjoyed some success in the civil aviation market, receiving considerable publicity with sales of hydroplanes to financiers Vincent Astor and Harold Payne Whitney. The enterprising Burgess also included a floating hangar of his own design in his aviation package for the millionaire flyer interested in "water plane sports." The media had a field day with the whole idea:

> It does not confine the activity of the machine to one particular locality, but enables moves to be made to suit the desires of the owner. If he so wishes, the summer months may be spent in the North, either on the Atlantic Coast or on one of the many inland lakes, whilst when winter makes climactic conditions uncomfortable for flying, the machine and its hangar may be sent down to the smiling Florida waters. What infinite possibilities for the future of the sport of aviation are here foreshadowed![11]

There were other orders for the Dunne derivative: a warplane for Canada was delivered but then abandoned after it was damaged in shipment; and allegedly, a military aircraft for Russia. The Burgess catalog listed an attractive flying boat with a Curtiss hull, designed "primarily for sportsmen who do

20

When the prototype G 38a D-2000 made its maiden flight on November 6, 1929, it was billed as the largest landplane in the world, featuring a mammoth wing with a chord of almost 33 feet and 6 feet thick at the root. Although by no means a true flying wing, it incorporated some of the desirable characteristics of such a design by locating the payload compartments and engines in an unbraced cantilever wing. (Courtesy Lufthansa Archives)

not wish to lose the sensations of the speed boat."[12] There was a BD Sportsman's Seaplane, as well as a Model BDH Reconnaissance Type which, because of its inherent stability, enabled the pilot "to fly long distances without fatigue and make observations at his leisure."[13] Prototypes for all of these were built, but the market was limited.

Perhaps the high point of Starling Burgess's romance with the Dunne design was his winning of the 1915 Collier Trophy for development of the Burgess-Dunne hydroaeroplane. With the outbreak of World War I, however, the market for purely civilian aircraft disappeared, and there was no military requirement for the Dunne machine.[14]

Starling Burgess accepted a commission in the U.S. Navy in 1917, and in the process severed all ties with the company that bore his name. The Burgess Company continued to produce conventional trainers, flying boat hulls, and airship cars for the Navy during the war, but a disastrous fire on November 7, 1918, destroyed one Burgess plant. The fire, and the end of the war a few days later, spelled the end of the Burgess Company. Burgess returned to the boat business, in which he worked with considerable success until his death in 1947.[15]

Shortly before Burgess shifted his interest from boats to airplanes, the Boland brothers of Rahway, New Jersey, began their investigations into tailless designs in a manner which, on the surface, appeared to be something less than scientific. In 1904, Frank and Joseph, the more mechanically inclined of the three brothers, established a service garage for bicycles, motorcycles, and automobiles in Rahway, with brother James running the business and taking care of the finances. In 1907, Frank tried unsuccessfully to build his own airplane without drawings, knowledge, or advice.

In 1908, Frank was joined by his brothers, with Joseph applying his considerable talent to designing and building a suitable eight-cylinder water-cooled engine for their next venture. A series of designs for tailless aircraft

In 1913, W. Starling Burgess secured American patent rights to build aircraft in the United States under the Dunne patents covering inherent stability. The U.S. Army's Burgess-Dunne S.C. No. 36 shown here was delivered in 1914 and was one of a number of Dunne aircraft produced from 1914 to 1917. The airplane was initially equipped with a single square flat-bottomed pontoon that was alternated with conventional landing gear during test flights.

evolved in a process which one aviation writer of the day described as "flying, smashing, altering, with the one object in view of proving that rudders as generally used are unnecessary, that ailerons and warping wings are only two methods of keeping right side up."[16] Frank Boland acted as test pilot and, through trial and error, ingenuity, and no little courage, finally did prove to the aviation world that the fledgling Boland Airplane and Motor Company could produce aircraft that could fly.

The key to the Boland airplane's ease of handling and maneuverability was a patented system of lateral control long known to sailors, called a jib. Rudders, ailerons, and wing warping were not part of this design. Lateral control was provided by elliptically shaped surfaces, or jibs, mounted between the outer ends of the top and bottom wings. Each jib was pivoted on an oblique axis from the lower front strut to the upper rear strut and was movable inward, in one direction only. The operation was similar to steering an automobile: a control wheel was turned in the desired direction, the jib on that side was pulled in, and the aircraft banked and turned. Control in elevation was provided by a curved control surface located 14 feet in front of the wings. Moving the control column forward caused the craft to go downward, and vice versa.

As the Bolands continued to test and improve their designs, word of their success spread. Orders for aircraft and engines began to arrive, as did the curiosity seekers and the serious investigators. In 1911, Wilbur Wright paid a visit to the Rahway shop to determine if the jib control infringed on Wright patents. It did not, and apparently Wilbur Wright praised the Bolands for their original work.

Frank Boland was killed in 1913 during an exhibition flight in Trinidad, a crushing blow to the Boland Company. Joseph took over control of the ven-

22

After two years of experimenting, the Boland brothers produced this tailless biplane, which flew quite successfully in 1910. Jibs used for turning the airplane can be seen at the wing tips. Since the pilot's feet were not used for any purpose during flight, they were inserted in "stirrups" on the outrigger, so that the pilot sat with knees high, like the driver of a racing automobile.

An improved version of the 1910 Boland flew at the Mineola fair grounds in 1914. A fabric-covered nacelle was added to protect pilot and passenger. An 8-cylinder, 60-hp Boland engine powered the biplane, which was made in both land- and seaplane versions.

ture, concentrating on development and manufacturing, while using other available talent for test flights and demonstrations. A tailless flying boat appeared in 1913, and in 1914 the newly formed Aeromarine Plane and Motor Company of Avondale, New Jersey, took over the exclusive manufacturing rights of Boland airplanes and engines. Joseph and James remained with the new organization for a time, Joseph continuing to work on engine and airplane developments. Unfortunately, little more was heard of the Boland tailless airplane and its unique jib control.

The Boland brothers were a relatively small, but extraordinary, part of early aviation history in the United States. Frank supplied the enthusiasm, ingenuity, and self-taught flying ability; Joseph provided the mechanical genius to transform ideas into some tangible, workable form; and James had the business sense so often lacking in ventures of that sort. Unfortunately, with Frank Boland's death, many of the ingredients necessary for success went with him.

With World War I came a temporary hiatus in the experimentation with tailless aircraft as nations turned to the more practical business of adapting the airplane to full scale warfare for the first time. In the decades that followed, however, the impetus provided by the tremendous growth in military aviation and associated technology contributed to a resurgence of interest in the tailless airplane, initially in Europe, then in the United States.

NOTES

1. Charles H. Gibbs-Smith, *Clément Ader: His Flight Claims and his Place in History*, p. 12 (France).

2. H.F. King, "Swing-Wing, Variable Incidence, Air-Cushion Hydrofoil," pp. 68–70 (France).

3. Charles H. Gibbs-Smith, *The Invention of the Aeroplane (1799–1909)*, p. 91 (General).

4. For an excellent, detailed account of the evolution of the *Taube* and all of its variations, see Colonel John A. deVries's *Taube, Dove of War* (Germany). Igo Etrich's own account of his early experiments with gliders is contained in his autobiography *Die Taube, Memoiren des Flugpioniers* (Germany).

5. José Weiss showed signs of being a dedicated family man. His manned aircraft of the 1909–1911 period were named *Olive, Madge, Elsie,* and *Sylvia* after daughters, and *Joker,* after one of his sons.

6. Major C.C. Turner, *The Old Flying Days*, p. 3 (General).

7. Percy B. Walker, *Early Aviation at Farnborough, Volume II: The First Aeroplanes*, p. 185 (United Kingdom).

8. Ibid., p. 176. Dunne's use of sweptback wings for attaining stability in pitch should not be confused with their modern use for transonic and supersonic flight. Supersonic flight was hardly one of Dunne's concerns.

9. Constance Babington-Smith, *Testing Time—The Story of British Test Pilots and their Aircraft,* p. 16 (United Kingdom). John Dunne's work at Farnborough is treated in considerable detail in Walker, *Early Aviation at Farnborough, Volume II,* pp. 163–283 (United Kingdom).

10. Alexander Dumas, "Le 'Stablavion' R. Arnoux," *L'Aérophile*, pp. 35–36 (France).

11. "Waterplane Sport in America," p. 716 (U.S., Non-Northrop).

12. Bartlett Gould, "The Burgess Story," *American Aviation Historical Society Journal*, 1967, 12(4): 278.

13. Ibid., p. 279.

14. In February 1916, the Curtiss Aeroplane and Motor Corp. acquired the services of Burgess and his organization. The Curtiss Co. took over the stock of the Burgess Co.; Mr. Burgess became a Curtiss director, remained in charge of the Marblehead plant, and continued his work with the Dunnes.

15. The story of W. Starling Burgess is told in excellent fashion in a series of five articles by Bartlett Gould, "The Burgess Story," *American Aviation Historical Society Journal* (General).

16. "The Boland Tail-Less Biplane," p. 156 (U.S., Non-Northrop).

Chapter 2

Europe between the Wars

As the world entered the roaring twenties, what has been called the "Golden Age of Aviation" began, and interest in tailless aircraft revived and spread. Many of the early proponents of the concept were gone; some had abandoned the idea for more practical and profitable designs; some, like J.W. Dunne, ceased their aeronautical activities, though their theories and experiments provided guidance and inspiration for those who followed (including Hill of England, Lippisch and the Hortens of Germany, and John K. Northrop of the United States, the man who would eventually carry the flying wing to its ultimate stage of development).

René Arnoux of France was one the early pioneers who had not lost his interest in tailless aircraft during the war. He resumed his experiments in the early 1920s, building a tailless biplane from surplus parts. The strange looking hybrid, which incorporated Arnoux's "flying plank" wing, flew successfully 12 times between February and April 1922, with some interest shown by the press. Unfortunately the airplane crashed, severely injuring the pilot, Fetu. It was rumored that Fetu had removed the stops restricting downward travel of the controllers, making the airplane unstable.

During this same period, Arnoux formed his own company, Simplex, and teamed up with a well-known French fighter pilot, Georges Félix Madon. Fourth ranking French ace of World War I with 41 victories, Madon became closely associated with Arnoux as his test pilot for several years, to the extent that "Arnoux" designs became "Madon" designs in the minds of many.

The first Simplex design, and perhaps the most controversial of the Arnoux line, was the Simplex-Arnoux tailless racer, constructed for the 1922 *Coupe Deutsch* race. The aircraft had a simple Arnoux "flying plank" wing, with full span controllers, tiny vertical fin and rudder, and was powered by a 320-hp Hispano Suiza engine. The machine was said to have a maximum speed of 236 mph, fast indeed for that day.

Press coverage of the revolutionary design increased as the September 30 race date approached. Arnoux, not known as a publicity seeker, was not even listed as designer. The airplane was now the *Simplex (type Madon Carmier)*,

French ace George Félix Madon, who had 41 dogfight victories in World War I, poses by the futuristic Simplex Arnoux racer of 1922. The pilot's vision forward and down was severely restricted by the Lamblin radiator perched on top of the fuselage and the expanse of the Arnoux "flying plank" wing.

The last of the Arnoux aircraft was this 1923 hybrid combination of a Hanriot HD 14 and miscellaneous spare parts, all put together with considerable imagination. It actually flew well according to official reports.

after the pilot Madon, whose name was now totally identified with Arnoux designs, and an engineer named Carmier, who had contributed significantly to the design. Regardless of who deserved credit for the design, it seemed a bit too risky for its purpose, and whatever chances it might have had in the upcoming *Coupe Deutsch*, disappeared shortly before the race. Madon crashed on September 24 during a landing attempt, demolishing the racer but sustaining only minor injuries himself.

This accident, coming as it did so soon after Fetu's biplane crash, did little to increase popular acceptance of the Arnoux design. There is little documentary evidence that Arnoux continued to produce designs under his name, although in 1933 he apparently collaborated with another advocate of tailless craft, Charles Fauvel. Reports do exist of test flights in 1923 of a Madon tailless aircraft that is obviously a derivative of the ill-fated 1922 Arnoux biplane.[1] The airplane appeared to be nothing more than a Hanriot HD 14 sawed in half, with a large single rudder added just aft of the cockpit. According to test pilot Madon, this arrangement resulted in extremely sensitive directional control. The upper ailerons were rigged to act as elevator trim tabs controlled by a hand wheel in the cockpit. The lower wing ailerons acted as elevators and ailerons.

The Madon airplane demonstrated satisfactory flying characteristics, required no special training for the ordinary pilot, and showed definite promise as a military aircraft. Interestingly enough, Madon was given credit as the inventor of the aircraft.

Not long after his 1923 demonstration flights, Madon gave up the tailless project, joined the Bapt round-the-world expedition for a few short months, and finally rejoined the army in July 1923. He died during an airshow at Bizerte, Tunisia, on November 11, 1924, when he experienced an engine failure at low altitude, and crashed after courageously maneuvering his aircraft to avoid the crowd.

Another visionary whose interest in the tailless aircraft began before the war was Alexander Soldenhoff. Born in Geneva in 1882, Soldenhoff immigrated to Germany in 1908 and began a professional career as a painter, writer, and decorator. Although he was an artist by trade, Soldenhoff had a consuming interest in aviation, particularly in the development of powered tailless aircraft. He obtained his first official patent for a tailless aircraft in 1912, and experimented extensively for many years with models and wind tunnel tests to perfect a practical, inherently stable, tailless monoplane. His first powered aircraft flew in 1927. The aircraft, designated A1, was a single-seat, swept wing aircraft powered by a 32-hp Bristol Cherub engine with a pusher propeller. After two test flights, test pilot Ernest Gerber experienced a strut failure in flight and made an emergency landing at Dubendorf airport in Switzerland.

Restricted from further flights by Swiss officials, Soldenhoff shifted his activities to Germany, where his second effort, the A2, was designed and constructed with the assistance of engineers Langguth and Friedman.[2] Completed in 1929, the A2 was test flown by the renowned German sailplane pilot, Gottlob Espenlaub, who also built and flew his own tailless designs. The two-seater A2 had conventional tricycle landing gear, pusher propeller, and two trailing-edge control surfaces on each wing. Successful flight test of this configuration encouraged Soldenhoff to build the third of his experimental aircraft, the A3.

A two-seater like its predecessor, the A3 had a tricycle landing gear with the single wheel aft, under the pusher propeller. This was the first Soldenhoff design powered by a French Salmson 9-cylinder, 40-hp engine, with which all of his later designs would also be equipped. Also appearing for the first time were two control rudders, one mounted about mid-span on each wing.

Alexander Soldenhoff's second tailless airplane, the A2 (D-1708), was flown in 1929 by noted German aviator, Gottlob Espenlaub. Two movable control surfaces can be seen on the trailing edge of each wing. (Courtesy Heinz J. Nowarra; SI Negative 80-20296)

Artist and designer Alexander Soldenhoff (right) poses with his test pilot Anton Riedeger (left) in front of Soldenhoff's third tailless design, the A3 (D-1923). Riedeger became Soldenhoff's principal test pilot and demonstrated considerable courage and rare aeronautical ability during his flights in these primitive models. (Courtesy Heinz J. Nowarra; SI Negative 80-20304)

Test pilot for the A3 was Anton Riedeger, who did all of the test flying on the A3, A4, and a later model, the A5. Riedeger flew the A3 for the first time on July 30, 1930, from Dusseldorf-Lohausen. Riedeger, an experienced commercial pilot, was pleased with the flight characteristics of the A3. Unfortunately, after a week of extensive test flights, Riedeger was seriously injured and the airplane was destroyed during an attempted crosswind landing.

Undaunted, Soldenhoff produced the A4, another design quite similar to the A3. The streak of bad luck continued, however, when the A4, with the intrepid Riedeger once again at the controls, crashed in a gusty crosswind and flipped over. Riedeger was again injured, though less seriously than before.

The last Soldenhoff machine to fly was his A5, a design similar to its predecessors, but with a conventional tricycle gear and distinctive discs, or endplates, at the wing tips. These plates could be changed in the search for a more efficient aerodynamic design. The A5 apparently flew well. Soldenhoff and Riedeger set off together in the two-seater on an aerial tour of Europe. The combination of the accident-prone but determined Riedeger and the deaf artist/designer Soldenhoff in the open cockpits of their flimsy experimental aircraft hardly inspired confidence in the successful outcome of the trip. An instrument takeoff in dense fog followed by occasional blind flying in the clouds over the Swiss Alps using the rudimentary instruments of the day added to the spirit of adventure as the two departed on the first leg of their tour in September 1931. Although the tour barely got underway before it was aborted for a variety of reasons, the fact that it started at all was a tribute to the enthusiasm and determination of both the pilot and the designer.

A later design, the S5, was constructed along lines similar to his previous models. It was never flown, and the project failed for lack of official Swiss support.

Considering Soldenhoff's lack of technical training, it is amazing that he made the progress that he did with his designs. The artist suffered, not sur-

The Soldenhoff A4 prepares for takeoff at Boblingen Field, Germany, in January 1931. Riedeger had no better luck with the A4 than he had had with its predecessor. A crash left the A4 inverted in the snow and Riedeger with minor injuries. (Courtesy Heinz J. Nowarra; SI Negative 80-20298)

Riedeger flies the A5. Many of the design features of Soldenhoff models would be observed in later tailless aircraft in other countries. (Courtesy Heinz J. Nowarra; SI Negative 80-18115)

prisingly, from lack of financial support and governmental interest. He by no means solved all the problems of tailless design, but his concepts provided the basis for many subsequent sport plane configurations, including the roadable airplanes of the 1930s.

In 1923, an innovative Englishman, Professor G.T.R. Hill, began his investigations into the questions of control and the problems of designing a safe airplane. Hill studied sea birds and concluded that they used wing warping and changes of wing camber rather than their tails for longitudinal control in normal flight. Consulting during this period with J.W. Dunne, Hill eventually designed a family of unusual tailless aircraft known as the Pterodactyls, after the prehistoric flying reptile.

Hill's appreciation for the dangers associated with stalling an airplane stemmed from his early days as a test pilot for the Royal Aircraft Factory at Farnborough, England, in 1916. He had studied the reports on Lilienthal's glider experiments, and knew of his death as a result of a stall in his glider. He was also deeply concerned over the tragic loss of about 50 lives a year in the Royal Air Force due to stall/spin accidents.

Professor Hill sought solutions to the stall problem over a number of years; his experiments eventually led to a non-stalling, tailless glider in 1924. It was a monoplane and featured movable wing tip "controllers" that provided longitudinal and lateral control regardless of the airplane's attitude. When operated together, the controllers acted as elevators; operated differentially, they acted as ailerons. Successful gliding tests with the aircraft led to powered flight of the first Pterodactyl a year later, which occurred on November 2, 1925. Subsequent flight tests proved the soundness of Hill's theories, for there was no definite stall, and good control was retained even at high angles of attack.

Professor Hill's 1934 Pterodactyl Mk. V was designed as a two-seater fighter for the Royal Air Force. The rear seat was for a gunner. Control was afforded by balanced flaps on the upper wing that operated together as elevators and differentially as ailerons. Wing tip rudders provided directional control and also acted together as air brakes. The machine was fully capable of aerobatics and inverted flight. (SI Negative 78-18249)

England's distinguished G.T.R. Hill designed this Westland-Hill Pterodactyl Mk. IA in 1928. This experimental tailless monoplane had pivoted wing tips that served as both ailerons and elevators and that remained effective regardless of the airplane's attitude.

During the next seven years, Westland Aircraft Works produced five models of the Hill-designed Pterodactyl, the last, the Mk. V of 1932, a two-seater fighter capable of 190 mph. Hill's Pterodactyls incorporated many novel features, including the first use of variable wing sweepback during flight, the use of spoiler air brakes and bicycle-type tandem-wheel landing gear with wing tip skids, and the first use of wing tip slats on a swept back wing. The Pterodactyl Mk. IV was the first tailless aircraft ever to be spun, rolled, and looped.

Although the Mk. V was the last of the Pterodactyl series, G.T.R. Hill continued to research tailless aircraft during a brilliant career as engineer and academic. It is a tribute to his genius as an innovator and designer that many of the Pterodactyl design features appeared in later variations of tailless aircraft and flying wings.

Flying the Atlantic in a giant airliner was also the dream of the Austrian engineer, Dr. Edmund Rumpler. Builder of the well-known *Taube* series of World War I fighters designed by Igo Etrich, Dr. Rumpler also saw the utility of a large wing to house passengers, cargo, and engines. He did see a limit to increasing the span and size of airplanes designed according to conventional practice, however. If aircraft progressed in size beyond a certain limit, Rumpler theorized, the weight of wings increased out of proportion to the increased size of the airplane; the larger the airplane became, the smaller the payload capacity and range.

Dr. Rumpler believed that the weight could be kept within reasonable limits if it were distributed evenly over the wing span instead of being concentrated in a single fuselage or hull. His plan was to arrange a number of small airplanes side by side and join their wings. The larger aircraft that evolved would have high load capacity and very long range. The airplane was not a tailless design. Rumpler shared only some of the theories advanced by the purists; he advocated eliminating the fuselage, but retained the tail surfaces.

Dr. Rumpler publicized his concept of a transoceanic airliner in 1926 and, over the next four years, worked on the detailed design while searching for financial backing in Europe and the United States for full scale production.

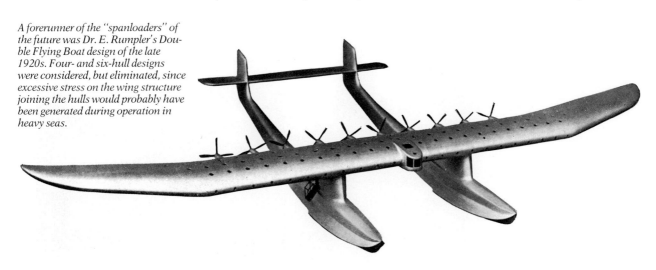

A forerunner of the "spanloaders" of the future was Dr. E. Rumpler's Double Flying Boat design of the late 1920s. Four- and six-hull designs were considered, but eliminated, since excessive stress on the wing structure joining the hulls would probably have been generated during operation in heavy seas.

The all-metal, twin-hulled flying boat was to have a single wing with a span of 289 feet and a height of 8 feet at its thickest point. Sixty-five tons of fuel would be carried in the twin hulls; fuel would be fed by pumps to the ten 1000-hp engines, which would give the gigantic craft a cruising speed of 185 mph.

The accommodations for the 35-man crew and 135 passengers were lavish. Cabins were to be situated in the wing interior at the leading edge. Cabins would seat six, each with a breathtaking view forward. A wide passageway extending the entire span of the wing would separate the passenger cabins from the engine compartments at the trailing edge. The passageway, over six feet high, would serve as a promenade deck as well as sound buffer for the passengers.

Dr. Rumpler planned to build an entire fleet of these boats to ply the oceans of the world. Like so many other similar schemes, however, the Rumpler Double Flying Boat was only a paper airplane. He failed to gain the necessary funds for the project at home or abroad and was not in favor with the German government after Hitler's rise to power. He did, however, sum up the fascination that he and so many others had with the "big wing" concept: "Give me wings large enough and sufficient motive power and I'll take the earth for an airplane ride."[3]

Dreamers, visionaries, and conceptual designers abounded in the field of flying wing design. Few could take the concepts and apply them to a design with popular appeal. One who overcame the odds was Charles Fauvel of France, the only designer seriously involved in early development of tailless aircraft whose name remained associated with the design and production of those designs half a century later. Fauvel's first powered tailless craft flew in 1933; today tailless gliders with the Fauvel name still fly in many countries around the world.

Fauvel's designs were similar in concept to those of his countryman, René

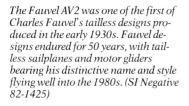

The Fauvel AV2 was one of the first of Charles Fauvel's tailless designs produced in the early 1930s. Fauvel designs endured for 50 years, with tailless sailplanes and motor gliders bearing his distinctive name and style flying well into the 1980s. (SI Negative 82-1425)

Arnoux. The two even collaborated on a tailless patent in 1930. Fauvel also favored the absence of sweepback, dihedral, and washout. Fauvel's wings did incorporate considerable taper, however, to the extent that wing tips were almost pointed. He did not favor wing tip rudders, but leaned toward single or double vertical fins and rudders on the after part of the wing center section.

Fauvel produced a number of powered and unpowered models during the 1930s, with varying degrees of success. The A.V.2 was a powered glider that enjoyed limited success in 1933. The engine was detachable and the wheels could be replaced by a skid for test flights of that configuration. The unpowered A.V.3 was tested during the summer of 1933, and demonstrated excellent flying qualities. The A.V.10 of 1934-1935 was the most successful in many respects, having been exhibited at the Paris Aero Salon and subsequently receiving the first certificate of airworthiness ever awarded to a tailless aircraft in France. The two-passenger airplane was powered by a 75-hp Pobjoy engine which, in June 1936, carried the unique aircraft to an altitude of 23,500 feet.

Fauvel's pre-World War II designs were not financial successes, but his theories on longitudinal stability in tailless aircraft were sound. After the war's end his name was associated with a series of tailless gliders and home-built airplanes that had great popular appeal.

The imaginative Horten brothers, Walter and Reimar, approached the ideal of the flying wing with their own powered aircraft of the 1930s and 1940s. All of the Horten craft were innovative and were distinguished by experimental shapes and diverse control systems. Their impact on flying wing design was significant, and special consideration will be given to Horten designs of World War II in a later chapter (see Chapter 4).

Three Horten gliders of the pre-war years were interesting precursors of their World War II designs. The first of these, the 1931 Ho I sailplane, consisted of a wing with a small cockpit canopy in the center secton. The craft was constructed of wood with fabric covering and incorporated a central, fixed landing skid. Having no vertical or tail surfaces, the Ho I was controlled by separate ailerons and elevators located at the trailing edge of each wing panel. Yaw control was obtained by the use of brake flaps above and below the leading edges near the wing tips.

The aircraft was licensed too late to enter the Rhön Gliding competition of 1934.[4] The Hortens towed it from Bonn to the Wasserkuppe in the Rhön mountains in western Germany. Unfortunately, Reimar damaged the skid on landing, putting the glider out of commission for awhile. Finally, in frustration, the brothers salvaged the metal hardware and burned the glider after only seven hours of flight time, convinced that a better design was possible.

Another wooden airplane, the Ho II, followed in 1934. Improvements over the Ho I included trailing edge sweep back[5] and a tandem wheel undercarriage with retractable nosewheel and faired rear wheel. Two trailing edge surface controls were linked so that the outboard controls primarily gave longitudinal control, and the inboard surface provided lateral control. Wing tip brake flaps were fitted for yaw control. First flown as a glider in 1934, the Ho II

Second in a series of significant pre-World War II designs by Germany's Horten brothers was this Ho II, built in 1934 as an unpowered glider, but later powered by an 80-hp engine. Two sets of elevon control surfaces were installed in each trailing edge. The D-10-131 is a special marking adopted for German gliders about 1937. The D is the international registration letter for Germany (Deutschland), the 10 represents the gliding district in which the craft is registered, and the 131 is its number within that district. (SI Negative 72-8627)

Another classic Horten design of the late 1930s was the Ho III, which attained an altitude of 23,000 feet in competition. Control surfaces were similar to those of the Ho II, except that an inner set, used as flaps, was added. (SI Negative 4405-A)

The Ho IIID was built as a powered glider and featured a propeller whose blades could be folded to reduce drag during unpowered flight. The propeller is shown in the folded position. Outer wing sections are missing. (Courtesy Vintage Sailplane Association; SI Negative 80-19284)

was equipped in 1935 with an 80-hp Hirth HM 60R engine that was submerged in the wing and drove a pusher propeller through an extension shaft. Hanna Reitsch, the famed German woman test pilot, flew the Ho II on November 17, 1938. Stability and control were considered marginal in some respects, but the aircraft could not be stalled or spun by any combination of control movements. The diminutive Hanna Reitsch described the cockpit as only possible for athletes, while the arrangement and operation of the retractable landing gear were considered as only possible for long-armed pilots.

Spurred on by a less than enthusiastic endorsement, but with some official interest, the Hortens constructed the more elaborate Ho III in 1938. Also designed as a sailplane, the Ho III resembled the Ho II but had increased span and aspect ratio and was of mixed construction, the center section being of welded steel tubes with plywood covering, and the outer sections being of wood. The trailing edge of each wing half carried three control surfaces to replace the two of the Ho II, the inner surface being used as a landing flap and the outer surfaces acting differentially as ailerons and together as elevators. Directional control was provided by tip-mounted drag rudders.

A second version of the design, the Ho IIIB, was built, and considerable experimental work was done with the two sailplanes. Dive flaps were tried on both upper and lower center section surfaces; automatic flaps were installed on the under surfaces to limit maximum diving speed; and the wing tips were rigged to rotate for lateral control. Other versions of the aircraft were built; the Ho IIIC was fitted with a small additional wing set forward of the main wing; the Ho IIID was built as a powered glider with a propeller whose blades could be folded to reduce drag during gliding.

With the beginning of World War II, the Hortens eventually attracted the government interest they required to continue their flying wing developments. Their efforts, like those of other believers in tailless aircraft in Germany, England, and the United States, turned to finding a wartime use for such an airplane.

The Horten brothers can be viewed as purists in their experiments with tailless airplanes in that all of their designs were distinguished by the total absence of any vertical control surfaces. Also dedicated to the idea of tailless aircraft but a firm believer in the requirement for vertical surfaces for directional stability and control, was their countryman, Alexander Lippisch.[6]

Few serious designers of tailless airplanes could claim the lasting impact on modern aircraft design that Lippisch had with his development of the delta wing, which is found in many military airplanes of the 1980s and in the Concorde and TU–144 supersonic transports. As a Berlin schoolboy of 14, Lippisch had the good fortune to witness a flight demonstration by Orville Wright in September 1909. Thus inspired, he followed the accounts of Dunne's and Etrich's experiments with inherent stability, and after military service during World War I, applied his interest to glider design. His first tailless glider was built in 1921, by Gottlob Espenlaub, the German glider enthusiast who would later collaborate with the Swiss designer Alexander Soldenhoff on his designs

The Lippisch-Espenlaub E2 was the first of over 50 swept-wing, tailless designs produced by Lippisch over the next three decades. Though this first effort was less than impressive, it at least was a starting point from which Lippisch began serious, systematic development of tailless designs. In 1924, he was designated Director of the Aeronautical Department of the Rhön-Rossitten-Gesellschaft (RRG, which later became the German Research Institute for Soaring Flight).

With limited resources at his disposal, Lippisch chose an unconventional, step-by-step method of developing his designs, testing the original concept first as a flying model, then as a man-carrying glider, and finally as a powered aircraft. Lippisch considered this approach would produce results in less time and with less expense than a wind tunnel research program. From this design philosophy evolved two famous series of tailless aircraft—the *Storch* (stork) and the Delta.

Between 1927 and 1932, eight *Storch* aircraft were designed by Lippisch, all of them high-wing monoplanes with sweepback. In 1926, a succession of large, free-flying models of various configurations, including canards and the "flying plank" design later adopted by Fauvel in France, led to the *Storch I* experimental glider, first test-flown in 1927 by Bubi Nehring. Lack of aileron effectiveness was evident in this and the *Storch II* and *III* that followed. The ailerons were redesigned to approximate the form of the Zanonia seed and Igo Etrich's *Taube*. Etrich himself recommended the configuration to Lippisch; his faith in the principle was reaffirmed when the 1929 *Storch IV* glider demonstrated impressive stability and control characteristics with Günther Grönhoff at the controls.

Designer Alexander Lippisch (right) poses with builder Gottlob Espenlaub (left) by their E2 glider of 1921. Plates at each wing tip were drooped to provide directional stability. Test flights were not impressive. (Courtesy U.S. Air Force)

The Lippisch Storch II *of 1927–1928 had free-swing end plate rudders at each wing tip. The craft suffered from poor directional stability, and subsequent versions had solid end plates with adjustable rudders. (Courtesy U.S. Air Force)*

Development work on the *Storch* series was temporarily interrupted in 1928 when Lippisch collaborated with Fritz von Opel and the rocket manufacturer Sander in performing rocket-powered flights of some Lippisch tailless models. These successful experiments were followed by a manned flight of a rocket-powered tail-first glider, the *Ente* (duck). Although these experiments also met with moderate success, Lippisch returned to his original interests in 1929. These experiments, and subsequent research on the basic principles of rocket propulsion, provided the foundation for later projects with rocket-propelled aircraft in the late 1930s.

In 1929, the *Storch V* appeared equipped with a small, 8-hp DKW engine for Lippisch's first attempt at powered flight with the *Storch* series. Following successful test flights by Grönhoff, a public demonstration of the *Storch V* was made at Tempelhof Airfield at Berlin in October 1929, with the expectation of obtaining some government financial backing.

None came, but the transatlantic pilot Captain Herman Köhl expressed interest in the idea of a tailless aircraft for flights across the Atlantic.[7] With this order in hand, Lippisch stopped work on the *Storch VI* and began the design of what would eventually become the renowned Delta series. Lippisch later worked on three more versions of the *Storch*; the *Storch VII*, powered by a 24-hp engine, won a prize for the first 300 km overland flight of a tailless aircraft when Grönhoff flew the aircraft from the Wasserkuppe to Berlin in 1931 in 1 hour, 55 minutes. The *Storch VIII* was a privately financed craft that could be flown either with or without tail surfaces attached. The *Storch IX* training glider appeared in 1933, and was successful enough to prompt two variations, the IX a and b.

Lippisch's methodical, step-by-step experiments had been quite successful with the *Storch* series, but the *Storch* was merely a foundation for further efforts to build a pure, all-wing aircraft. From the *Storch*, with its sweptback leading and trailing edges, came the Delta, also a sweptback wing but with one essential difference: the trailing edge, from wing tip to wing tip, was a straight line. This triangular wing allowed a thick midsection, with the potential for storing all loads inside the wing.

Following his customary routine, Lippisch proceeded from drawing to flying model to full-scale glider, and finally in June 1931, the powered Delta I was flown on the Wasserkuppe. Again, Günther Grönhoff's test flights were so successful that another Templehof demonstration was conducted; and again, the Lippisch aircraft was clearly a success, with accounts of Grönhoff's aerobatic skill with the revolutionary airplane appearing in the press in Europe and the United States.[8] Unfortunately, no financial backing materialized.

For the next several years, Lippisch, serving with the RRG (in 1933 reorganized under the title Deutsche Forschungsanstalt für Segelflug [DFS, German Research Institute for Soaring Flight]), produced dozens of designs for tailless aircraft; some never left the drawing board, and some made it to the model stage. Others, like the Delta, eventually flew and underwent countless modifications as tests revealed deficiencies in stability and control. The Delta series progressed through the Delta IVC, at which point the series designation was changed to DFS 39. The DFS 40, or Delta V, was the last of the series to fly, in 1939.

As the decade came to a close and Germany prepared for war, Lippisch transferred to the Messerschmitt Company in January 1939, where he again became involved in the application of rocket propulsion to tailless aircraft.

Interest in tailless aircraft was not confined to western Europe and England during the period between the wars. Designers in the Soviet Union demonstrated an appreciation for the idea and an understanding of the benefits and problems associated with the design. The idea even found some expression in Poland, though they met with extremely limited success there.

In the years between the wars, the Soviet Union provided a congenial atmosphere for a series of important experiments with designs for tailless aircraft. Even in the difficult economic conditions of the 1920s, the Bolsheviks sought to demonstrate their air-mindedness through aeronautical research

The Delta I of 1931 is shown in company with two Junkers G31 transports. The Delta I was powered with a 30-hp Bristol Cherub engine. Trailing-edge hinged surfaces at the outer section of the wing were used as ailerons; inner surfaces served as elevators.

The Delta I is shown in flight over Templehof Airport at Berlin in September 1931.

and development. Through the Central Aero-Hydrodynamics Institute (TsAGI) and various design contests, the Soviets gave concrete support to imaginative designers such as B.I. Cheranovskiy. Soviet aviation historians credit Cheranovskiy, an aeronautical engineer, for pioneer work in the design and construction of flying wings.

As early as 1921, Cheranovskiy began his BICH series of tailless sailplanes and powered parabola-shaped aircraft. The BICH-2, completed in 1924, had the pilot submerged in the wing and the elevators and ailerons arranged across the trailing edge. It flew 27 powered flights and was acknowledged in the USSR as the world's first successful flying wing. If this date is accurate, it would place the BICH-2 a few years before similar tailless monoplane designs of Soldenhoff, Lippisch, and Hill.

Cheranovskiy's designs progressed through the BICH-20 model of the late 1930s, and included single- and twin-engine designs, parabolic and triangular wings, and some experimentation with rocket power using the F.A. Tsander OR.2 rocket engine. Conventional engines used included the British Bristol Lucifer and the Blackburn Tom Tit.

The growth of gliding clubs in the mid-twenties and thirties, with recognition and support of the Soviet Air Force, provided both the incentive and the setting for Cheranovskiy and others to test their designs. The Ninth All Union Meet of 1933 featured gliding trials of four tailless models, three designed by Cheranovskiy and one by Kostenko. Cheranovskiy's entries included his BICH-11, 12, and 13. A specially arranged program of flight tests was conducted during the meet, with about 40 flights made by the BICH series, and 30 by the LAK-1, a tailless glider from the Leningrad Aero Club. The nature of the flight tests was strictly controlled, records were scrupulously kept, and results were analyzed with a view toward improving the flight characteristics of the designs.

The highlight of the meet was the performance of the BICH-13, which became the first tailless glider to soar in the USSR. The aircraft exhibited satisfactory longitudinal directional stability, always of paramount consideration. Stepanchenok, one of the four pilots who flew the BICH-13, observed: "Insofar as the established customs of the pilot are concerned, the steering of the 'Parabola' does not differ in any way from the steering of gliders of ordinary construction."[9]

Despite the enthusiasm over the BICH-13 and the successful performance of the gliders, participants and technical observers realized that construction and study of experimental gliders would have to be taken up by the professionals in the construction bureaus and research institutions. Glider performance and design and the experience of the participants were not up to those generally encountered at the Rhön Gliding competitions in Germany.

One of the Soviet Union's leading designers of conventional civil aircraft was also responsible for the design of a practical, military tailless airplane in the mid-1930s. During his distinguished career, K.A. Kalinin designed some 16 aircraft types, many of which showed considerable imagination. Between 1924 and 1934, Kalinin designed a number of successful civil aircraft includ-

Designed about 1930, the BICH-7A was powered by a 100-hp Bristol Lucifer engine and was capable of 100 mph cruising speed. Though underpowered, the parabola-shaped wing apparently had excellent flying qualities. (SI Negative 81-2799)

B.I. Cheranovskiy's BICH-11, constructed in 1932, appeared to be a conventional tailless aircraft of the period, although a detailed assessment of the control surfaces is not possible due to the poor quality of the photograph. Vertical rudders turned outward only, and could not be operated simultaneously. (SI Negative 81-2805)

ing the K-4, the first civilian aircraft ever manufactured in series production in the Soviet Union. In 1934, he turned his efforts to a tailless airplane for the military. The aircraft that evolved, the K-12, was a strange looking craft with a trapezoidal wing, wing tip rudders, and trailing edge elevators and ailerons. It was supposed to be a three-place bomber with gunners' positions at the front and rear.

The K-12 first flew in 1936 and demonstrated satisfactory flying qualities. Nicknamed *Firebird* by its designer, the airplane made its first public appearance at Tushino Airport on August 18, 1937, sporting a paint scheme that was at least unusual. The K-12 went into series production in 1938, and the Russians claimed it was the first tailless bomber in the world. Successful though it may have been, however, it came to the usual end for tailless aircraft; the reasons were only stated differently; Kalinin, at the peak of his career, "fell victim to the arbitrary and vicious procedures arising from Stalin's cult of personality." He was placed under arrest and his design bureau was disbanded.[10]

The BOK-5 (above) was a product of the Experimental Design Bureau. It was supposedly built as a flying scale model for the much larger Kalinin K–12 (right), but showed little resemblance to that airplane. The fabric skin of the K–12, nicknamed Firebird, *was painted a garish red for effect. The unusual airplane was billed as the world's first tailless bomber. (SI Negatives 82–938; 82–940)*

Since Kalinin's death in 1938, there has been little tangible evidence of interest in the USSR in tailless aircraft until the emergence of the delta wing following World War II. The Soviets seemed to have experienced the usual problems with stability and control encountered by their contemporaries in western Europe and America, and on the surface do not appear to have made any extraordinary breakthroughs in flying wing design.

Eastern European interest in tailless aircraft design during the pre-war period was not limited to the Soviet Union. There are several examples of such activity in Poland. As early as 1923, tailless designs appeared, initially at the First Polish Glider Contest. Of the amateur designs, two were tailless. One of these, the *Zabus* (froggy), the work of Captain Franciszek Jach, seemed reasonably conventional in concept, lacking only a vertical fin and rudder. Appearances were deceiving, however, since the control system was decidedly unconventional, even for a tailless glider. The elevator control surface was operated by the pilot's feet, and each aileron by a separate hand lever! The machine, flown by its designer, crashed after 16 seconds in the air on its only flight.

Also entered in the contest was the *Dziaba*, an aircraft so bizarre in concept and appearance that had it not been seriously damaged by wind while being carried to the starting point, a mishap on its maiden flight would not have been a surprise. It featured a variable-camber wing with a small horizontal stabilizer mounted in front of the wing on two rods. The stabilizer was operated by the camber-changing mechanism inside the wing. There were no vertical surfaces initially, although apparently two were added later. The pilot altered wing camber differentially, or on both sides of the wing together, to control the aircraft's roll or pitch. There was no landing gear; the aircraft was strapped to the pilot, who was supposed to run until airborne. The glider was repaired before the end of the contest, but the lack of wind precluded any attempt to fly.

The furturistic JN1, named after its designer Jaroslaw Naleszkiewicz, had a successful maiden flight in July 1932. It was a true tailless craft, with trailing-edge elevators and ailerons, and wing tip mounted vertical fins and rudders, both of which could be deflected to act as air brakes. Despite its success in the air, the project went no further.

Gustaw Mokrzycki's PZL22 was described as unorthodox when it was completed and readied for flight in 1934. Mokrzycki, Professor of Flight Mechanics and Aircraft Building at the Warsaw Technical University, was a far-sighted individual with a flair for the unconventional. Influenced by Lippisch's tailless aircraft from the late twenties, Mokrzycki designed a small wooden aircraft, which wind tunnel tests predicted would have good stability and flying qualities.

The airplane had a delta wing, upon which was situated a plywood nacelle with open cockpit. Control surfaces consisted of elevons and a vertical rudder hinged at the rear of the nacelle, with an American Menasco B-6 six-cylinder air-cooled engine and fixed undercarriage. Due to its unconventional nature, flight tests were not officially sanctioned and the plane was relegated to obscurity.

The dearth of successful tailless designs in Poland was not due to a lack of highly skilled aircraft designers who were willing to create imaginative designs. Rather, a combination of factors was involved: adverse political and economic circumstances, lack of wide support for its aircraft industry, bureaucratic indifference and resistance to the unorthodox (the latter situation was common in even the most highly industrialized countries).

As Hill, Lippisch, and the Hortens spearheaded serious activity involving tailless aircraft in Europe during the 1920s and 1930s, interest in the United States was minimal until the 1930s, when the idea became quite fashionable. Designs by the dozens appeared; some flew once, some often, many not at all. None attracted the requisite financial support or had the market appeal to qualify as successful commercial ventures. Not until the end of the decade did a design appear with all the necessary elements: sound design, government interest and support, and a market.

NOTES

1. "Tailless Airplane," Report No. 6826-W, Military Attaché, Paris, and "Tailless Aircraft," Report No. 6923-W, Military Attaché, Paris (France).

2. Friedman is reported to have left Soldenhoff in the early 1930s and gone to the United States where he worked for Jack Northrop; this story cannot be verified. See Giorgio Evangelisti, *Macchine Bizarre; Nella Storia dell Aviazione*, p. 106 (Switzerland).

3. "Edmund Rumpler, Airplane Expert," *New York Times*, September 10, 1940, p. 23 (Germany).

4. For an interesting account of early German soaring competitions and the test and development of gliders such as those of the Hortens, see Dr. Walter Georgii, *Ten Years Gliding and Soaring in Germany*, pp. 278–283 (Germany).

5. A sweptback wing had an inherent disadvantage. The need for high angle-of-attack attitudes during low-speed takeoff and landing conditions put both wing tips on the ground if a relatively high landing gear was not used, adding unwanted weight and structure.

6. More than half of the 90-odd aircraft that Lippisch designed in his lifetime were tailless. More than 30 reached the flying stage; of the remainder, some were tested in a wind tunnel and some were built in mockup form. See Alexander Lippisch, *The Delta Wing: History and Development* (Germany) for Lippisch's personal account of his brilliant career in aeronautical research, during which he proved the feasibility of the tailless aircraft.

7. On April 1928, the first east-to-west crossing of the Atlantic was made by Captain Köhl and two others in a Junkers monoplane, the "Bremen," from Ireland to Newfoundland.

8. In 1932, Günther Grönhoff suffered a fatal accident in a high-performance sailplane during the thirteenth Rhön Soaring Contest.

9. A.I. Salman, *Tailless Gliders of the Ninth All-Union Meet*, p. 16 (USSR).

10. N.D. Anoshchenko, editor, *History of Aviation and Cosmonautics, Vol. I*, p. 15, published in translation in NASA TT F-11, 427, November 1967 (USSR).

Chapter 3

America Discovers the Tailless Airplane

Until the 1930s, most of the developmental work with tailless aircraft had been conducted in Europe. The Wasserkuppe in the Rhön mountains in Germany particularly provided a perfect environment for the likes of Lippisch, the Hortens, Espenlaub, Grönhoff, and others to conduct the glider experiments they considered essential for flying wing development.

During the Depression, however, American engineers, inventors, and tinkerers came to appreciate the potential of tailless aircraft. With government impetus, industry and private citizens alike joined in a new-found urge to produce safe airplanes, roadable airplanes, and, understandably, in a record-breaking era, airplanes that would go farther and faster with greater payloads. It was perhaps inevitable that many far-sighted designers would see in the designs for tailless aircraft or flying wings the solutions to their problems.

One of the first American designers to capitalize on the "flying wing" mystique was Vincent J. Burnelli. In the 1920s, Burnelli produced two biplane transports with large, airfoil-shaped fuselages that contributed a considerable portion of the airplane's lift. His goal was to develop a more efficient airplane that could carry a large payload. Although Burnelli referred to his lifting body transports as "flying wings," his production aircraft invariably retained some kind of a tail, frequently supported by upswept booms that extended rearward.[1]

Burnelli's first monoplane, the CB-16, appeared in 1928. This aircraft and subsequent Burnelli types produced into the 1940s had certain features in common. The engines were close together and ahead of the cabin structure. The airfoil fuselage section, which provided 50 percent lift at cruising speed, housed the passenger cabin and the pilot's and mechanic's compartments. More than 60 percent of the weight and strength of the aircraft structure surrounded and protected the passenger cabin section for maximum resistance to telescoping. Burnelli maintained that his lifting design had unparalleled safety, economic, and operational advantages over conventional transport designs. His design philosophy was supported by many prominent civil and

Vincent J. Burnelli was known for his unattractive, but functional "lifting fuselage" transports of the 1920s and 1930s. His RB-2 of 1924 was capable of carrying 6000 pounds of freight, a remarkable feat in its day. (SI Negative 46749-a)

military aviation experts well into the late 1940s, but he failed to gain the political and economic backing that would have ensured public acceptance of his unconventional designs.

Despite Burnelli's claims to a virtual monopoly on the lifting body design, it is interesting to observe similar efforts carried on in France concurrently with Burnelli's work in the 1920s and early 1930s. Louis de Monge built a clean, lifting body monoplane with a cantilever wing in 1924, at the same time Burnelli was producing the RB-2 biplane. The de Monge 7.4 was built as a flying scale model of a proposed transatlantic airliner. In 1925, the Dyle and Bacalan shipyard at Bordeaux acquired the rights to the de Monge design and subsequently produced a variety of civil and military lifting body aircraft covering the range from twin to four-engine configurations. As the models were scaled up, however, clutter appeared in the form of struts, gun mounts, and cockpits, and performance suffered proportionally.

Shortly after Burnelli produced his first "flying fuselage" monoplane, an unusual machine with a superficial resemblance to the Burnelli appeared in the sky over the Mojave Desert, California. Jack Northrop's 1929 Flying Wing had a wing center-section thick enough to enclose the crew and the engine. Since it had a tail carried on two slender tailbooms, the aircraft was not a true flying wing, although it was widely touted as such in aviation magazines of

48

Burnelli's 1935 UB-14 represented the ultimate in construction of his airfoil fuselage design. The airfoil fuselage provided 50 percent of the total lift at cruising speed, while providing seating capacity for two pilots and 14 passengers. Two Pratt & Whitney Hornet radial engines provided 680 hp and a maximum speed of 235 mph.

the day.[2] Nonetheless, the airplane was obviously unconventional, having been built primarily as a flying laboratory to test structural innovations and unusual arrangements of various components of the airplane.[3]

The Northrop 1929 Flying Wing was designed by Jack Northrop and W.K. Jay during the latter part of 1928. Its early development and tests were carried on by the Avion Corporation, financed in part by newspaper publisher George Hearst, who was president of Avion, with Jack Northrop as vice-president. Northrop experimented with both a pusher arrangement of the Mark III Cirrus engine, specially inverted by Menasco Motors, Inc. of Los Angeles, and a Menasco A-4 four-in-line inverted engine driving a tractor propeller. In either configuration, cooling air passed through a large tunnel extending entirely through the wing from the front opening in the engine cowling to an opening just ahead of the trailing edge on the lower side of the wing. This cooling arrangement proved satisfactory, and a material reduction in drag was effected by enclosing the engine.

Initial flight tests were conducted at Muroc Dry Lake on the Mojave Desert with test pilot Eddie Bellande at the controls. Later flights were made from the United Air Terminal, Burbank, California. The aircraft demonstrated normal flight characteristics in every respect, and general performance was above average. Maximum speed was approximately 25 percent better than

Powered by two 3-cylinder, 35 hp Anzani engines, the de Monge 7.4 carried two side-by-side seats and luggage space in the wing center section. The French de Monge (later Dyle and Bacalan) aircraft of the 1920s were more technically advanced than their American Burnelli counterparts.

The 1926 Dyle and Bacalan D.B.10 applied the lifting body principle to military requirements. The D.B.10 was designed as a night bomber with pilots, forward gunner, navigating and bomber compartments, and twin 480 hp Gnome and Rhone Jupiter engines located in the thick center section of the wing. Lifting body characteristics could be found in a full range of Dyle and Bacalan military and civil aircraft types in the 1920s and 1930s.

Jack Northrop's 1929 Flying Wing was touted as such, but it still relied upon conventional rudders, ailerons and elevator for control. The all-metal airplane employed a newly developed type of structure in which the reinforced duralumin skin provided both covering and most of the structural strength of wings and tail surfaces. In this photograph the right hand cockpit has been covered up for the test flight.

The 1929 Flying Wing is shown in its twin-seat, tractor propeller configuration. The design was patented May 10, 1929 (U.S. Patent #1,929,255); experimental license was approved May 31, 1929 (Reg. #216H).

Jack Northrop discusses flight test plans with test pilot Eddie Bellande. In the pusher configuration, the propeller was connected to the engine by means of a seven-foot shaft extending between the two cockpits. Original retractable landing gear, designed by Northrop and built by Menasco Motors, was later replaced by a fixed gear in the Flying Wing. (SI Negative 74-03466)

any other design of like power and capacity. Much of the engineering data obtained during flight tests of the airplane contributed directly to the design of Northrop's first real flying wing 10 years later.

On September 22, 1930, Northrop advised the Civil Aeronautics Authority that flights with the airplane would be discontinued pending wind tunnel and laboratory tests. No further records are available for the first of Jack Northrop's flying wings. Few of the southern California aviation pioneers of the 1920s shared Jack Northrop's budding enthusiasm for the flying wing. There was one man, however, who not only believed in the concept, but may have been responsible for selling Jack Northrop on the idea.

Anthony (Tony) Stadlman was a Czechoslovakian who had immigrated to the United States in 1905 at the age of 20. In 1910, he began a career in aviation that ultimately involved him in practically every phase of the business: maintenance, construction, design, and an abbreviated but eventful stint as pilot. In 1918, Stadlman joined Loughead (pronounced Lockheed) Aircraft Manufacturing Association with the Loughead brothers, Allan and Malcolm, and a young draftsman just out of Santa Barbara High School, John K. Northrop. This association led to the development of the monocoque fuselage used so successfully in the Lockheed Vega that was to follow years later.

In 1923, three years after the dissolution of the Loughead firm, Stadlman and Northrop worked together for Donald Douglas in Santa Monica, California. For years Stadlman had been intrigued by the early efforts of J.W. Dunne to develop a successful tailless aircraft. Stadlman continued his research and study of tailless aircraft during his tenure at Douglas. Stadlman and Northrop became good friends, with Northrop eventually sharing Stadlman's enthusiasm for tailless aircraft. Working together, the two engineers built a set of wings for a tailless aircraft, a project that was never completed.

In 1926, with the anglicized spelling of Loughead now legalized, Lockheed Aircraft Corporation was back in business once again, with Allan Lockheed, Stadlman, and Northrop working together to build the famous Vega. Preoccupation with the Vega left little time to explore the potential of the flying wing. But in 1928, Northrop left Lockheed to form the Avion Corporation, and his 1929 Flying Wing soon followed. Stadlman left in 1929 to devote more time to his own flying wing designs.

Finally, in August 1929, "Tailless Tony" Stadlman enjoyed a brief but well-deserved flurry of publicity for his concept of the flying wing cargo and passenger aircraft of the future. Newspapers in San Francisco, Los Angeles, and Chicago, in August and September 1929, proclaimed Stadlman's progress in the design and construction of a flying wing that would revolutionize air transportation. Tony posed for photographs holding a model of his tailless design, a design that he and Jack Northrop had discussed and worked over during countless hours together during their Douglas and Lockheed years.

Unlike Northrop's 1929 Flying Wing, Tony Stadlman's design never got airborne. He did go on to have a very successful career in aircraft construction, but, until his death in September 1982 at age 96, he remained disappointed over the circumstances that kept him from realizing his dream of the

Anthony (Tony) Stadlman poses in 1929 with a model of his design for a tailless aircraft. There were certain obvious similarities between the Stadlman and Northrop 1929 Flying Wings. (Courtesy American Hall of Aviation History Collection, Northrop University)

A derivative of early Burgess and Dunne designs, the 1930 Arrowhead Safety Airplane was also inherently stable, weighed only 850 pounds and landed at a low 22 mph. (SI Negative 81-2832)

true flying wing. He could take some measure of satisfaction, however, from the knowledge that his ideas on tailless aircraft were appreciated by the one man whose name became synonymous with the flying wing.

A throwback to the era of Burgess and Dunne was the 1930 Arrowhead Safety Airplane. The similarity to the Burgess-Dunne designs of 1914-1916 was not coincidental, since an assistant designer on the project was one J.W. Davis, formerly of the Burgess Aircraft Company of Marblehead, Massachusetts. The builder was a former U.S. Marine Major B.L. Smith, who described his design as a flying wing that he hoped would be "economical and safe, in which pilots can be taught to fly in a short length of time at low cost."[4] The design claimed the interest of Glenn H. Curtiss, with whom Davis was connected in real estate development. Curtiss, whose interest in a roadable airplane went back to 1911, died before the first flight of the airplane, and although the Arrowhead made 34 flights by the end of 1930, interest waned and another "foolproof" airplane faded away.

> Safe flying for everybody emerged from the chrysalis of past dreams and became a living, vibrant actuality today when a new type of airplane before a throng of notables at Glenn Curtiss Airport, North Beach, Long Island, convinced the most skeptical experts that it could not dive or stall or spin—the causes of nearly all accidents.[5]

This rather dramatic press release from the Merrill Aircraft Company of New York City on February 11, 1931, announced the public demonstration of yet another "flying machine that could be landed safely under all circumstances, even with utterly inexpert piloting." The key to the aircraft's stability and control lay in its wings.

Designer Albert Merrill explained: "If we move the stabilizer forward, progressively increasing its size until it becomes a lower wing located somewhat behind the upper wing, i.e., with 'stagger' and angularity to the upper wing, i.e., 'décalage' we have a ship that is equally stable in any position."[6]

The two wings of the aircraft were not integrated with the fuselage, and the entire biplane wing structure could be tilted up or down by the pilot to a maximum angle of 14 degrees. Pitch control of the airplane was thus obtained by altering the angle of the wings relative to the fuselage rather than by altering the angle of the entire fuselage relative to the ground as is generally done with the elevator. Both wings moved as a unit; no alteration of the relation of upper and lower wings was possible. By limiting the lower and upper limits of wing travel with mechanical stops, safe flight was more or less assured within the range of practical flying.

According to Merrill: "So long as you fly within these limits nothing can stall or nose the machine and this means safety!" If the occasion arose when it was necessary to exceed the limits of wing movement, as in an emergency or to perform aerobatics, an elevator was available for control. There was, however, no fixed horizontal tail surface.[7]

Albert Merrill had been experimenting in aeronautics since 1894, when he first became associated with Octave Chanute, Samuel P. Langley, and Otto Lilienthal, all members of the Boston Aeronautical Society. After a near-fatal

Twelve years of research and testing by Albert Merrill led to this experimental movable-wing biplane, renowned for its safety features. In the upper photograph, the wings have been rotated so that they are at the highest angle of incidence, with the bottom wing forward, and the top wing aft. In the lower photograph, the wings have been rotated to the other extreme, i.e., the lowest angle of incidence. The bottom wing is aft, the top wing is now forward. Safe flight was assured between these two extremes.

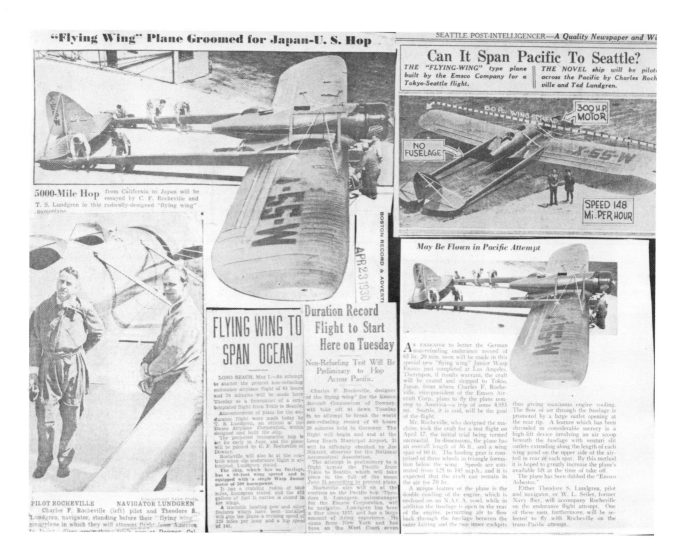

This montage of newspaper clippings reflects the publicity accorded Charles Rocheville's projected transpacific record attempt in his Emsco B-8 Flying Wing in 1930. (SI Negative 81-11257)

flying accident in 1911, Merrill became convinced that the conventional control system was wrong, and he devoted many years to designing, building, and testing experimental aircraft to prove his theories. The first of these was a tailless, tractor biplane with a pronounced stagger. Though not a complete success it did show distinct possibilities; inherent stability was obtained within a limited flying range.

Merrill's efforts to design a longitudinally stable, yet fully controllable, airplane continued during his tenure as a faculty member at California Institute of Technology. Tailless gliders were built to test his theories of control. One such glider prompted an exchange of correspondence in 1924 between Professor Merrill and rocket pioneer Robert H. Goddard, who at the time was performing the research that led to the world's first liquid propellent rocket in 1926. Merrill prevailed upon Goddard to furnish drawings for a 60-pound thrust rocket for one of his tailless gliders, the purpose of which would be to extend the glider's soaring endurance while waiting for the "next gust." In response, Goddard recommended a light reciprocating engine as a power source. Undaunted, Merrill repeated his original request, but Goddard never did the drawing.

A more conventional combination of power plant and airframe evolved in 1926 with Merrill's first movable-wing biplane. Further research on various wing combinations led to refined biplane models in 1928 and 1931, and a monoplane followed soon thereafter.

Despite the "gasps of wonder" which public demonstrations of Merrill's fool-proof airplane generally evoked from the audience, financial support never really materialized for the project. After an absence from Cal Tech, Merrill returned there and remained until his retirement. He died in 1952, respected by his peers as a pioneer aviation enthusiast and professional aerodynamicist.

Not all designers were seeking the safe, fool-proof airplane. Charles F. Rocheville and Clare K. Vance sought exceptional range, endurance, and payload, and in so doing, followed in the footsteps of Burnelli. Rocheville was a designer, inventor, entrepreneur, and pilot. Among the many innovative aircraft designs he produced was his 1930 Emsco B-8 Flying Wing, designed while he was vice president of Emsco Aircraft Corporation. A twin-boom configuration was used to connect a single-fin empennage to a 60-foot wing, upon which perched a streamlined nacelle with tandem cockpits. Equipped with reverse tricycle landing gear, the aircraft employed an unusual "blown wing" system, in which air was inducted aft of the engine cowling, carried through the wing, and ejected out of slots set one-third of the way forward of the trailing edge.

Clare Vance's flying wing carried 1200 gallons of fuel in its thick center section, sufficient for a non-stop range of 7500 miles. Vance designed and built the craft from models whittled out of wood while he flew the mail across the mountains. (SI Negative 79-11309)

Dr. Snyder's first aircraft was known as the Dirigiplane, Monowing, and finally Arup S-1, at various stages of its development. Rudders are at the after edges of the vertical stabilizers; elevator extends across the wing trailing edge; ailerons are at the top of the vertical stabilizer, forward.

Auxiliary ailerons were added to each wing tip of the Arup S-2 to supplement those on the trailing edge of the wing. First flown in April 1933, Arup S-2 had a top speed of 97 mph, stalled at an amazingly low 23 mph. (SI Negative 81-2542)

Rocheville intended to improve the existing non-refueled endurance record of 65 hours 20 minutes; he would follow this feat with an attempted nonstop flight from Japan to America, a distance of almost 5000 miles. Despite favorable flight tests, the project was terminated in 1930 for financial reasons before any record attempts could be accomplished.

Two years later, renowned air mail pilot Clare K. Vance unveiled his own version of a flying wing that bore a superficial resemblance to the Emsco aircraft. The Vance airplane was not as technologically advanced as the Emsco, but seemed well suited as a long-haul freight carrier. Vance claimed a top speed of 200 mph and fuel capacity for a 7500 mile range. After a successful series of test flights, Vance competed unsuccessfully in the 1932 Bendix Trophy race before his death in December 1932. The airplane was subsequently modified and was entered in, but did not complete, the 1933 and 1934 Bendix races.[8]

A podiatrist from South Bend, Indiana, was responsible for one of the more distinctive and successful tailless designs of the Depression. Dr. C.L. Snyder, intrigued with the flying qualities of a felt heel lift that he had idly tossed through the air one day in 1926, pursued his idea from the primitive model stage to unpowered and powered gliders, and finally to several highly successful disc-type aircraft.

Like Junkers, Soldenhoff, and Rumpler, Snyder's goal was to develop of the flying wing for air transport purposes. He envisioned an aircraft with a wing 15 feet thick with a 100-foot span and a 100-foot chord. The passengers were

Arup S-4 (foreground) demonstrates the practicality of a low aspect ratio wing. Both Arup S-2 (background) and the S-4 were frequently used as flying billboards during their accident-free careers. (SI Negative 81-2549)

to be seated in the wing with a clear view forward through the plastic leading edge of the wing. Snyder's early glider experiments led to the formation of the Arup Manufacturing Corporation in 1932 to refine his initial experimental configuration to a practical aircraft. Aided by the engineering skills of Raoul Hoffman[9] and with Glenn Doolittle (racing pilot Jimmie Doolittle's cousin) acting as test pilot, Dr. Snyder produced three more variations of the basic disc-shaped Arup S-1 powered glider. Of the three, Arup S-2 and S-4 proved to be more durable and practical, making hundreds of flights during the mid-1930s, including impressive demonstration flights for the NACA, CAA, and the Army.

The Arup experienced an accident-free service life. Some of its pronounced advantages over more conventional aircraft were greater lift and safety, increased cruising range, lower takeoff and landing speeds, and stall-proof flight characteristics. Dr. Snyder's Arups were not commercial successes, however. He had inadequate working capital, inexperienced management, and an aircraft that just did not "look right."

Raoul Hoffman, Dr. C.L. Snyder's engineer at Arup, left that company in 1933 and moved to Florida where he designed an Arup-type aircraft for a Chicago industrialist. The Hoffman flying wing, like the Arups, had performance figures that were guaranteed to appeal to those citizens who wanted to replace the family automobile with an "air flivver." Unfortunately, Hoffman's aircraft caught fire in flight from a broken fuel line and crashed, killing the pilot.

Built in St. Petersburg, Florida, this unusual tailless aircraft resembled the Arup disc designs. A 1934 design by former Arup engineer Raoul Hoffman, the wing was a semicircle to which floating tip-controllers were added to serve as ailerons. Elevators were located in the wing's trailing edge.

Batwing Aircraft Company, headed by Walter F. McGinty, constructed this tailless model in the late 1930s. Vertical surfaces at the wing tips served as rudders and airbrakes. Wing-mounted elevons acted as elevators and ailerons. The craft was similar in appearance to Waldo Waterman's Arrowbile, but was not roadable. A twin-engine design was projected but not built.

Walter F. McGinty of Batwing Aircraft Company also had an eye on the "air flivver" market. His X-1, a two-place tailless aircraft, featured a hydraulic extension of the nose gear to facilitate landing and taking off in a restricted space. Powered by a 40-hp Pobjoy engine, the aircraft was reported to have gotten just one foot off the ground at the end of a 6000-foot runway!

Neither Arup, Hoffman, nor McGinty developed the first truly functional flying automobile. The credit for this remarkable achievement is generally given to Waldo D. Waterman of California, who for many years had visualized the development of a simple, safe, and cheap airplane for the average private pilot. Waterman felt the solution lay in a design based on the tailless concept.[10] In 1932, he built an aircraft that was not only the first successful tailless monoplane in the United States, but was the first step toward a practical design for a tailless aircraft that could also be adapted to a flying automobile.

Waterman's 1932 prototype, nicknamed "Whatsit" for its unconventional nature, led to the 1935 "Arrowplane" designed and built for the U.S. Department of Commerce Safety Airplane competition. Powered by a Menasco C-4 95-hp engine, it was flown from Santa Monica to Washington, D.C., in July

1935, winning an award for Waterman. Once the airworthiness of the design had been proven, Waterman turned to the task of adapting the design for surface use. The first "Arrowbile" was completed and flown by Waterman on February 21, 1937. It proved to be stable, difficult to spin or stall, and possessed all the maneuverability required for normal flying. Equally important, the airplane conformed to laws for operation on the highways. Waterman's financial problems and poor health, and World War II, interrupted the orderly development of the "Arrowbile," but a final variant, the "Aerobile" appeared in 1957. The "Aerobile" was a three-place machine with a liquid-cooled Franklin engine and a single-piece wing. A one-of-a-kind aircraft, the "Aerobile" was flown successfully many times before it joined the "Whatsit" at the National Air and Space Museum in 1961.

John D. Akerman's tailless aircraft of 1936 deserves a passing mention if only to illustrate the wide diversity of factors that led to construction of such aircraft. Akerman, a professor in the Department of Aeronautical Engineering at the University of Minnesota, did not design a tailless aircraft for inherent stability or safety of flight, nor did he want a flying automobile or transoceanic airliner. He designed his tailless airplane to provide employment under the Public Works Administration work program for several airplane mechanics and some aeronautical engineering students!

Akerman's selection of a tailless design was motivated by his opinion that a real tailless aircraft had never been built in the United States or England. He discounted the work of Dunne, Hill, and Waterman, because the wings were so swept back that the wing tips were, in effect, two tails. Akerman acknowledged the work of Germany's Alexander Lippisch with the delta concept, and incorporated the delta shape in his airplane.

The Akerman design consisted of wing tip rudders, elevons, and center section flaps that were used in conjunction with the elevons for pitch control. The center section flaps, which were controlled by a lever in the cockpit, could also be used to trim the airplane for balanced flight. The wing, which was a modified delta, had a fixed leading edge slot.

One brief, harrowing flight was made by Professor Akerman at Wold Chamberlain airport in Minneapolis, Minnesota in 1936. Once airborne, the aircraft appeared to fly normally in straight and level flight at an altitude of 15 feet. Unfortunately, a news cameraman following along the runway created the possibility of a collision, so Akerman prudently cut the engine and landed. University officials were highly upset, fearing that the professor had exposed the University to possible liability by flying the experimental aircraft without proper qualifications. It was the beginning and the end of the Akerman tailless airplane. There were no more flights; the airplane was placed in storage, and another brief episode in the history of tailless aircraft came to a close. As a tribute to the pioneering efforts of Professor Akerman, the airplane was refurbished and donated to the Smithsonian Institution in 1970.

In 1937 the Management and Research, Inc. Model H-70-71 (NX-20399) tailless monoplane was manufactured for the U.S. Department of Commerce. It was one of many prototypes that appeared briefly in the thirties. The air-

Waldo Waterman's Arrowbile (right) was completed in February 1937, and was successfully flight tested. Waterman had to design a gear reduction system to transmit power to the rear wheels, a declutchable propeller, and detachable wings. He was also required to conduct extensive road tests (below). The Arrowbile also featured a Studebaker automobile engine, radiator, dashboard instruments, and body trim.

Professor John D. Akerman conducts taxi tests in his experimental tailless aircraft in 1936. During its single test flight, the radical design demonstrated normal takeoff characteristics, satisfactory horizontal flight, good lateral control, and good stall characteristics during landing.

Test pilot James B. (Jimmie) Taylor inspects the tailless Management and Research Model H–70–71 monoplane at Floyd Bennett Field, New York, on April 15, 1938. The aircraft had crashed on January 27, 1938, and had been subsequently rebuilt by Tuscar Metals, Inc. prior to resumption of the flight test program at Floyd Bennett Field. (Courtesy Rudy Arnold; SI Negative 81–13688)

plane was a derivative of the 1936 Stearman-Hammond Y, a product of the Bureau of Air Commerce light plane development program. The wing was nearly rectangular, with two pairs of flap-type controllers fitted in the straight trailing edge. A pair of rudders were mounted over each wing. Powered by a Menasco 95-hp engine, the aircraft allegedly had a top speed of 100 mph.

The airplane had an undistinguished flying career. Although official Civil Aeronautic Administration certificates indicate NX-20399 was owned by Management and Research, Inc. until its destruction in August 1945, the aircraft was referred to in the press, and in some Department of Commerce papers, as the Tuscar Metals, Inc. Model H-71. Regardless of proper ownership, the airplane proved difficult to fly, and required the skilled hands of one of America's most distinguished test pilots, Jimmie Taylor, at the controls during much of the flight test program. By November 1944, it had accumulated about 50 to 60 hours of flying time, and less than a year later, was totally destroyed in a crash in August 1945, thus ending its service life without making any significant impact on flying wing design.

Notwithstanding the efforts of Waterman, Snyder, Hoffman, and others, tailless aircraft were not accepted in the marketplace. Neither government nor industry displayed the sustained interest or provided the timely support that would have ensured some success.

NOTES

1. In April 1948, Burnelli testified before the U.S. House of Representatives Appropriations Committee on the merits of a "lifting body" transport for U.S. Air Force use. He testified: "The fundamental principle of the flying wing is based on body lift. It does not matter how the configuration is. So long as the body lift is a part of the system, it can be called a 'flying wing'. The pure flying wing is idealism."

In a later exchange during the hearings, in response to a question as to whether he was the inventor of the flying wing, Burnelli replied: "According to the Smithsonian Institution and the Patent Office, I am. They are experts." The Smithsonian denied that they had so credited Burnelli.

2. Regarding longitudinal and directional control for the aircraft, Northrop knew it might have been possible to provide the necessary stability by using enlarged sweepback and movable wing tips, as in the Dunne or Hill types. He reasoned the efficiency of such an arrangement would be poor, and because of his lack of previous design experience with such an arrangement, the resultant controllability of the whole airplane would be very questionable. Consequently, he used outriggers extending to the rear of the wing to solve the problem.

3. The design is best described in Jack Northrop's own words:

> The design, when completed, turned out to be about as queer a looking machine as one could wish to see. Those who have been associated with it for a year and a half have begun to get used to the appearance, but a newcomer is generally at a loss for words of comparison, and it is suspected that we very rarely hear the true opinion of those who see the machine, as it generally is muttered under one's breath.

See John K. Northrop, "The Flying Wing," pp. 46–49 (U.S., Northrop).

4. Cecil R. Warren, "The Arrowhead Safety Plane," p. 13 (U.S., Non-Northrop).

5. Merrill Aircraft Co. press release, "Merrill Aircraft Demonstration: Flight at Glenn Curtiss Airport," February 11, 1931, p. 1.

6. Albert Merrill, *The C.I.T. 9 Preliminary Report*, p. 1, (U.S., Non-Northrop).

7. Ibid., p. 2.

8. Flying the night mail across the mountains of California, Vance missed clearing a ridge by 10 feet and died in the resulting crash. Few pilots of the time could have matched Vance's 10,000 hours in the air, more than 2500 at night, accumulated during years of flying the mail under the most demanding conditions. See Truman Weaver, *Sixty-Two Rare Racing Airplanes from the Golden Years of Aviation*, p. 66 (U.S., Non-Northrop), for details on subsequent development of the Vance flying wing.

9. Raoul Hoffman was a German engineer who had previously worked for Emil M. (Matty) Laird, designer of the Laird Solution and other famous racing airplanes of the thirties. Hoffman also worked on the giant L.W.F. Engineering Corporation's Owl transport.

10. According to Waterman, one intriguing feature of the tailless design was that by the elimination of the tail structure, some reduction in weight, head resistance, and cost would result, and that through the reduction in weight and head resistance, aerodynamic efficiency would be gained. The fact that the tailless airplane without its wings would take the form of a streamlined coupe and that the design lent itself admirably to the efficient use of the pusher propeller, which in turn greatly increased visibility and made possible certain safety features, convinced him that the development of a plane of this type, with the ultimate idea of its becoming a flying automobile, was a logical step.

Chapter 4

The War Years

With the outbreak of World War II in 1939, the outlook for flying wing development improved immeasurably. On both sides of the Atlantic, governments were more than willing to gamble funds and manpower in a search for the right combination of weapons and aircraft that could mean the difference between victory and defeat in the air war ahead. Most of the governments that were at war took a few tentative steps in the direction of tailless fighters, but only one aircraft of the type, the Messerschmitt Me 163, was used in combat. In the United States, only Jack Northrop worked vigorously to build a flying wing, but it was not until a year after the war that the first of his giant aircraft made its maiden flight. In Germany, despite the exigencies of war, the Hortens continued to create a series of imaginative flying wing designs that culminated in the world's first turbojet-powered flying wing. The Lippisch-designed Me 163 became the world's first operational tailless fighter.

Following their success with the prewar Ho III series, the Hortens designed and built the first model officially sponsored by the German government. In the 1941 Ho IV, the Horten brothers doubled the aspect ratio of the Ho III to about 22:1. The glider featured a plywood-covered steel tube inner section containing the cockpit, in which the pilot assumed a semi-prone position to reduce drag as much as possible. This "praying mantis" position, in which the upper part of the pilot's body was horizontally inclined 30 degrees, was restful on long test flights, one of which exceeded nine hours. The wings were made of wood with fabric covering except for the outer six feet, which were made of aluminum. Using a retractable type of skid landing gear, the Ho IV took off on a wheel attached to a wooden skid. After takeoff, the wheel dropped automatically when the skid was retracted. There were no vertical surfaces on the wing, and a complex control system was employed, consisting of dive brakes that moved out at right angles to the wing surface, drag rudders, and three elevons along each trailing edge.

A variant of this aircraft was the Ho IVB, which incorporated a laminar flow airfoil with a plastic leading edge. The airfoil section was based on data obtained from wind tunnel tests of a captured P-51 Mustang fighter. Unfortu-

Arranged from left to right are models of four significant Horten designs: the pre-war Ho II and Ho III, the 1941 Ho IV, and the single-seat, 1942 Ho V.

nately, the Ho IVB suffered from bad stalling characteristics and eventually crashed after a spin, killing the pilot. Nonetheless, the basic Ho IV, developed for distance soaring, attained a very high performance level, having been tested in extensive flight trials totalling more than 1000 hours.

The Ho V, built in 1937, was the first of the Horten craft designed from the outset as a powered airplane and was the first Horten wing of sufficient size and capacity to demonstrate the commercial or military value of this type. The 1937 Ho V had two side-by-side cockpits and was powered by two Hirth HM 60R 80 hp-engines. This version was rebuilt in 1942 as a single-seater and was extensively flight tested in 1943. The Ho V, which in many respects resembled Jack Northrop's N-1M and N-9M flying wings of the same period, had a simple control system with two moving surfaces at each trailing edge, landing flaps beneath the center section, and spoilers at the wing tips.

A second version of the Ho V was constructed largely of plastic using considerable sandwich material. Plastic sheeting was used for wing covering and rib webs, plastic laminate for main spar booms and stringers, and wood for rib booms. On its maiden flight, this aircraft was badly damaged in a rough landing made in high winds. A third version of the Ho V, a glider tug, was proposed but never built.

Even more unconventional than most Horten designs, the Horten Parabola had a quarter-moon shape with two parabolas meeting at the wing tips. The wing was relatively thick at the center, and the outer panels tapered to the tips without dihedral. Only one of this model was built, and it was intentionally destroyed after moisture warped the very light structure.

The Ho VI that followed had the high aspect ratio of the Ho IV, but had a wingspan of slightly over 78 feet, 13 feet greater than that of the Ho IV. With an aspect ratio of 32.4:1, the glider was built strictly for research and was not considered practical for private ownership. According to Walter Horten, the Ho VI behaved extremely well in tests, although it was too advanced for ordi-

Initially constructed as a two-seater, the Ho V was rebuilt about 1942 as a single seater. Two moving control surfaces were on each trailing edge with landing flaps beneath the center section. (Courtesy Heinz Nowarra)

nary soaring practice and demanded great skill from the pilot.

Two models of the Ho VI were built, one of which was destroyed. The other was captured by the Allies and eventually delivered to the Northrop Aeronautical Institute in the United States for study and evaluation.

A more powerful successor to the twin-engined Ho V was the Ho VII, which was equipped with two 240-hp Argus AS 10C engines. Directional control of the aircraft was accomplished with wooden drag bars, mounted on rollers behind and parallel to the spar tip. Moving the rudder pedals moved one of the bars out of the wing tip to cause drag, a concept that proved unsatisfactory in flight. The Ho VII, designed to familiarize Luftwaffe pilots with flight characteristics of flying wings, was considered by Walter Horten to be the brothers' most successful aircraft. Reimar Horten tells the following anecdote concerning single engine performance of the Ho VII:

> Göring wanted a demonstration of the single engine performance of the Ho VII. Heinz Scheidhauer flew to Oranienburg (Berlin) and made several low passes in front of the Reichsmarshal. The temperature of the day was 14 degrees F and Scheidhauer was unable to restart the dead engine with the compressed air starter following the demonstration. In preparing for a single engine landing he discovered that the landing gear would not lock down, since the hydraulic pump was installed on the dead engine. With the gear half extended he made a single engine go-around, then discovered that the emergency compressed air gear extension system did not work either, since the air supply was depleted in the unsuccessful engine start attempts. The Ho VII ended up on its belly in the landing.[1]

Dr. Horten adds: "It's a shame. He had an hour of fuel left, and could have flown around for a while, and charged his air bottle with the operating en-

Shown on the ground (right), the Ho VI was a research glider with an extremely high aspect ratio of 32.4:1. Constructed of wood and metal, the craft was considered by Walter Horten to be the highest performance sailplane of its day. The bird-like aircraft soars dramatically over the German countryside (below). (Courtesy Vintage Sailplane Association; SI Negatives 80-19283, 80-19277)

gine." But Göring was satisfied.[2] By March 1945, one Ho VII was completed and undergoing tests, another was nearing completion, and eighteen more were on order.

The most ambitious of the Horten wartime projects was the mammoth Ho VIII, an aircraft with a 158-foot wing span, and six BMW 600-hp engines driving pusher propellers. It could accommodate about 60 passengers in the wing center section. With an anticipated range of about 3700 miles, the airplane appeared to be slated for the postwar commercial market, but could possibly have been used as a military transport. Construction was not completed by the end of the war. Many years later, Reimar Horten designed an-

Dr. Walter Horten considered this Ho VII with two 240 hp Argus engines to be the Horten brothers' most successful craft. It was to be used to familiarize pilots with the characteristics of powered tailless aircraft. Only one was completed and test flown about March 1945. (Courtesy Heinz Nowarra)

The world's first turbojet-powered flying wing, the Ho IX V2, is prepared for flight tests somewhere in Germany in January 1945. (SI Negative SI 77-14586)

other tailless transport for the *Argentina Institute Aerotecnico*. Faintly reminiscent of the defunct Ho VIII, the I.A. 38 was about two-thirds the size of the Ho VIII, was initially powered by four 450-hp Gaucho engines and had a large compartment beneath the wing center section that could hold up to six tons of cargo. The aircraft eventually flew on December 9, 1960, but development was hampered by engine cooling problems, and the program was eventually terminated.

By far the most advanced Horten design, and the first one intended for combat use, was the Ho IX jet fighter. Patterned after the conventionally powered Ho V, the radical Ho IX first flew as an unpowered glider in the summer of 1944. The aircraft consisted of a welded steel tube center section and wood for the outer panels with plywood covering, a method of construction that was basic to all Horten craft. Reimar Horten described the construction:

> The inexperienced workers available in 1944–45 could more easily be trained to work with wood, as long as the design was kept simple and primitive. Control rods and wires were inside the spar, fuel was kept in the space in front and behind. Fuel resistant glue and varnish were used, and fuel was pumped right into the wood structure without any kind of liners or bladders. Glue could be mixed with sawdust and applied over varnished surfaces to fill imperfections. The wing skin was up to 17 mm thick; with a more refined construction, 6 mm would have been sufficient.
>
> The wood construction had some additional benefits; for instance the aircraft was almost invisible on radar. The wood panels even diffused the returns from the top mounted engines sufficiently to make radar gun sights useless. A second advantage was the minimal damage a 20 mm shell would do when it exploded inside the wing. A hole would be made, and a few ribs damaged, but the aircraft could still fly. A similar explosion inside the metal wing of a Me 109 would deform the wing so that the aircraft could not fly.[3]

Steel plates protected the upper surface of the Ho IX wing from the hot jet engine exhaust. The entire trailing edge of the wing consisted of three control surfaces on each side, with outer and center surfaces giving lateral and longitudinal control, and the inner surfaces acting primarily as landing flaps. Directional control was provided by one large and one small air brake flap located above and below the outer wing. The large air brake flap did not operate until the smaller flap had fully extended, resulting in smoother control than with previous systems. Unique features of the pilot's cockpit included a seat catapult escape device and a control stick, the pivot point of which could be adjusted to increase mechanical advantage for high speed flight.

The second model, designated Ho IX V2, was completed in late 1944. Equipped with two 1890-pound thrust Junkers Jumo 004B turbojet engines, the world's first turbojet-powered flying wing flew in January 1945. The famous German soaring pilot Erwing Ziller was at the controls. While initial flight tests were encouraging, tragedy occurred after only two hours of accumulated flight time. Ziller was killed during an unsuccessful single-engine landing. Nonetheless, with the enthusiastic support of Reichsmarshal Hermann Göring, preparations were made for mass production of the aircraft by Gothaer Waggonfabrik A.G. Accordingly, the third prototype was designated

The Gotha Go 229 (Ho IX) as it appeared after capture by United States forces at war's end. The turbojet engines exhausted over the upper surfaces of the wings, which were protected by metal plates. The sturdy tricycle landing gear retracted into the wing, the center section of which was built up from welded steel tubing, with the outer section made of wood with plywood covering. Outer wing sections are missing in these photographs. (SI Negatives 72-3579; A38635-a)

Go 229 (Ho IX V3) and was built at the Gotha factory. The aircraft was virtually completed when the workshops were overrun by Allied forces, thus terminating any further development of the series. The completed Go 229 was ultimately sent to the National Air and Space Museum in the United States and will eventually be restored. Several other Horten wings were under construction as the war drew to a close, but none reached the flight stages.

The Horten brothers made technical achievements through initiative, imagination, and tenacity. Although none of their designs were used in combat, their contribution to the growing body of knowledge on the intricacies of flying wing design was considerable, and they must be ranked with the leading pioneers in the field.

Like the Hortens, Alexander Lippisch spent the war researching the military applications for tailless aircraft. While the Horten designs were not produced in sufficient quantity to have any significant, lasting impact, one of Lippisch's designs was the most startling and revolutionary aircraft of World War II.

The DFS 194 was built in 1937. Lippisch conducted ground tests with a Walter rocket engine installed in 1940, followed by the first rocket-propelled flight in August of that year. Eventually, the world's first rocket-powered fighter evolved, the Me 163A, derived directly from the Lippisch Delta IVC-DFS39.

A remarkable accumulation of highly imaginative designs continued to pour out of Lippisch's Department "L" at Messerschmitt during the early years of World War II. Fighters, bombers, and trainers, all tailless, came equipped with piston engines, turbojets, or rocket engines, or combinations thereof. Some reached the model or mockup stage but none, other than the Me 163A or its derivatives, ever reached flight test.

In May 1943, Lippisch became Director of the *Luftfahrtforschungsanstalt Wien* (LFW, Aeronautic Research Institute, Vienna) where he began research on the development of supersonic aircraft. Efforts centered around the use of the ramjet engine as the propulsion unit. Project P12 was conducted under the most arduous circumstances, with Allied bombing a constant threat. Shortages of strategic materials and skilled engineering personnel hampered the orderly progression of research programs. Nonetheless, the P12 and P13 reached the model stage, with wind tunnel and free-flight tests showing enough promise to warrant construction of a ramjet-powered manned aircraft.

With the end of the war imminent, the project had only reached the manned glider stage. A full-size glider model of the P13 ramjet interceptor was constructed to investigate low speed characteristics of the aircraft. Designated DM-1, the glider was not finished by the end of the war. However, at the instigation of Dr. Theodore von Kármán,[4] construction of the DM-1 was completed and it was shipped to the United States for testing.

The DM-1 was tested in the National Advisory Committee for Aeronautics (NACA) Langley full-scale wind tunnel in 1946.[5] Eight different configurations of the model were tested, with modifications of the wing leading edges,

Originally built in 1937 as an experimental prototype of a tailless fighter, the Lippisch-designed DFS 194 was later modified for installation of a liquid-fuel rocket engine. The DFS 194 was subsequently used as a test bed for the Walter engine, flying at speeds up to 342 mph; successful flight tests led to increased priority for development of the Me 163, world's first rocket-powered fighter. (Courtesy U.S. Air Force)

Alexander Lippisch's work with tailless aircraft during the 1930s led directly to the most revolutionary operational fighter of World War II, the Messerschmitt Me 163 Komet. Shown here is one of the B-series prototypes, the Me 163BV2, which made its first rocket-powered flight on June 24, 1943. (Courtesy National Archives)

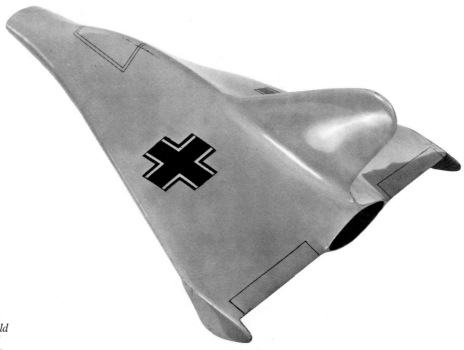

Project P12, shown (right) in model form, was to be an experimental aircraft equipped with a ramjet engine. Since ramjet engines do not produce thrust at zero speed, the aircraft would have to be accelerated to flying speed either by a "piggyback" arrangement or rocket assisted takeoff. The Lippisch DM-1 (below) was constructed as a glider to test the low speed flying qualities of a ramjet-powered interceptor. Wind tunnel tests were conducted in the United States after the war, but the aircraft was never flight tested. (Courtesy U.S. Air Force; SI Negative A4404-c)

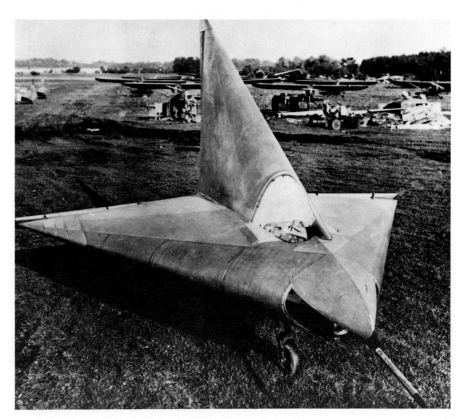

the vertical and horizontal stabilizers, and the control surfaces made to determine lift, drag, and stability characteristics. Initial tests were disappointing; lift coefficient was low, drag was high, directional stability was unsatisfactory, and the craft was considered unsafe for flight tests. In the final analysis, however, after suitable modifications, results indicated that delta wing airplanes with 60 degree sweepback and sharp leading edges could be designed to have acceptable stability characteristics at subcritical speeds.

The DM-1 was Lippisch's last tangible effort for a dying cause. In 1946 he moved to the United States where after a few years of government service, he joined Collins Radio Company as an expert on special aeronautical problems. In 1966, he founded Lippisch Research Corporation and developed the X-113A Aerofoil Boat.

Alexander Lippisch died in 1976. He did not have an aircraft company named after him, only one of his designs was produced in quantity, and even it did not bear his name. But his experiments paved the way for the thousands of aircraft bearing the distinctive Lippisch imprint that have routinely flown in the high speed regime originally explored by Lippisch.

A general discussion of German designs for tailless aircraft and flying wings must include a brief description of some designs that were still on the drawing board at the conclusion of World War II. Encouraged by the successes of the Horten series and the spectacular performance of the Lippisch-inspired Me 163 Komet, German designers produced a series of futuristic designs in the final chaotic days of the war. If the old maxim that says if an airplane looks right, it will fly right is true, then very few of those unconventional designs would have lifted off the runway. Among the many improbable combinations of sweepback, sweepforward, variable sweep, asymmetrical arrangements, ventral and dorsal fins, and butterfly tails, there appeared a few seemingly practical configurations, some with characteristics that would appear in the post-war designs of other countries.

In the latter part of 1944, the high command of the Luftwaffe issued an urgent requirement for an improved single-engine jet fighter with performance equal to or surpassing that of the twin-engined Messerschmitt Me 262. Specifications required that the new fighter be powered by a single Heinkel-Hirth 109-011A turbojet, have a level flight speed of 621 mph at 23,000 feet, a service ceiling of 46,000 feet, and be armed with four MK 108 30-mm cannons.

Among the more plausible proposals submitted in response to the Luftwaffe requirement was the Messerschmitt P.1111, a wood and metal tailless fighter that resembled a streamlined, sleek Me 163. Powered by the 2866-pound thrust Heinkel-Hirth 109A-011A turbojet, the aircraft featured wing-mounted controls consisting of elevons, inboard split flaps and outboard leading-edge slats, and theoretically was capable of speeds over 600 mph.

The Heinkel response to the request for proposals was a step or two further away from the conventional direction of the Messerschmitt submissions. The Heinkel P.1078 was originally projected in three versions designated P.1078A, B, and C. The P.1078C, the preferred version, was a jet-propelled tailless aircraft with the cockpit situated over the single air intake, with cannon located

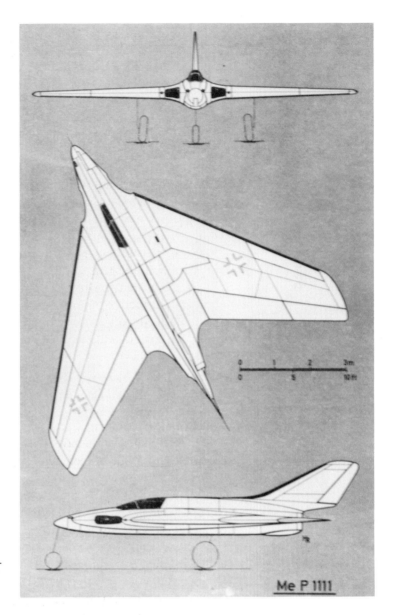

Me P 1111

German aerodynamicists showed a preoccupation with tailless aircraft during the closing days of WW II. Representative of the scores of futuristic designs was the Messerschmitt P.1111, a fairly realistic looking jet fighter in the 600 mph category.

on each side of the cockpit. The wing tips were drooped like those on Northrop's N-1M.

Other Heinkel designs of the 1944-1945 period included the P.1079, a two-seat night-fighter with two turbojet engines installed, and the P.1080, a single-place tailless fighter built around two ramjets delivering an estimated 3440 pounds of thrust at 621 mph. Takeoff thrust was provided by four solid-fuel rockets.

In the same class with the Messerschmitt and Heinkel designs, but a bit more exotic, were the Blohm and Voss P.212 and the Junkers EF 128.

In the best tradition of Dunne and Hill, British interest in the tailless aircraft concept also persisted throughout the war, and was evident in the designs of Handley Page, Armstrong Whitworth, General Aircraft Ltd., and de Havilland. A rather undistinguished model of the period, with a decidedly checkered service life, was the Handley Page Manx. Dr. Gustav V. Lachman designed a craft which, like its feline namesake, bore only the vestige of a tail, a single vertical fin on the rear of the centrally mounted fuselage. Wing-tip vertical fins and rudders, two pusher in-line engines, slats, elevons, and split flaps, completed the configuration. The airplane was delivered for testing in 1939, but it was found to be 3300 pounds overweight. Its weight was reduced and the joints of the main spar were partially reworked because of deterioration of the glue. Taxi tests in 1942 resulted in damage to the nose gear. Repairs and further modifications to the basic design ensued. There were several unsuccessful attempts to fly; on one occasion, the aircraft hit a bump on the runway and rose to a height of 12 feet.

Finally, the Manx flew what could be called its maiden flight on June 11, 1943. It was an inauspicious beginning; the pilot aborted the flight after ten minutes due to a lost canopy. The flight was symptomatic of a test program that was plagued by fits and starts, accumulating about 17 hours flight time in some 30 flights. The airplane was eventually scrapped in 1952, due to fading interest in the concept following the extended development program.

A slightly more orthodox approach to tailless aircraft was taken by General Aircraft Ltd., which had been interested in the development of tailless aircraft since 1934. During the war, the company, which merged with Blackburn Aircraft, Ltd. in 1949, planned to build four tailless gliders having differing planforms with various degrees of backward sweep; all wings had common attachment points for anchorage on a standard nacelle. Designed from 1943 to 1947, three were built under the designation of G.A.L. 56. The fourth of the series, designated G.A.L. 61, more closely approached the all-wing concept in that it was equipped with retractable landing gear and, in the absence of fins and rudders, directional control was achieved by drag rudders. The only appendage was a small pilot's canopy.

Captain Eric M. Brown, R.N. (retired), former Chief Naval Test Pilot at the Royal Aircraft Establishment, Farnborough, England, flew over 480 different types of aircraft during a brilliant career. The G.A.L. 56 did not rank at the top of his list of aircraft that were pleasurable to fly:

> It was one plane in which I found I could not relax for a second, beginning right away with takeoff. You could not lift it off the ground through the slipstream of the towing aircraft before the latter was airborne, which was the normal method, because as soon as it was clear of the ground effect—the cushion of air between wing tip and ground—the centre of pressure suddenly shifted and the machine dived straight back into the ground, to bounce on its very springy undercarriage wildly across the airstrip. And it had the most incredible stalling characteristics. When you eased the nose up to slow the speed down, the plane suddenly took charge and continued to rear nose up until it was in a tail slide. Even pushing the stick right on to the dash made no difference. Then suddenly the stick movement would take effect and you would be pitched forward to fall almost vertically. General Aircraft decided to

The Manx was typical of many ill-fated tailless aircraft projects undertaken by most of the participants in World War II. Built in Great Britain by Handley Page Ltd., the Manx featured two pusher in-line engines, wing tip vertical fins and rudders, and a vertical fin on the aft fuselage for stability. Taxi tests began in February 1940, and the test program stretched on with frequent interruptions until termination in 1946 after about 17 hours of flight.

Representative of the G.A.L. 56 gliders was this G.A.L. 56/03 Maximum V, with 36.4 degrees wing sweepback and nose flaps. The wing/fuselage attachment of the G.A.L. 56 incorporated a device whereby wing dihedral could be adjusted on the ground. Two sets of split flaps were fitted, one set hinged at the 50 percent chord line and the rear set at 70 percent chord. Only one set could be used at a time, the change-over being effected on the ground.

investigate this awful phenomenon after we had finished our tests. Their chief test pilot, glider expert Robert Krönfeld, went into a spin and was killed. The stalling characteristics also made landing very tricky.[6]

Another variation on the standard theme was a proposal by the renowned G.T.R. Hill, who had designed the Pterodactyl. While serving as British Scientific Liaison Officer at the National Research Council (NRC) in Canada in the mid-1940s, Hill proposed a research glider for the study of the control and stability of the tailless aircraft. A far cry from the Hill tailless designs of the 1920s, the NRC experimental glider was rather conventional with the usual

With the assistance of England's Professor G.T.R. Hill, designer of the famous Pterodactyl series, Canada's National Research Council developed this experimental tailless glider. First flown in 1946, the glider exhibited good flying characteristics, although it lacked rudder power at low speeds. The wing tips, including elevon, fin, and rudder, could be rotated to prevent tip stalling and improve lateral control at low speeds.

elevons, flaps, fins, and rudders at the wing tips, and a retractable tricycle landing gear. After initial flights in 1946, the aircraft flew some 105 hours, of which 18 hours were in free flight. In September 1948, the glider was towed about 2300 miles across Canada. Flight characteristics were good, although there was a lack of rudder power at low speeds. Work on the project was terminated by 1950.

Of the many tailless aircraft projects that reached the advanced development stage during the mid-1940s, two British designs stand out: the Armstrong Whitworth A.W. 52 jet-powered flying wing, for its visionary approach to the jetliner of the future; and the de Havilland D.H. 108 tailless research aircraft, which became the first British aircraft to exceed the speed of sound. Although these aircraft flew after the war, their designs reflect the advanced thinking of British designers during the latter stages of the war.

The Armstrong Whitworth project consisted of a logical progression of experiments, commencing with wind tunnel model tests, followed by a glider that was a half-scale model of a 34,000-pound powered aircraft. This in turn was to be half the size of a projected airliner that would weigh about 180,000 to 200,000 pounds. The object of the designs was to combine the merits of the tailless design with the advantages of the laminar-flow wing. This arrangement could theoretically result in an aircraft with a total parasite drag about one-third of that of a conventional aircraft.

Following successful wind tunnel tests, design work started on the A.W. 52G glider in May 1942, and it was finally towed into the air for the first time three years later, in March 1945. Built mainly of wood, the two-place craft was controlled by wing tip elevons that were hinged to the trailing edges of "correctors" hinged to the wing. Correctors provided trim in pitch and also corrected the pitching moment resulting from flap operation. Spoilers fitted to the upper surface of the wing and a vertical fin and rudder at each wing tip completed the control arrangement. An anti-spin parachute was housed at the base of each rudder. Boundary-layer control was provided over the outer section of the wings by the suction of the boundary-layer air into a slot located in front of the elevons. This prevented the breaking away of the air flow over the wing and delayed wing tip stall at low speed. Wind-driven pumps were mounted on each main landing gear leg to provide power for the boundary-layer control.

Flight tests of the A.W. 52G proceeded well enough to confirm theoretical calculations. The next step in the development plan was the production of two A.W. 52 jet-powered research aircraft with a design weight of about 34,000 pounds. Configuration of the powered aircraft closely resembled that of the glider version, with the obvious addition of two 5000-pound thrust Rolls-Royce Nene turbojets buried in the wing center section on either side of the cockpit. Boundary-layer control suction was provided by the turbojets, with the suction slots in the wing connected by ducts to the engine air intakes. Designed for speeds of 400-500 mph, the aircraft also had an ejection seat for the pilot only, retractable tricycle landing gear, pressurized cockpit, and thermal deicing of the wings using jet exhaust.

The test pilot for Armstrong Whitworth, E.G. Franklin, flew the first A.W. 52 (TS 363) on November 13, 1947. The second aircraft, TS 368, fitted with Rolls-Royce Derwents, flew almost a year later, on September 1, 1948. Although the A.W. 52 was an impressive attempt to further the state of the art,

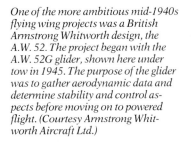

One of the more ambitious mid-1940s flying wing projects was a British Armstrong Whitworth design, the A.W. 52. The project began with the A.W. 52G glider, shown here under tow in 1945. The purpose of the glider was to gather aerodynamic data and determine stability and control aspects before moving on to powered flight. (Courtesy Armstrong Whitworth Aircraft Ltd.)

These two photographs of the jet-powered A.W. 52 in flight clearly show many of the distinctive design features of the craft. The trailing edge of the center section of the wing had a Fowler flap that was dished to pass under the protruding turbojet tail pipes. Vertical fins and rudders at the wing tips provided directional control. At the base of each rudder was a compartment for an anti-spin parachute.

the test flights were disappointing. Laminar flow was not achieved, and landing and takeoff distances exceeded those experienced with a conventional aircraft of similar wing loading. Elevator control of the aircraft was extremely sensitive.

The first aircraft was lost on May 30, 1949, due to an asymmetric flutter that caused the pilot to abandon the aircraft in flight. Although the second model subsequently underwent a research program on airflow behavior on sweptback wings at the Royal Aircraft Establishment at Farnborough, until September 1953, Armstrong Whitworth abandoned further development efforts. Investigation established that the structure had failed under the tremendous loads experienced at airspeeds of about Mach 0.9.

While Armstrong Whitworth conducted their A.W. 52 tests with an eye on the jetliner of the future, engineers and designers at the de Havilland Aircraft Company, pursued the same goal using a completely different approach. In October 1945, under the guidance of Chief Designer Ronald Bishop, the de Havilland design team selected the acorn-like fuselage of a de Havilland Vampire jet fighter, attached a rakish vertical fin and rudder on the aft end, and drew up a pair of shapely, swallow-like wings to complete the arrangement. Power was provided by a de Havilland Goblin 4 turbojet engine generating 3750 pounds of thrust.

Designated the D.H. 108, and appropriately called the Swallow, the first of three versions, TG 283, flew on May 15, 1946, with de Havilland's son Geoffrey at the controls. The first model, fitted with Handley Page slots fixed in the open position, was designed to determine low-speed characteristics of the swept wing, while the second, TG 306, was equipped with retractable slots and was intended to assess high-speed swept wing characteristics. The Swallow project was marked by moments of spectacular triumph and tragedy for de Havilland and British aviation in general.[7] Tragedy struck on the evening of September 27, 1946. Geoffrey de Havilland died when his D.H. 108 disintegrated during high speed flight.

A third aircraft, VW 120, was built along the same lines so that the high-speed program could continue. Fitted with a Goblin engine of higher rating, the aircraft also incorporated power-boosted controls, a sharper nose, and a lower cockpit with strengthened canopy. It was in this aircraft that test pilot John Derry set a world's 100-km speed record of 605.23 mph on April 12, 1948. A few months later the D.H. 108 became the first British aircraft to exceed the speed of sound. On September 6, 1948, John Derry put the D.H. 108 into a dive at 40,000 feet at full power and held the dive until the needle on the Machmeter passed the number "1." True air speed was calculated to be about 700 mph.[8]

Flight tests continued with the two remaining D.H. 108s at Farnborough until 1950. On February 15, 1950, VW 120 crashed, killing the pilot, J.S.R. Muller-Rowland. A few months later, the first aircraft, TG 283, crashed during stall trials, killing the pilot G.E.C. Genders.

Despite the accidents that plagued the program, the graceful D.H. 108 brought a most welcome measure of prestige to British aviation with its out-

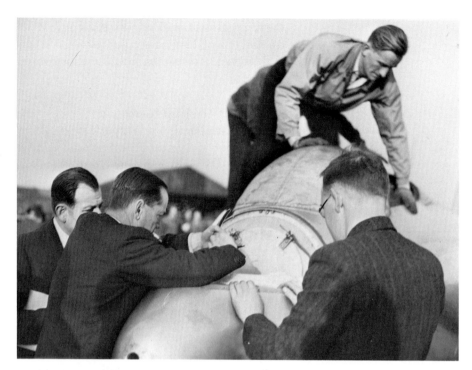

John Derry, famous de Havilland test pilot, is shown climbing into the cockpit of a D.H. 108 moments before takeoff for his record-breaking flight on April 12, 1948. Derry was killed on September 6, 1952, when the de Havilland D.H. 110 which he was flying broke up during a flight demonstration at Farnborough. (Courtesy de Havilland Aircraft Co.)

The third de Havilland D.H. 108, VW120, was flown by John Derry to a new world's closed course speed record of 605.23 mph on April 12, 1948. VW120 was also the first British aircraft to exceed the speed of sound. (Courtesy de Havilland Aircraft Co.)

standing performance. Perhaps of more importance, the flight test program provided invaluable data that convinced de Havilland engineers that a tailless airliner was not a practical proposition. The result was a more orthodox approach to the design of the world's first civil jet transport, the de Havilland D.H. 106 Comet.

Japan's interest in tailless aircraft during World War II was minimal compared with that of the other warring powers. Efforts centered around the glider designs of the Kayaba Works and the Mitsubishi attempts to copy the German Messerschmitt Me 163 rocket fighter.

The Kayaba gliders were developed to investigate the characteristics of tailless aircraft, and other than a 1938 private venture, the HK-1, were sponsored by the Japanese Army. The HK-1 was designed by Dr. Hidemasa Kimura based on an idea by pioneer aviator Kumazo Hino, the first person to fly an airplane in Japan, in 1910. Tests with the HK-1 led to Army interest, and Dr. Kimura, later to become Professor of the Science and Engineering Department, Nippon University, during the postwar years, responded with the KU-2. Working with Kayaba's Chief Designer Shigeki Naito, Kimura designed a single-seat model that flew 270 flights between October 1940 and May 1941.

Dr. Kimura, in collaboration with designer Joji Washimi, next produced a more advanced version of the KU-2 in 1941. The KU-3 was a two-place experimental craft with no vertical control surfaces. The leading edge of the wing was "cranked," incorporating sections of different angles of sweepback, with three control surfaces arrayed along the trailing edge of each wing. Over 60 flights were flown before the lone KU-3 crashed in 1941.

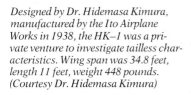

Designed by Dr. Hidemasa Kimura, manufactured by the Ito Airplane Works in 1938, the HK–1 was a private venture to investigate tailless characteristics. Wing span was 34.8 feet, length 11 feet, weight 448 pounds. (Courtesy Dr. Hidemasa Kimura)

昭和 16 年 2 月   Feb., 1940

The KU-2 (above) and KU-3 (right) were designed in 1946 by Dr. Kimura for the Japanese Army. The vertical fin and rudder of the KU-2 were replaced in the KU-3 by a horizontal control surface. Both gliders used ailerons and elevators in the trailing edge. (Courtesy Dr. Hidemasa Kimura)

Dr. Kimura carried the KU-3 design one step further. A powered version, the KU-4, was designed, but abandoned by the Japanese Army before it was built. It marked the end of any significant tailless aircraft development in Japan until 1944.

The appearance of American B-29 Superfortresses over Japan in 1944, produced an urgent need for a high performance interceptor. Inspired by the Me 163 Komet, Mitsubishi engineers, using a German Walter HWK 109-509 rocket motor and an instruction manual for the Me 163B, designed the J8M1 *Shusui* (swinging sword) for the Japanese Navy, and the Army version, designated Ki-200. A glider version, the MXY-8, was also developed to provide data

These MXY-8 Shusui *gliders were used to train pilots to fly the J8M1 rocket interceptors. Glider training took place at Kashiwa Air Base in Japan. The Japanese Army called the glider "Shusui* Light Glider;*" later on heavy gliders, about the same weight, structure, and appearance of the rocket fighter, were programmed. (Courtesy Dr. Hidemasa Kimura; SI Negative 81-14325)*

on handling characteristics of the J8M1 and to be used for rocket pilot training. A prototype glider was flown in early 1945, and subsequently placed in production. Similar training gliders were planned for the Army's Ki-200.

A special corps of potential rocket pilots began training at Kashiwa Air Base in the spring of 1945, conducting test and training flights in preparation for the day when the rocket-powered fighters would be available. Unfortunately, that day never came. The J8M1 first flew on July 7, 1945, but an engine failure shortly after takeoff resulted in a disastrous crash, killing the test pilot. There were no more flights prior to war's end, although J8M1 production was underway, and a J8M2 and an advanced Ki-200, designated Ki-202, were planned.

While the Hortens and Lippisch were making considerable progress in flying wing research and development in Germany, the idea was pursued vigorously in the United States only by Jack Northrop. A few other tailless prototypes appeared briefly, two of which should be mentioned before proceeding to Jack Northrop's wartime designs. These configurations were unique even in a field of aircraft design where the unusual was commonplace.

Ten years after the first Arups appeared in the 1930s, another disc-shaped oddity could be seen flying around the Connecticut countryside. The Vought V-173 "Flying Pancake" was the brainchild of Charles H. Zimmerman, who built his flying wing while employed as an engineer with the National Advisory Committee for Aeronautics (NACA). NACA's light-plane research study of 1933, which provided the incentive for other tailless designs in the 1930s, also inspired Zimmerman to design a passenger-carrying aircraft that would land and take off like a helicopter and once airborne, convert to conventional flight. Perhaps influenced by the Arup design, Zimmerman built test models that received NACA endorsement.

In 1937, Zimmerman turned to Chance Vought for the sponsorship that he

The all-movable, or "flying" tail of the V-173 "Zimmer-Skimmer" is quite evident in this view of the disc-shaped aircraft. During its successful flight test program, the "Flying Pancake" experienced several crashes, but sustained little damage because of its very low landing speed. Test pilots were unable to spin the aircraft and were amazed at its rapid deceleration as it was pulled into a tight turn.

needed. With U.S. Navy funding, the V-173 was constructed as a prototype for a high performance fighter, eventually designated XF5U-1. Powered by two 80-hp Continental engines, the fabric and wood V-173 was flown for the first time on November 23, 1942, by Vought chief test pilot Boone T. Guyton. He described the flight as "one of the most interesting I had made in my career."[9] Control forces were so heavy that it required two hands to control the aircraft during the short 13 minute flight!

The V-173 enjoyed a successful flying life with 131.8 hours flown by Guyton, Richard Burroughs, and U.S. Navy test pilots.[10] During the flight test program, which extended to March 1947, the XF5U-1 fighter prototype was designed and built. Powered by two Pratt & Whitney R-2000-7 radial engines, the V-173 look-alike was designed to fly as fast as 500 mph and also have exceptional handling at low speeds. The aircraft became a victim of the jet age, and never progressed beyond the taxi test phase.

George W. Cornelius, who began his experiments on variable incidence wings in the middle 1920s in California, continued his innovative trends when he displayed a tailless aircraft with a forward swept wing in September 1943, at Dayton, Ohio. The aircraft, called the "Mallard," also featured a variable incidence wing, with two outboard wing panels that could vary their angle of incidence about a fixed spar attached to the fuselage. Fore and aft movement of the control stick by the pilot varied the angle of the wings in unison, causing a pitching movement. Moving the stick laterally varied the incidence angle of the wings differentially, producing a rolling moment in the same manner as produced by ailerons.

The wings automatically adjusted themselves to absorb or offset unbalancing forces caused by turbulent air, preventing the sudden displacement of the airplane from its flight path. Although the airplane flew successfully, it was experimental in nature and was never produced.

George Cornelius of Dayton, Ohio, was a staunch advocate of the swept-forward wing concept, which lent itself well to this experimental tailless aircraft of the 1940s. Cornelius claimed that the combination of variable incidence wing and forward sweep resulted in an aircraft that was virtually stall-and spin-proof. (SI Negative 80-1745)

The Cornelius XFG-1 was designed as an expendable, pilotless glider to fuel bombers in flight. Incidence of the swept-forward wings could be adjusted on the ground between three and seven degrees. (SI Negative 81-12068)

Cornelius tried a more specialized application of his concepts to the expendable fuel transport glider, the XFG-1. Built in 1944 for the U.S. Army, the glider was designed to provide a supplementary fuel supply for long range bombers. While being towed through the air by a fuel hose, the glider would theoretically pump about 700 gallons of fuel to the tow plane, after which the hose and pilotless aircraft would be released to eventually crash. Only two models were built for test purposes, the first of which crashed during a spin, killing the pilot. Requirements for the glider ended with the end of World War II.

Many of these tailless aircraft and flying wings preceded, and in some cases overlapped, the efforts of Jack Northrop during World War II. Aside from a few instances of public acceptance in the marketplace on a limited basis or a government requirement during the war, the success of the concept was very limited. The reasons for failure were diverse—poor design, inexperienced management, inadequate financial backing, public and bureaucratic indifference, and for Lippisch and the Horten brothers, being on the losing side in a war.

Given a basic understanding of the people and events that shaped the early history of the flying wing, we are in a better position to appreciate the single-mindedness and dedication of Jack Northrop and the enormity of his accomplishments as we discuss what, in terms of flying wing design, must be called the "Northrop years."

NOTES

1. Jan Scott, letter to Donald Lopez, May 31, 1981 (Germany).

2. Ibid.

3. Ibid.

4. Dr. von Kármán and other aeronautical experts from the United States were briefed by Lippisch in Paris in May 1945, resulting in American interest in the project.

5. The triangular- or delta-wing configuration was not brought to the attention of the U.S. Air Force by Dr. Lippisch or by the arrival of the DM-1. A similar aircraft, based on a design concept of Michael Gluhareff, had been proposed by the Ludington-Griswold Co. of Saybrook, Connecticut, in 1944. The properties of triangular wings had also been studied by NACA's R.T. Jones, who, with Mr. H. Soule, examined wind tunnel tests and theoretical analyses made at the Langley Aeronautical Laboratory up to a Mach number of 1.75. For an excellent summary of the origins of the delta wing in Europe and the United States, see Richard P. Hallion, "Lippisch, Gluhareff, and Jones: The Emergence of the Delta Planform and the Origins of the Sweptwing in United States," pp. 1-10 (Germany).

6. Captain Eric M. Brown, *Wings on My Sleeve*, p. 117 (United Kingdom). Austrian born Robert Krönfeld, one of the finest soaring pilots in the world, established numerous world's performance records for gliders in Europe in the 1920s and 30s. Krönfeld moved to the United Kingdom in 1939, joined the Royal Air Force and participated in experimental testing of gliders during World War II. Krönfeld was renowned as an exceptional test pilot, aircraft designer, research scientist, and author on soaring flight.

7. The roster of pilots who at one time in their illustrious careers flew the D.H. 108 reads like a Who's Who of British test pilots. Geoffrey de Havilland, John "Cat's Eyes" Cunningham, John Derry, and John Wilson all had a try at Britain's first supersonic airplane. John Wilson fondly

recalls the aircraft as "exhilarating and challenging" and remembers John Cunningham's "brilliant, intuitive airmanship" when he recovered from an inverted spin while exploring the low speed handling characteristics of the D.H. 108.

8. In a 30 degree dive from 40,000 feet, the D.H. 108 would attain a speed of Mach 1.0 at full power. Terminal Mach number for the D.H. 108 was Mach 1.0 at 30,000 feet, at which point the aircraft was uncontrollable. Control was regained as the aircraft decelerated through Mach 0.98. John Derry was later killed when the second D.H. 110 Sea Vixen prototype broke up during a flight demonstration at the Farnborough air show in September 1952.

9. For an interesting account of the flying qualities of V-173, read Arthur L. Schoeni's "Vought XF5U-1 Flying Flapjack" (U.S., Non-Northrop).

10. A review of V-173(S/N 02978) aircraft flight log reveals a total of 190 flights from November 23, 1942, to March 31, 1947. Former Federal Aviation Administrator and Chief Executive Officer of Pan American World Airways Najeeb E. Halaby is listed for one familiarization flight as a test pilot. Not listed is Charles A. Lindbergh, who was alleged to have flown the "Zimmer–Skimmer," as it was affectionately known.

PART II

THE NORTHROP YEARS

Chapter 5

N-1M: Northrop's First Flying Wing

> Only one of the many advantages to be gained through such development has inspired our work, namely improved efficiency of the airplane. Therefore, we have concentrated our efforts on an all-wing aircraft by which I mean a type of airplane in which all of the functions of a satisfactory flying machine are disposed and accommodated within the outline of the main supporting airfoil.[1]

Jack Northrop became interested in the development of the cleanest possible airplane early in his career as an aircraft designer. In 1923, as an engineer for Donald Douglas in Santa Monica, California, Northrop continually explored advanced designs for aircraft, seeking new ways to eliminate drag and the severe penalties in aircraft performance it imposed. Even then, he envisioned an airplane without protruding surfaces that did not contribute in some way to lift. He even undertook the design of a tailless, all-wing glider as a "pastime" project, but never finished the aircraft, due to other commitments and lack of funds. In 1927, Northrop designed the incomparable Lockheed Vega as the best possible compromise that could be made with known and proven elements. Even this aircraft, with its conventional arrangement of wing fuselage and tail, gave hints of the unconventional concepts that were beginning to form in Jack Northrop's mind. One summer day in 1927, the distinguished Arctic explorer Captain George Hubert Wilkins sat in his hotel room in San Francisco agonizing over the choice of an aircraft for his forthcoming third trip across the icy expanse of the North. As he gazed out his window, he saw the sleek silhouette of an airplane—a Vega. He described in almost poetic, mystical words the beauty of the scene:

> I had firmly fixed in my mind the plan of flying alone when across my distant vision flashed the most efficient-looking monoplane I have ever seen. It was a fleeting glimpse, but I saw instantly and at a distance its distinctiveness. The machine was broadside to me. I marked its beauty of streamline, angle of incidence, and attack of the wing in level flight. The speed and the angle gave me a first impression that the machine was descending from a height, but its constant position above the horizon soon showed it to be flying level. As it turned

Captain George Hubert Wilkins (right) and his pilot, Ben Eielson (left) pose by the Northrop-designed Lockheed Vega in which they flew non-stop across the Arctic Sea on April 15, 1928. Wilkins and Eielson became the first men to fly over the top and bottom of the world. Far ahead of its time aerodynamically and structurally, the Vega was also appreciated by many for its beauty of design.

Noted for its multicellular construction, Northrop's 1929 Flying Wing, with its twin booms and tail structure, was a cautious step toward his first true flying wing design in 1939.

towards me I realized the full beauty of its design. It apparently offered no head resistance except for the engine, leading edge and a slim landing gear. It had no flying wires; no controls exposed—nothing but a flying wing.[2]

With his ultimate goal still in mind, Northrop left Lockheed in 1928, and formed a small company, the Avion Corporation, in the Burbank/Glendale area, to further explore the idea of a tailless craft. His 1929 Flying Wing evolved, an aircraft unusual in appearance and performance, but more noted for its unique all-metal, stressed skin, multicellular construction. Although financial considerations forced suspension of further development of the airplane, its unique structure paved the way for major Northrop contributions to aviation in the perfection of all-metal construction.

In 1932, Northrop formed a new Northrop Corporation at El Segundo, California, in partnership with Douglas Aircraft. As Northrop continued to design and produce airplanes of a conventional nature, he found another opportunity to test his ideas with a wind tunnel model in 1937. He was assisted in his project, designated Model 25, by Edward H. Heinemann, who in his own right would have a profound impact on the design of military aircraft in the United States.[3] Without any significant financial support, the project was abandoned after wind tunnel tests showed that it needed a tail.

In 1938, the Northrop Corporation became the El Segundo division of Douglas, with emphasis on production design. More interested in experimental design, Jack Northrop resigned, and in 1939 formed his own company once again, Northrop Aircraft, Inc. Business came in the form of contracts for construction of Consolidated PBY subassemblies, a Norwegian order for 24 Northrop-designed N-3PB patrol bombers in March 1940, followed by a contract for coproduction of Vultee-designed Vengeance dive bombers. Northrop finally had the financial wherewithal, facilities, and ultimately, government interest, to enable him to pursue his interest in research and development and more specifically in the flying wing. As Northrop progressed through the early design stages of his first true flying wing, he sought the advice and technical expertise of one of the world's leading aerodynamicists, Dr. Theodore von Kármán, Director of the Daniel Guggenheim School of Aeronautics at the California Institute of Technology (GALCIT),[4] and von Kármán's assistant, Dr. William R. Sears. Also available were all of the technical data and information in foreign aeronautical literature and NACA reports.[5] Northrop and his assistant chief of design, Walter J. Cerny, conducted extensive wind tunnel tests with a number of flying wing models. The result was an aircraft incorporating the latest thinking on buried engine design, new airfoil sections of low drag and improved stability, and the use of various high-lift devices, spoilers, and flaps.

Northrop viewed the diminutive N-1M (Northrop Model 1 Mockup), with its 38-foot wing span, as a flying scale mockup, perhaps one-third or one-half full-scale size. To achieve the efficiency and economy possible with a pure all-wing design, Northrop envisioned a commercial cargo airplane of a minimum 70-foot span, providing a maximum thickness of about 6 feet. With wing thickness growing in proportion to increase in span, a thickness of 15 to

20 feet would ultimately be possible. Depending on whether the use of the aircraft would be military or commercial, gun turrets, passenger cabins, and other special loads could be accommodated by bumps or projections that would not alter the basic characteristics of the aircraft.

The National Air and Space Museum is fortunate to have in its collection one of the original models built by Jack Northrop to investigate his theories of flying wing design. Constructed of balsa wood, tissue paper, and cardboard, the delicate structure bears a strong resemblance to the N-1M and incorporates many of the control surfaces evident in the real aircraft. Hinged wing tips, cardboard flaps that serve as rudders, and the elevons provide control and balance. The model was tested in hand-launched free glides to test its stability and flight characteristics.

The N-1M that evolved from many design studies and model tests was the first such tailless configuration to appear in the United States. The experimental aircraft was distinguished by the absence of any of the unusual appendages; the pronounced anhedral, or downward droop, of the wing tips gave the airplane a distinctly bird-like appearance. Aircraft configuration could be varied on the ground between tests to permit in-flight evaluation of the many variables associated with wing sweep, dihedral, and the all-wing design. In effect, the N-1M was the forerunner of today's "variable geometry" airplanes.

Control of the N-1M was accomplished using many of the same techniques and methods employed by the Hortens in Germany and other European designers. Elevons operated together for pitch control and differentially for roll control. Rudder control was accomplished initially with a plain split flap or "clamshell" at each wing tip. Actuated independently by the rudder pedals, they opened to produce drag, which, in turn, induced yaw. Both split flaps could also be opened simultaneously to increase gliding angle or reduce airspeed, thus serving in the role of air brakes.

The N-1M was of wooden construction, and thus easily adaptable to the many changes in configuration to which it was subjected during the flight test program. The aircraft was initially powered by two submerged 65-hp Lycoming 0-145 four-cylinder, horizontally-opposed engines driving two-bladed pusher propellers by means of extension shafts. The engines, which were later replaced by 117-hp six-cylinder, air-cooled Franklin engines driving three-bladed propellers, were cooled by means of slot-type intakes in the leading edge of the wing.

Engineering and construction of the N-1M took exactly one year, beginning in July 1939. The first flight of the N-1M, nicknamed the "Jeep," was in July 1940, and indeed was an accidental one, as pilot Vance Breese bounced the airplane into the air during a high-speed taxi run on Baker Dry Lake, California.

It took only several days of abbreviated test flights to prompt Jack Northrop to report encouraging results to Gen. H.H. "Hap" Arnold, Chief of the Air Corps. Northrop reported the airplane was both statically and dynamically stable about all three axes, with normal stick forces and good controllability,

This early experimental model was used by Jack Northrop to test his ideas about the flying wing. Constructed of balsa wood covered with tissue paper, the model weighs only three ounces, with a span of 33 inches. The left wing is signed by John K. Northrop and E.V. Chandler, the builder. The right wing has the initials and dates "D.K.L., 12/2/39" and "E.B., 12/4/39," patent attorneys to whom the model was shown on those dates.

One of Jack Northrop's early sketches of his first true flying wing reflects much of his thinking on the concept—no fuselage, buried engines, no external fins, rudders, or auxiliary surfaces, and a thick airfoil with room for aircrew, power plants, accessories, and plumbing. (SI Negative 74-03474)

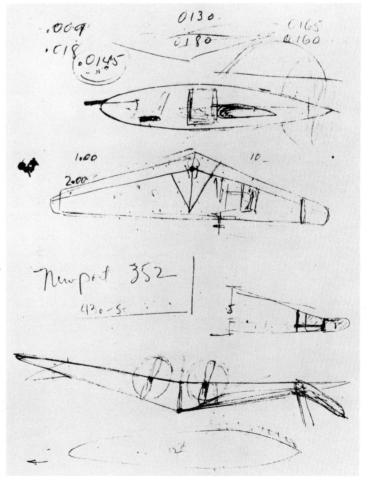

All of the N-1M's original distinctive design features are evident in these views of the aircraft at rest on Muroc Dry Lake in June 1941. Droop of the wing tips, with split flap rudders installed, could be adjusted on the ground; sweepback, dihedral, center of gravity location (by changing angle of sweepback), and control surface arrangement were also adjustable. The faired tail wheel, which prevented excessive rollback on the ground, also provided some measure of directional stability. The metal bump on the top of the canopy was added to accommodate the pilot's head.

laterally and longitudinally. The aircraft was considerably shy of adequate rudder control using the trailing edge split flap rudders, but Northrop was optimistic about a solution.

The N-1M's test program provided valuable data for its successor, the N-9M, but it was not without problems. Choosing suitable power plants became the first, and most enduring dilemma, one that would plague many of Jack Northrop's piston-engined tailless designs.

At an early stage in the test program, it was determined that the Lycoming engines were totally inadequate for the N-1M. Moye Stephens, Northrop's company secretary and test pilot who took over the flight test program from Vance Breese, recalls that the Lycoming engines could not get the 4000-pound airplane any higher than ground effect during flights at the dry lake:

> In the initial flights with the Lycoming engines the ship would climb to about five feet and the increased induced drag associated with attempts to force it higher would bring it down to a landing. Continuous flight called for maintenance of a precise angle of attack. Any increase in the angle of attack and the ship would land. Any decrease in the angle of attack and the ship would land. The situation was complicated by a "dead area" in elevator effectiveness. In order to nose down it was necessary to move the wheel forward a disturbing amount with no response, and then the elevons would suddenly take over. In order to keep from banging into the ground it was then necessary to traverse the dead elevator area in the opposite direction to find the start of effectiveness. This was moderately unsettling while flying along five feet off the ground. I temporarily overcame the difficulty by use of the longitudinal trim flap: a control surface spanning the trailing edge of the center section. With this adjusted to create a nose heavy condition, flight was maintained with a constant back pressure on the wheel. To nose down it was simply necessary to ease off the back pressure.[6]

Dr. Theodore von Kármán quickly came up with a solution for the problem. Realizing that the extremely thick wing was creating an airflow separation that was not coming together until aft of the wing, he suggested extend-

Jack Northrop poses by the N-1M, while Moye Stephens beams from the cockpit.

The flat surface of Muroc Dry Lake was the ideal site for early test flights of the "Jeep," shown here cruising at an altitude of 10 feet.

Moye Stephens and the N-1M are shown during an early test flight over the California desert. Despite Jack Northrop's claims that the N-1M had 33 percent less drag than a conventional aircraft of similar size and carrying capability, the N-1M was underpowered, and performance suffered.

ing the trailing edge of the elevons into the closure of the airflow. The solution apparently had the desired effect.

Early test flights were made in a straight line over the length of the dry lake, generally at the maximum ceiling of the aircraft, about ten feet. On one of these flights, Stephens lost one foot of a propeller tip on the desert floor. Despite the extreme vibration which broke a rear spar, Stephens landed the N-1M without further damage.

Replacing the Lycomings with 117-hp Franklins almost doubled the horsepower. The engines still had to be operated considerably in excess of the manufacturer's limitations to achieve anything approaching satisfactory flight. Overheating became chronic, and much time was lost in attempting to reduce oil and cylinder head operating temperatures to acceptable limits. By May 1941, Jack Northrop had come to the conclusion that the difficulty lay in engine design, since tests had shown sufficient pressure drop across the engines to cool them if they had been properly finned. Northrop considered the necessity of eventually changing engines once again, possibly using a new Lycoming six-cylinder engine of 150 hp. Apparently the switch never took place, since the N-1M was received by the National Air and Space Museum in 1950 with Franklin engines still installed.

Engine problems notwithstanding, Northrop concluded that the flying wing as demonstrated by the N-1M was a practical idea, and entirely normal operation of the Flying Wing was no longer a problem. Although Northrop leaned toward a medium-range airplane as the next logical step, officials of the Army Air Corps (which officially changed its name to Army Air Forces on June 29, 1941) were turning to the possibility of a long-range airplane based on the flying wing principle. Requirements for an airplane with a range of 10,000 miles, cruising speed of 300 mph, service ceiling of 40,000 feet, and a bomb load of 10,000 pounds were soon being discussed in the context of a flying wing design. Northrop's feasibility studies eventually led to a conference with Air Force Materiel Division representatives in September 1941 to consider an experimental airplane with the desired military characteristics. The design that evolved was an incredible 140,000-pound behemoth—a far cry indeed from the tiny 4000-pound N-1M, which only two short years before had still been on the drawing board! Equally ambitious was an anticipated delivery date 24 months from contract approval.

As plans materialized for the long-range, heavy bomber, and as N-1M flight testing proceeded apace under tight security conditions in the desert, an ironic sequence of events occurred, hardly more than a footnote in the story of Jack Northrop's flying wings. For the Horten brothers in Germany, however, these events were a turning point in their own personal struggle to prove the flying wing concept.

Although the Air Force decided to classify all information pertaining to the Flying Wing in June 1941, routine publication of patent drawings had already occurred in the *Official Gazette* of the U.S. Patent Office on May 13. After media speculation forced an official release of information by Northrop and the Air Force, the patent drawings and an N-1M photograph eventually appeared in the international aeronautical journal *Interavia* on November 18, 1941.

When the Horten brothers were interrogated after their capture by Allied forces in May 1945, they referred to the appearance of the N-1M photograph and drawings in *Interavia* as a stroke of good fortune. They used the article to "sell" the German Aviation Ministry on a more intensive program of development of the flying wing as a military aircraft in anticipation of American progress along these lines. The end result was the world's first turbojet-powered flying wing, the Horten Ho IX (Go 229), which flew in January 1945.

By November 1941, according to Jack Northrop, 200 flights had been flown with the N-1M, which varied in time and altitude from a few seconds and 2 or 3 feet, to more than an hour and 7500 feet.[7] During this time, Moye Stephens flew the N-1M with numerous combinations of wing tip deflection, dihedral, and sweepback. Initially it was thought that having the wing tips deflected downward would contribute to directional stability. It was soon found that they had little if any effect in this regard, but did lessen lift noticeably. Consequently, they were straightened.

With an aircraft of such radical design, stability was one of the primary concerns. In some configurations tested, yawing the aircraft, that is, moving the rudder pedals to cause motion about the vertical axis of the aircraft, and then releasing the controls, induced an oscillation called "Dutch roll."[8] The oscillations were intense enough that Moye Stephens wondered if they would reach a point beyond which they would be impossible to stop. Stephens found

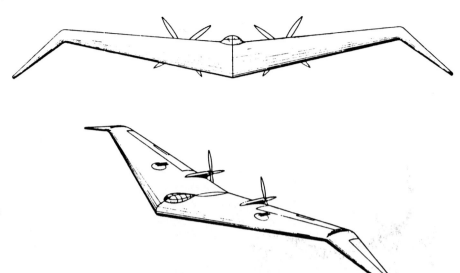

These patent drawings (right) were filed by Jack Northrop on November 20, 1940. Later published in the aeronautical publication Interavia *on November 18, 1941, the drawings received considerable attention in Germany. The result was increased government support for the Horten brothers' flying wing series such as the Ho V (below).*

"the burden of an unsatisfied curiosity in this connection not overly irksome." Eventually, with an alternative configuration of the aircraft, induced "Dutch roll" damped out after three or four oscillations.[9]

Of equal importance was the longitudinal stability of the flying wing. Again, Moye Stephens defined the problem:

> The ship was longitudinally unstable with the minimum degree of sweep-back: the configuration in which the trailing edge of the wing formed a straight line from wing tip to wing tip. It was the configuration which resulted in the rearmost positioning of the center of gravity. The instability was evidenced at low speed and under acceleration.
>
> In landing, the ship exhibited positive stability during the approach: increasing nose heaviness with decreasing speed. But following the flare-out,

The drooped wing tips were eventually straightened on the N-1M, as these two views of the aircraft illustrate. With maximum tip deflection and sweepback, and the N-1M at rest on the tricycle landing gear, the wing tips were only one foot off the ground. Raising the nose during takeoff lowered the wing tips until they touched the ground while the tail wheel was still six inches in the air. Skinned wing tips during landing or takeoff occasionally resulted. (Courtesy G.H. Balzer)

A control column and wheel seem out of place, dominating the narrow confines of the cockpit of the N-1M. The hand-printed labels near the controls along the right side of the cockpit lend a homemade, temporary air to the cramped cockpit, in keeping with the experimental state of the aircraft. (Courtesy G.H. Balzer)

A 1942 photograph of the design team behind many of the Northrop flying wings: Walter J. Cerny, Assistant Chief of Design, supervisor of the N-1M project; John K. Northrop, President and Chief Engineer of Northrop Aircraft, Inc.; and Dr. William Sears, Chief of Aerodynamics. (SI Negative 74-03482)

John Myers and the N-1M are towed to altitude by a C-47 transport on what may have been the last flight of the N-1M. At sufficient altitude, the N-1M was released so that Myers could perform spin tests.

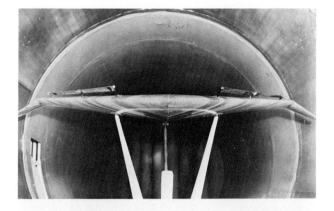

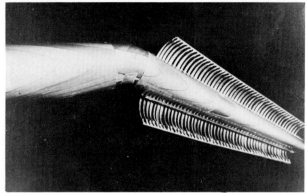

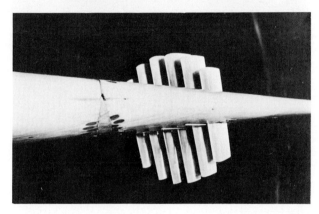

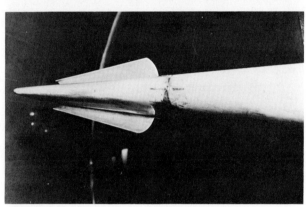

Throughout the N-1M development program, wind tunnel tests of alternative control configurations were conducted: the N-1M rigged with an auxiliary airfoil (upper left); leading edge, left wing tip with extended scoop rudder (upper right); straightened right wing tip with a multiple surface type rudder (lower left); front view, right wing tip with spoiler rudders (lower right).

increasing elevator stick force reversal resulted in an eventual full forward control position to maintain the holding-off altitude.

In steep turns nose heaviness was exhibited initially; but, as the Gs were increased, a point was reached at which the ship would want to root into the turn necessitating forward control pressure to prevent it from doing so.

Sweeping the wings back to the rearmost position moved the center of gravity forward and achieved longitudinal stability.[10]

After much adjusting, experimentation, and flight testing, a configuration was found in which longitudinal, directional, and lateral stability were acceptable: straight wing tips, minimum dihedral, and the greatest degree of sweepback.

Throughout the test program, investigation of the controllability and stability of the N-1M was frequently hampered by poor performance and engine problems. The aircraft was overweight and underpowered, factors that required unusual approaches to some of the everyday problems associated with flight testing.

Toward the end of the N-1M test program, Jack Northrop decided to relocate the N-1M from Muroc to Northrop Airport in Hawthorne, California, adjacent to the site of the Northrop plant. From Moye Stephens' viewpoint, operating the N-1M from the narrow confines of Northrop Airport was an unacceptable situation. "The loss of one cylinder on takeoff could result in the

NORTHROP
1ST FLYING W[...]

A portion of the Northrop team—"the gang that made it possible"—assembles in front of the "Jeep" on September 22, 1943. Pilot Moye Stephens sits in front of the N-1M nose wheel, flanked on the left by Jack Northrop, and on the right by Dr. Theodore von Kármán and Walt Cerny.

start of an N-1M avenue into the heart of downtown Hawthorne!"[11] The large expanse of Muroc Dry Lake was obviously the better test site.

Jack Northrop would not take "no" for an answer. The N-1M, with Vance Breese at the controls, was towed by a C-47 to Mines Field (now Los Angeles International Airport) since the N-1M was incapable of attaining sufficient altitude to make the flight. Several test flights from Mines Field were conducted by John Myers, and the aircraft was returned to Muroc.

An accurate flight history of the N-1M, including the final days of test flying, is difficult to document. Official Northrop and Army Air Forces records of flight test activity have been lost. In late 1941, Jack Northrop made frequent reference to "over 200 flights" in a number of articles that appeared under his byline. Moye Stephens, with the benefit of his personal pilot's log, has a different perspective:

My logbook lists 28 flights to this point. I know that I failed to record some of my earliest flights, but I doubt that the number would exceed five or six. The only other pilot to fly the N-1M prior to November 1941, was Vance Breese, and I doubt that his flights totaled more than ten or twelve.

Toward the end of May 1942, I had my disagreement with Jack Northrop as to the suitability of N-1M flights from Hawthorne and was relieved of experimental test flying. Two or three weeks later, Vance Breese was towed from Muroc to Mines Field behind a C-47, an arrangement made necessary by the N-1M's inability to top the intervening mountainous terrain. Prior to this time I had added 17 flights to the November 1941, figure of 28 for a total of 45.

Johnny Myers made his first flight in the N-1M on June 23, 1942, from

110

Regards to the Gang that made it possible
John K. Northrop

:INEERS
THE JEEP"

Mines Field. He reported that something was wrong with the ship; and on June 25th, at the request of Walt Cerny, I made a flight from Mines to look into the problem. I reported that, as far as I could tell, everything was normal. Johnny made another flight and still insisted something was wrong. Cerny requested that I make another check. I made the flight on June 26th and agreed that Johnny was quite right but pointed out that the miserable performance, excessive temperatures, and the necessity of drastically over revving the engines were the nature of the beast; that it was the basis of my refusal to fly the ship out of Hawthorne.

Johnny made several flights from Mines; and, shortly after August 14th, the ship was trucked back to Muroc. I made my last flight in the N-1M on August 14th from Mines before it was taken away. It brought my logged flights to a total of 48.

Johnny recalls that he made the last flight from Muroc toward the end of 1942 or in early 1943. It was probably shortly after January 9, 1943. On that date Col. F.R. Dent made a flight in the N-1M from Muroc. It was Dent in a C-47 who towed Johnny in the N-1M from Muroc to the Hawthorne area for a landing at Northrop to complete the final flight.

Only two pilots in addition to Breese, Myers, Dent, and myself flew the N-1M: Col. M.S. Roth (May 14, 1942) and Northrop production test pilot R.H. Ranaldi (June 26, 1942). They made one flight each. It is my sincere belief that the N-1M made considerably less than 100 flights in its lifetime, and that there is no way it could have completed 200 by November of 1941. It should be pointed out that it was laid up for a number of lengthy periods such as the occasions of the engine change, a number of cooling duct reworks, rebuilding the rear spar of the right wing following my loss of a portion of a right propeller blade, etc. The ship was trucked back and forth a number of times between

111

Hawthorne and Muroc, Baker, and Rosamond dry lakes which was time consuming. Also, the test flight mechanics and I were tied up during the period of December 30, 1940, to March 8, 1941, on the test program of the Northrop N-3PB (seaplane patrol bomber built for the Norwegians).[12]

In 1945, the N-1M was given to the Army Air Forces for eventual display. Official Air Forces records indicate it was preserved and placed in temporary storage on June 6, 1946, at Freeman Field, Indiana. On July 12, 1946, the N-1M was delivered to the Museum Storage Depot at Park Ridge, Illinois.

Despite performance and engine problems, the N-1M was a success as a flying laboratory designed to investigate the flying qualities of the pure flying wing design. By frequently altering the configuration of the aircraft the Northrop team was able to redesign the N-1M; unacceptable flying qualities were eventually eliminated, and the soundness of Northrop's concept was proved.

It was not enough for Jack Northrop to be convinced. If a practical military or commercial version of the flying wing was to evolve, it was obvious that the interest and financial backing of government or the airlines had to be obtained. The country moved toward war, and a military application of the flying wing assumed priority. Jack Northrop's conviction, his reputation as an aircraft designer, and his talent for selling his ideas to the right people, provided the necessary stimulus to keep the program moving.

Northrop and General Arnold were close friends. Arnold appreciated Northrop's reputation as an innovative designer, and was receptive to his ideas. Once favorable flight-test reports were passed along to General Arnold and the N-1M had been given some exposure to the military, General Arnold supported the flying wing, and Jack Northrop was on his way to realizing his dream. From the N-1M would come the N-9M and other wartime designs, the cornerstones upon which Northrop would build the ultimate in flying wing designs.

NOTES

1. Address by John K. Northrop, "Development of the All-Wing Aircraft" (U.S., Northrop).

2. George H. Wilkins, *Flying the Arctic*, pp. 197–198 (U.S., Northrop).

3. The flight deck of any U.S. Navy aircraft carrier in the late 1950s was crowded with an array of fighters and bombers that was eloquent testimony to Heinemann's foresight, determination, and imagination. A close friend of Jack Northrop, Ed Heinemann did not agree with Northrop's concept of a pure flying wing. Ironically, Heinemann received the 1953 Collier Trophy for development of the first supersonic fighter for the U.S. Navy, the F4D Skyray, which was a tailless aircraft.

4. Dr. Theodore von Kármán came to the United States in the mid-1920s after a distinguished career in aeronautical research in Germany. He became director of GALCIT in 1930, and during World War II, directed the Army Air Force jet propulsion and rocket motor program at Caltech. Dr. von Kármán laid the foundation for aerodynamic design leading to supersonic flight. He served with distinction as an aeronautical engineer, a university professor, and an industrial and government consultant, and received many honorary degrees and medals, as well as most of the awards given in aerodynamics and fluid mechanics.

5. In the 35th Wilbur Wright Memorial Lecture, "The Development of All-Wing Aircraft," delivered in London in 1947 (U.S., Northrop), Jack Northrop credited the Horten brothers with considerable contributions to developing the flying wing. Referring to the description of Horten developments in the technical reports emanating from Germany since the close of the European war, Northrop said:

> In many instances the Horten conclusions were surprisingly similar to our own. Their work was not carried so far, however, and I doubt that they had the sympathetic and responsible governmental backing and the resultant opportunities for development accorded to us.

6. Moye Stephens, *Northrop N-1M Test Program*, p. 2 (U.S., Northrop). Stephens and the adventurer, traveler, and writer Richard Halliburton began a vagabond journey by air in a C3B Stearman named "The Flying Carpet." Their exploits made an engrossing adventure story (Moye Stephens and Richard Halliburton, *The Flying Carpet*, New York: Garden City Publishing Co., 1932). Stephens, whose flying career was a virtual history of California aviation, was taught to fly in 1923 by none other than Eddie Bellande, Jack Northrop's test pilot on his 1929 Flying Wing. All information on the N-1M flight characteristics in this chapter attributed to Moye Stephens was obtained from the cited report during a taped interview of Stephens (J. Myers, M. Stanley, and M. Stephens, taped interview with E.T. Wooldridge, Los Angeles, California, February, 1982 [U.S., Northrop]), and Moye Stephens, letter to E.T. Wooldridge, May 17, 1982 (U.S., Northrop).

7. Jack Northrop summarized Flying Wing development in a letter to Mr. J.C. Mingling, Army Air Force Material Division, Wright Field, Dayton, Ohio, dated November 3, 1941. Northrop referred to over 200 flights and operations at 7500 feet with the N-1M. Both of these numbers are considered erroneous by many associated with the program. The matter of flights will be covered later. With regard to altitude Moye Stephens had the following comments:

> I don't remember climbing the ship to more than a couple of thousand feet above ground level. At Muroc this would have been an altitude of around 4000 feet. In order to climb, it was imperative to use full throttle. In view of the N-1M's slow rate of climb, climbing to altitude would have meant drastically exceeding the Franklins' limitations on engine speed and operating temperatures for a prolonged period. As a consequence, contrary to the usual circumstance, a lower altitude appeared more healthful than a higher. In any case, there is a question as to whether or not the N-1M could have reached 7500 feet. That altitude would have permitted flights to the Los Angeles area without the aid of a C-47.

See Moye Stephens, letter to E.T. Wooldridge, May 17, 1982 (U.S., Northrop).

8. A "Dutch roll" is a natural condition of flight in which the right and left wings rise and fall alternately. The wing tips trace a circular path in a plane that lies somewhere between the horizontal and the vertical.

9. Stephens, *Northrop N-1M Test Program*, p. 4 (U.S., Northrop).

10. Ibid., p. 5.

11. Ibid.

12. Moye Stephens, letter to E.T. Wooldridge, May 17, 1982, p. 2 (U.S., Northrop).

Chapter 6	# Wings of War

Like the Horten brothers and Alexander Lippisch in Germany, Jack Northrop found ample opportunity to apply the concept of a tailless aircraft to the practical requirements of war. Northrop's reputation as a brilliant innovator and the fact that this company was not initially overburdened with production commitments made him a logical choice to develop new aircraft designs. New mission requirements, new technologies, and Northrop's preoccupation with the concept of the flying wing led to a family of aircraft with unusual physical characteristics.

A number of aircraft propulsion systems were used in tailless aircraft, including conventional piston engines, turbojets, rockets, and pulse jets. A family of aircraft emerged with names as distinctive as their shapes and missions: Black Bullet, Rocket Wing, Power Bomb, Bat, Jet Bomb, and Flying Ram. Northrop test pilots had more than their share of thrills and narrow escapes as they flight-tested unproven engines and airframes in the skies over southern California. At the same time, across the Atlantic, German pilots tested the same concepts under equally hazardous circumstances, in designs by Lippisch, Horten, and Messerschmitt.

The first of Northrop's World War II family of tailless designs was the XP-56, also called the Black Bullet. This aircraft was designed at the outset of the war in response to an Army request for new designs that would counter foreign advances in fighter aircraft technology (Request for Data R-40C). Northrop's competitors for a production contract were the Consolidated-Vultee XP-54 and the Curtiss XP-55 Ascender, which, like the Northrop entry, were pusher designs that incorporated rear-mounted engines driving multi-bladed propellers. All three aircraft were originally scheduled to use the new Pratt & Whitney liquid-cooled X-1800-A3G engine, but cancellation of that project forced Northrop to use the Pratt & Whitney R-2280-29 air-cooled Double Wasp for the XP-56.

The XP-56 was a composite of a number of radical design features. The overall effect was an airplane that, by any contemporary standards, did not "look right." With the benefit of hindsight, it could be said that the failure of

John Myers prepares the first XP-56 (42-1786) for a test flight in late 1943.

the program was predictable. The XP-56 was the first all-magnesium, all-welded airframe in history; Northrop developed the "heliarc" welding process that assembled the strong, lightweight structure. The air-cooled engine was completely submerged in the stubby, bullet-like fuselage, driving two concentric counter-rotating pusher propellers, located a short distance aft of the cockpit. An emergency bailout by the pilot seemed guaranteed to produce disastrous results. Consequently, an explosive cord was wrapped around the engine gearbox so that in an emergency the aft portion of the aircraft, including propellers, could be blown away before the pilot left the airplane.

The XP-56 was a tailless, sweptwing, with both dorsal and ventral fins mounted directly in front of the propellers. Elevons were located at the midpoint of the trailing edge, and the wing tips were deflected downward, serving the dual purpose of fin and rudder. On the second of the two XP-56 models, air-operated bellows rudders were incorporated. Each wing tip housed a horizontal duct through which air was free to travel while the aircraft was moving. When the pilot moved the rudder pedals, a valve was actuated that diverted the airflow to a bellows, which assisted in operating split-flap rudders at the wing tips.

The first XP-56 (42-1786), which had been trucked out to Muroc Dry Lake, made its first flight on September 6, 1943, with test pilot John Myers at the controls.[1] The first flight was made at an altitude of four feet, at a speed of 140 mph. After the second flight that day, Myers complained of a directional control deficiency, not surprising since the dorsal fin was reminiscent of those on

115

Northrop's XP-56 was designed in competition with the Consolidated Vultee XP-54 and Curtiss XP-55 Ascender. The XP-54 (top) featured an electrically operated seat that functioned as an elevator for the pilot to gain access to the cockpit. The Curtiss entry, the XP-55 (middle), was developed from a wood and fabric lightweight mockup, the CW-24B (bottom), and was fitted with a controllable nosemounted control surface. (Courtesy U.S. Air Force)

116

the infamous Granville Gee Bee racers of the 1930s. The small vertical fin on the first aircraft was capped with a larger stabilizer that improved the yaw problems. Taxi and flight tests were resumed on October 8.

After successfully taxiing across Muroc Lake twice at high speed, Myers made a straight flight at an altitude between 10 and 15 feet with no apparent difficulty. This flight was followed by a high speed taxi run on the return trip across the lake and the flight was repeated. On the return taxi run following this flight the left main tire blew out about half way across the lake while the airplane was traveling at approximately 130 mph.

At that point, as Myers so eloquently put it, "The aircraft wanted to fly upside down and backwards, and finally did!"[2] The XP-56 began to somersault across the desert floor. After one backward flip, during which the airplane rose about 75 feet in the air, the pilot's seat supports failed, and the seat and Myers were catapulted clear. The XP-56 crashed on its upper surface and was totally destroyed. Myers, fortunately had been wearing a polo helmet for protection, and suffered only minor injuries.

A second airplane (42-238353), with a new larger dorsal fin and bellows rudders, first flew from Roach Lake on March 23, 1944, attaining an altitude of 2500 feet. The second aircraft eventually flew a total of 10 flights, during which a number of stability and control problems were experienced. Wing heaviness was attributed to a torque reaction resulting from improper propeller operation. The chief difficulty experienced was in longitudinal and directional instability.

The limited success of the flight test program did not result in great enthusiasm on the part of Army officials to continue the development program as the war ended. Limited potential and the arrival of the turbojet engine on the scene contributed to the cancellation of the program.

In retrospect, Jack Northrop admitted that the application of the flying

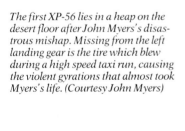

The first XP-56 lies in a heap on the desert floor after John Myers's disastrous mishap. Missing from the left landing gear is the tire which blew during a high speed taxi run, causing the violent gyrations that almost took Myers's life. (Courtesy John Myers)

The second XP-56 (42-238353) was easily distinguished from its predecessor by an enlarged vertical fin and the air bellows-operated rudders at the wing tips for greater yaw control. Designed for speeds well over 400 mph, the XP-56 never measured up to performance specifications and was plagued by a variety of other problems during its abbreviated flight test program.

wing concepts to this particular design was not the proper solution. It was a design he was not very proud of; as he candidly admitted, "I think it was a bust."[3]

The second XP-56 was shipped to the Army Air Forces (AAF) storage depot at Park Ridge, Illinois, on December 20, 1946, and was later sent to the National Air and Space Museum. In 1982, it was transferred to Northrop Corporation for future restoration.

On August 13, 1941, in Germany, test pilot Heini Dittmar flew the first rocket-propelled fighter, the Messerschmitt Me 163V1 *Komet*. Two months later, on October 2, 1941, with Dittmar again at the controls, the *Komet* became the first aircraft to pass a speed of 1000 km per hour by reaching 1003 km per hour (623.85 mph, Mach 0.84). The Me 163 eventually became the world's first operational rocket-powered fighter.

In September 1942, a year after Dittmar's flight, Jack Northrop produced a feasibility study for America's first rocket-powered military interceptor. An Army contract followed, calling for construction of three gliders to test the aerodynamic qualities of the configuration, and to serve as flying mockups for the XP-79 aircraft. In an unpowered configuration, the gliders were designated MX-334. The third aircraft, when it was eventually fitted with an Aerojet rocket engine, was then designated MX-324. The first aircraft had skids that were eventually augmented by a detachable four-wheel dolly that was jettisoned immediately after takeoff. This configuration finally gave way to a streamlined tricycle landing gear on the second and third aircraft.

Installation of a fixed nose gear on the centerline of the aircraft would have required extension of the shock strut through the pilot's cockpit, an unacceptable situation. Thus, the nose gear installation was offset to the left, a configuration that caused the pilot no problems during landing.

All three aircraft were plywood with a welded steel tubing center section. The control system consisted of elevons operated by the pilot's control bar, and rudders and airbrakes combined, called "brudders." Air bellows were operated and controlled by foot pedals for rudder action, or a cockpit control handle for brakes.

The pilot was to fly in the prone position, a concept practiced earlier by the Hortens. These accommodations permitted a wing structure thinner than the more conventional plan, and enabled the pilot to withstand considerably more gravity acceleration, reducing the strain imposed on him by violent maneuvers.

Northrop and his chief aerodynamicist, Dr. William R. Sears, designed the aircraft as a pure flying wing with no vertical fin. Controversy developed when calculations showed that a vertical tail would be required for stability at the high speeds contemplated.

Sears reluctantly agreed to add a wire-braced vertical fin made of plywood, on the condition that he be allowed to saw off part of it if flight tests showed that the aircraft did not need a tail. Following the tests, however, the tail remained in place.

John Myers conducted the first unpowered glider flight of the MX-334 on

America's first rocket-powered aircraft, the Northrop MX-324/334, was designed at the Army Air Forces Materiel Center, Wright Field, Dayton, Ohio, and subsequently built by Northrop using non-critical materials.

A closeup of the MX-334 cockpit reveals the V-shaped support upon which the prone pilot rested his chin during flight.

Alex Papana (left) world champion aerobatic pilot, and designer/racing pilot Harry Crosby (right) engage in a bit of "hangar flying" during a lull in flight tests. Papana and Crosby shared flight test duties with John Myers on most of the Northrop experimental flying wings during the war.

Harry Crosby (right) poses with a feathered friend by his CR-3 racer prior to the 1936 Thompson Trophy race. Crosby's new CR-4 (below) undergoes maintenance for the 1939 National Air Races. Crosby designed and helped build the CR-4 and flew the racer to a fourth place finish in the Thompson Trophy race. Another wartime test pilot for Northrop, Max Constant, placed fourth that year in the Bendix Trophy race.

Harry Crosby stands in the MX-334 during a lull in unpowered gliding tests in early 1944. Access hatches on the top and bottom gave Crosby a unique opportunity to add scale to the glider as it rested on the parched, cracked surface of Muroc Dry Lake. In the photograph at right, the aircraft is buttoned up. Crosby is lying in place, tow lines are attached, and another test flight is about to begin.

October 2, 1943. The intervening months between this first gliding flight and the first powered flight the following July were occupied by numerous test flights in which the stability and control characteristics of the three gliders were investigated by John Myers, and fellow Northrop pilots Harry Crosby[4] and Alex Papana.[5] AAF test pilots also participated in the flights conducted at the Flight Test Base at Muroc, Dry Lake, Harper's Lake, California, and Roach Dry Lake, Nevada. In the rather bland prose of official Army flight test reports, there is little evidence of the moments of stark terror experienced by company pilots Alex Papana and Harry Crosby at the controls of the tiny gliders.

Army pilots concluded that the glider was indeed flyable and controllable about all three axes. Aileron effectiveness was good, but fell short of current requirements for fighter aircraft. With regard to directional control, the time lag between operation of the rudder pedals and movement of the air-operated control surfaces was so great that the arrangement was considered impractical for that type of aircraft. Despite these limitations, the overall handling characteristics of the MX-334 were considered as good as or better than those of any other flying wing aircraft tested by the Army pilots to that date.

Test pilots sometimes described the tragedies and misfortunes that mark their daily lives in language entirely different from the engineering jargon of formal reports. Alex Papana and Harry Crosby flew many flights in the MX-334 gliders that deserved a few extra superlatives in their description. In 1980, former Northrop test pilot Max R. Stanley, a colleague of Crosby and Papana, described these experiences to a symposium of the Society of Experimental Test Pilots.

Two harrowing experiences occurred during this program. The first involved Alex Papana as pilot. Upon reaching the test altitude, Alex reached for the tow-line release, but inadvertently pulled the lever which jettisoned both the upper and lower escape hatch covers. The absence of the stream-lining effect of the hatch enclosures resulted in a dramatic increase in airplane drag and brought on very severe aircraft buffetting. Through a combination of pilot skill and good luck, Alex successfully landed on the lake bed after what must have been a hair-raising descent. As you know, the title of this session of the symposium is "Past Test Programs—Lessons Learned." I think the lesson to be learned from Alex's experience is that if you must pull something, be damn sure you pull the right thing.

The other harrowing experience occurred a few days later with Harry Crosby as the pilot. Immediately following towline release, Harry flew into the propwash of the P-38 tow plane . . . his glider pitched up, stalled and rolled off into a spin from which it recovered in a stable, shallow glide. The problem, however, was that it was flying inverted, and there was Crosby on his back in a prone position aircraft and unable to reach the controls. The escape hatch, which normally was on the bottom of the airplane, was now overhead. Somehow Harry managed to jettison the hatch and crawl through the opening to the top of the wing, which really was the bottom of the wing. He sat there for a moment contemplating his predicament. After deciding there was nothing he could do, he released his grasp, slid off the wing, and deployed his parachute. When he looked around he was amazed to see his still up-side-down glider flying in circles around him and descending at about the same rate he was. Although both the glider and the pilot landed at about the same time and in about the same place, they did not collide and Harry escaped without injury. The glider was damaged beyond repair.[6]

Despite the loss of the second MX-334 glider at Muroc, the test program proceeded in an orderly fashion through late 1943 and early 1944, until it was time for Northrop technicians to install the 427-pound Aerojet rocket motor in the squat, tailless aircraft. The motor nozzle, protruding through the trailing edge of the thin wing, was the only outward evidence of the engine's presence, although the actual motor, four pressure tanks, two propellant tanks, and hydraulic and electric control equipment were carefully fitted into the wing. One of the considerations in the design of this airplane was protection of the pilot from the monoethylaniline fuel and red fuming nitric acid oxidizer. The fuel tank was installed on one side of the pilot and the oxidizer tank on the other side. A heavy neoprene curtain was installed on each side of the pilot to protect him from any rupture of tanks or lines.

Beginning on June 20, 1944, exhaustive ground tests of the rocket motor were conducted at Harper Dry Lake, culminating in taxi tests on the desert floor by Harry Crosby. By the evening of July 4, the craft and Crosby were ready for their momentous flight.

Finally, almost three years after the successful maiden flight of the German Me 163, Harry Crosby eased himself into the prone position in the cramped cockpit of the MX 324. With his head resting in a specal sling behind the large glass windshield, Crosby had a clear view of the long tow line and the P-38 Lightning that was to tow him up to release altitude off the cracked, dry surface of Harper Dry Lake near Barstow, California. Early in the morning of July 5, 1944, P-38 pilot Martin Smith[7] towed Crosby and his strange-looking craft over the dry lake at about 8000 feet. Crosby tripped the towline release, braced himself in the narrow confines of the cockpit, and pressed the propulsion trigger on the control stick. Ignition of the 200-pound thrust Aerojet XCAL-200 rocket motor produced acceleration that, though hardly comparable to that of an afterburner in a modern jet fighter, at least proclaimed

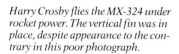

Harry Crosby flies the MX-324 under rocket power. The vertical fin was in place, despite appearance to the contrary in this poor photograph.

The XP-79B (right) is shown in the shop prior to painting. Some details of the cockpit, including headrest, flanked by control handlebars, are visible through the canopy. The so-called Flying Ram (below) was distinguished by twin vertical fins, two turbojet engines, and wing tip inlets for bellows-type rudders like those on the second XP-56. The XP-79B was the fourth turbojet-powered aircraft to fly in the United States.

America's belated entry into the era of rocket-powered flight. A short flight of over four minutes ended with a gentle landing on the dry lake bed.

Following Crosby's July 5th flight, other powered flights of the Rocket Wing were conducted. Some of these featured the early use of telemetry to transmit flight test data by radio to ground-based recorders. Despite the progress in the test program, however, the lack of more powerful rocket engines and a redirection of priorities resulted in termination of the project. Attention shifted to more unconventional approach to adapting the principles of the flying wing to aerial combat — the XP-79B.

The XP-79 was to have been an all-magnesium, rocket-powered, prone-pilot fighter-interceptor capable of speeds over 500 mph, with an exceptional rate of climb, and outstanding operational ceiling. It was to have been powered by an Aerojet 2000-pound thrust rocket using red fuming nitric acid and monoethylaniline (aniline) as propellants. Northrop engineers understood the corrosive effect of red fuming nitric acid on the magnesium fuel tanks in the aircraft. Thus, the protection of the fuel tanks from battle damage was of overriding importance. Allowing the acid and aniline to mix anywhere other than in the combustion chamber would have been catastrophic. To protect the propellants from battle damage, the fighter was a welded magnesium alloy monocoque structure with skin varying in thickness from three-quarters of an inch at the leading edge to one-eighth at the trailing edge. As in the MX-324 design, the pilot was to fly in the prone position.

Continuous delays in the development of a suitable rocket motor ultimately led to a decision to abandon that phase of the project and proceed with a turbojet-powered modification. In March 1943, plans were made to add two Westinghouse 19-B (J30) axial flow turbojets to the craft and its designation became XP-79B.

At this juncture the XP-79B acquired a new mission and a new nickname, the Flying Ram. Original specifications for the XP-79 do not mention ramming enemy aircraft as a mission requirement, but pilots associated with the MX-324 program recall that ramming was indeed the primary mission of the XP-79B. In Jack Northrop's words, "It was designed as a projectile, with the thought that it could be used to intercept and knock wings or tails off other airplanes. Rather than shooting at them, this airplane was going to slice sections off the other airplanes to destroy them."[8]

It is possible that the unusually high impact strength resulting from the magnesium construction might have provided Air Force planners with a rare opportunity to explore a concept of aerial warfare seldom practiced except *in extremis*. In retrospect, a tactic of such a desperate nature would seem unwarranted in view of the fact that in 1945 the U.S. Air Force had total command of the skies in every theater of war and mid-air collisions as a tactic would seem highly unrealistic. It is doubtful that many U.S. pilots had the skill or motivation to maneuver their aircraft in such a precise manner to collide with their opponents and return home intact.

Despite its debatable wisdom, the concept was approaching reality by mid-1945. In June 1945, the test aircraft, with its two 1150-pound thrust J30 turbojets installed and sporting two vertical fins had been delivered to Muroc Dry Lake for taxi tests. In September, the ill-fated XP-79B was ready for flight.

On September 12, 1945, just 10 days after the end of World War II, the XP-79B (43-52437) flew for the first and last time. The pilot was Harry Crosby, who had narrowly escaped death in the MX-334 glider, and was by then contemplating a more placid life on his ranch in California. Now, he again found himself in a situation beyond his control. Jack Northrop described the flight:

> The takeoff for this flight was normal, and for 15 minutes the airplane was flown in a beautiful demonstration. The pilot indicated mounting confidence by executing more and more maneuvers of a type that would not be expected unless he were thoroughly satisfied with the behavior of the airplane. After about 15 minutes of flying, the airplane entered what appeared to be a normal slow roll, from which it did not recover. As the rotation about the longitudinal axis continued the nose gradually dropped, and at the time of impact the airplane appeared to be in a steep vertical spin. The pilot endeavored to leave the ship but the speed was so high that he was unable to clear it successfully. Unfortunately, there was insufficient evidence to fully determine the cause of the disaster. However, in view of his prone position, a powerful, electrically controlled trim tab had been installed in the lateral controls to relieve the pilot of excessive loads. It is believed that a deliberate slow roll may have been attempted (as the pilot had previously slow rolled and looped other flying wing aircraft developed by the company) and that during this maneuver something failed in the lateral controls in such a way that the pilot was overpowered by the electrical trim mechanism.[9]

With the loss of the sole XP-79B, the program was cancelled.

Coincident with the MX-334, project, Northrop attempted to design an unmanned flying wing. Influenced by the British experiences with the German "buzz bombs," the AAF contracted with Northrop for development of the flying wing JB-1 Power Bomb.

Equipped with a pre-programmed guidance system, and powered by two turbojet engines, the Power Bomb was to be a ground-launched craft capable of striking a target some 200 miles away.

Under Project MX-543, 13 JB-1s were ordered but only two were built; the others were redesigned and redesignated JB-10. The first of the JB-1s was a manned glider to test the flying qualities of the basic design. The bat-like configuration consisted of a magnesium and aluminum alloy wing with a magnesium alloy center section containing a pilot's compartment and two bomb containers, one on either side of the pilot.

The first series of test flights of the glider began in 1944 with Harry Crosby at the controls, a year before his death in the XP-79B. Using aircraft tows to get airborne and ascend to release altitude, Crosby put the revolutionary aircraft through a successful test program. Following this unpowered phase, the second JB-1 was equipped with two 400-pound thrust General Electric B1 turbojet engines, which were modified turbo-superchargers. The unmanned craft was launched by means of a rocket-assisted sled that carried the Power Bomb down a 400-foot track to attain a takeoff speed of 160 mph.

Before a complete development program could be conducted for the JB-1

The JB-1 manned glider (right) was built to flight test the design of the turbojet-equipped Power Bomb that followed. Two hitches were attached to the tips of the two bomb containers, one of which is visible in the right foreground. The jet-powered JB-1 (below), designed with wing containers for two 2000-pounds bombs, is poised for a ground launch from a 400-foot track.

Constructed of aluminum and magnesium using Northrop's patented "Heliarc" welding process, the JB-10 was launched from a track-mounted sled by electrically-fired Tiny Tim rockets.

A JB-10 is shown undergoing tests at Eglin Field, Florida, near the end of World War II.

Power Bomb, official interest switched to the use of the pulse jet engine. Consequently, the JB-1 program was modified in late 1944, and Northrop was asked by the Army to design the JB-10 Jet Bomb (a modified JB-1) using a Ford Motor Company version of the German V-1 buzz bomb engine. The engine, designated PJ-31-1, was located in a cooling shroud in the wing center section. One 1825-pound warhead was positioned on each side of the engine.

Theoretically capable of striking targets at a range of up to 185 miles, the JB-10 was ground launched from a Northrop-developed rocket-sled arrangement. Four Tiny Tim rockets propelled the flying wing on its launch down the track to a speed of 220 mph required for pulsejet engine operation. Cruising speed was to have been about 425 mph.

Test launchings of the JB-10 were conducted in 1945 at Muroc and at Eglin Field, Florida. Only 11 JB-10s were constructed by the end of World War. However, over 1000 Northrop-designed sleds were built for launching other guided missiles, such as the JB-2. The program was terminated at the end of the war.

One concept that had its genesis in late 1945 deserves consideration, although it does not fit conveniently into the categories of flying wings designed for tactical purposes during World War II, nor does it belong to the postwar family of flying wings. The Northrop X-4, nicknamed the Bantam, or Skylancer, was a swept wing, tailless research aircraft designed to investigate stability and control problems at transonic velocities of about Mach 0.87. By the spring of 1946, Jack Northrop was by far the leading proponent and most experienced designer of tailless aircraft in the United States, and the obvious choice to develop the tiny X-4 for the AAF and NACA.

Drawing on previous experience with the ill-fated XP-79 program, the Northrop design team, under the leadership of Arthur I. Lusk, produced a rather rakish-looking aircraft that bore a decided resemblance to the British de Havilland D.H. 108 Swallow, which preceded the X-4 by more than two years. Two X-4s were built; the first (46-676) flew on December 16, 1948, with Northrop pilot Charles Tucker at the controls. Various mechanical problems limited test flights to three in six months, a disappointing performance record that the plagued X-4 No. 1 never overcame during its brief 10-flight history. It remained for X-4 No. 2 (46-677) to carry the brunt of the flight test program, one that stretched interminably from first flight on June 7, 1949, through late 1953.[10]

In the 102 flights of the second X-4, Northrop, NACA, and U.S. Air Force test pilots explored the transonic regime to determine the effectiveness of the tailless design at high subsonic Mach numbers. Flight tests vividly demonstrated that above Mach 0.76, yawing and rolling motions persisted, elevon effectiveness decreased markedly, and at Mach 0.88, the pilots encountered an uncontrollable oscillation about three axes, with an undamped porpoising motion above Mach 0.9.[11]

Viewed purely from the standpoint of contributions to the war effort, the record of success of the wartime flying wings was hardly impressive. Harry Crosby lost his life; Alex Papana and John Myers very nearly lost theirs; none

Small and highly maneuverable, the X-4 (right) was powered by two 1600-pound thrust Westinghouse J30 turbojets fitted in the wing roots. Wing control surfaces consisted of outboard elevons and split flaps designed to serve as speed brakes and landing flaps. The speed brakes, shown in the extended position on the second X-4 (46-677) (below) were extremely effective for speed control during flights at high subsonic speeds.

of the projects really came close to operational service, with the possible exception of the JB-10; it experienced two partially successful test flights in 10 attempts. Notwithstanding the negative aspects of the programs, however, there was probably some transfer of technical data and expertise from these programs to the N-9M and XB-35 aircraft which were then undergoing concurrent development.

NOTES

1. A Harvard law school graduate and flying addict since high school, John W. Myers acquired his pilot's license in 1929. At the beginning of World War II, he left his law practice to take up test flying, eventually joining Northrop in 1942. The irrepressible Myers flew almost all of the Northrop flying wings, including first flights of the N-9M, XP-56, and MX-334 glider.

2. John Myers, Max Stanley, and Moye Stephens, interview with E.T. Wooldridge, Los Angeles, California, February 1982 (U.S., Northrop).

3. John K. Northrop, interview with E.W. Robischon, Santa Barbara, California, July 23, 1968, (U.S., Northrop).

4. Airline pilot, aircraft designer, frequent participant in the National Air Races of the 1930s, Harry Crosby came to Northrop in 1943. A highly competitive individual, Crosby demonstrated tremendous flying skill, versatility, and courage in his two years of test flying the wartime flying wings.

5. Of all the flying wing pilots, Alex Papana had the most extraordinary background. Born in Bucharest, Rumania, the son of an Army General, Papana eventually became one of the world's leading sportsmen and pilots. He was tennis champion of Rumania, holder of several motorcycle and automobile racing records in Europe, Olympic bobsled champion at Lake Placid in 1932, holder of several Rumanian aircraft speed and altitude records, and three-time world aerobatic champion. A superb airman, Papana joined Northrop as a test pilot in 1944.

6. Max Stanley, "The Flying Wing," pp. 242–243. (U.S., Northrop).

7. On January 26, 1946, Captain Martin L. Smith was one of three pilots who flew Lockheed P-80A Shooting Stars across the United States on a record breaking flight. Captain Smith's time was 4 hours, 33 minutes, 25 seconds. In April 1946, Captain Smith set a new national record of 29 minutes, 15 seconds, for a flight between New York and Washington, D.C., flying his P-80A at an average speed of 438.9 mph.

8. Richard A. Thurston, "John K. Northrop Oral History Transcripts," (U.S., Northrop).

9. John K. Northrop, "The Development of All-Wing Aircraft," Address before the Royal Aeronautical Society, p. 000 (U.S., Northrop).

10. In 1982, X-4 No. 2 was obtained by Northrop Corp. from the U.S.A.F. Museum for eventual restoration. The first X-4 was given to the U.S. Air Force Academy in Colorado Springs, Colorado, for display.

11. Melvin Sadoff and A. Scott Crossfield, *A Flight Evaluation of the Stability and Control of the X-4 Swept-wing Semitailless Airplane*, p. 13 (U.S., Northrop).

Chapter 7   N-9M: Prelude to the Flying Wing Bombers

The next step on the development path from the N-1M to a heavy, long-range bomber was a flying model that was the aerodynamic equivalent of the larger flying wing. Such was the N-9M, a 60-foot scale model about one-third the size of the projected XB-35 in every comparable dimension, and designed to provide flight test information from which the maneuverability, controllability, and performance of the XB-35 airplane could be predicted. Four N-9Ms, the N-9M-1, N-9M-2, N-9MA, and N-9MB, were eventually built.

Construction and test of the flying mockup, for delivery in 360 days, were approved by the Secretary of War on October 3, 1941.[1] The aircraft bore a distinct resemblance to its smaller predecessor, the N-1M. With two 260-hp Menasco C6S-4 engines buried in the wing, the 7000-pound N-9M was designed for an endurance of 3.2 hours with 100 gallons of fuel, and had a design ceiling of 21,500 feet. Controls consisted of elevons, rudders, and trim tabs. An hydraulically operated, retractable tricycle type landing gear was provided, and supplemented by a fourth retractable wheel extending from the trailing edge just aft of the canopy to protect the propellers in the event of an extremely tail-low landing.

Cockpit space was at a premium, with various pieces of test equipment, switches, and gauges using up what little space was available. Seat and rudder pedals were not adjustable, quite unusual for an airplane of that size and maneuverability. As in the N-1M, the usual control stick was replaced by a control column and wheel, an awkward and cumbersome arrangement for the size of the cockpit, but appropriate for its role as a bomber mockup.

The first flight of the N-9M-1 was on December 27, 1942, three months later than specified by contract. Over the next five months there were 45 flights. With a few exceptions, most were terminated by mechanical failures of one sort or another, with the Menasco engines the primary source of problems.[2] Consequently, very little data relative to drag, stability, and control were obtained. After about 22.5 hours of accumulated flight time, the N-9M crashed approximately 12 miles west of Muroc Army Air Base on May 19,

133

The first of the four N-9Ms had unusual split flap drag rudders whose hinge lines were oriented fore-and-aft. The aircraft was designed for a maximum speed of 257 mph at 7000 feet.

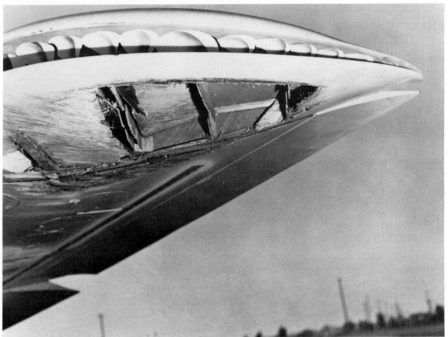

Photographs taken after a minor accident with the N-9M-1 afford a unique opportunity to examine the wing tip rudders. In the photograph above the right hand rudder is open, the left hand rudder almost closed. At right the underside of the left hand rudder has been torn away and the rudder is partially open, revealing teeth that have been painted in the cavity. (Courtesy G.H. Balzer)

Two photographs show the remains of N-9M-1 after Max Constant's fatal accident on May 19, 1943. The view at right is from in front of the aircraft, looking aft. The two propeller shaft housings are evident, with the cockpit in the middle, canopy missing, antenna mast at the rear. The view below is from aft of the airplane looking forward. Part of the left hand drag rudder, complete with teeth, is in the left foreground. (Courtesy G.H. Balzer)

1943. The pilot, Max Constant, was killed as he attempted to recover the aircraft from a righthand, 60 degree nose-down spin.[3] Apparently, Constant made every attempt to stop the spin, since the left hand spin chute had been deployed, and the flaps appeared to be partially lowered. There was definite indication that the pilot had attempted to leave the aircraft; the cockpit enclosure had been released, the propeller brakes had been applied, and Constant had unfastened his safety belt. Whether he was prevented from bailing out by lack of time or by some unknown physical circumstance was not determined.

It appeared that the N-9M might have dangerous spin characteristics that could not be controlled by normal use of the control surfaces; perhaps the spin chutes were inadequate in size or improperly placed on the airplane for quick recovery. Further investigation in the NACA spin tunnel was required.[4]

The loss of the first N-9M was followed a month later by the first flight of N-9M-2 on June 24, 1943. A minor setback was experienced when the cockpit canopy came off in flight and, despite a successful landing, slight damage to a landing gear door, radio mast, and yaw meter resulted. Nonetheless, by mid-September 1943, the first reliable drag data were being obtained on N-9M-2; they indicated the drag of the XB-35 at cruising speed would be approximately 7 to 12 percent greater than that estimated from wind tunnel test results.

The N-9M-2 generally exhibited satisfactory longitudinal and lateral stability and control in high speed and cruising ranges. Some difficulty in obtaining satisfactory directional control was experienced. Of more concern, however, was the occurrence of severe reversal of elevator control forces at high lift coefficients. Due to premature separation of the airflow over the top surface of the wing as the stall was approached, flow conditions over the elevons caused them to trail upward producing a force reversal on the elevator control. This may have been the reason for the difficulty which led to the crash of the first N-9M.

By April 1944, the N-9M-2 had completed 33 flights for a total flying time of 23 hours. Data obtained on the flights were constructive and contributed to performance predictions for the XB-35, then in the design phase.

On June 28, 1944, Army pilots flew acceptance flights on the N-9MA. This model contained practically all of the design features that were to be used in the XB-35 aircraft. In addition to the split trailing edge and pitch control flaps that served as devices for increasing lift and drag, a leading edge slot was installed near the tip of each wing to lessen stall tendencies at high angles of attack. Flight characteristics of the N-9MA gave firm indications that the characteristics of the XB-35 bomber would also be satisfactory. Ground handling was excellent; the aircraft was very maneuverable and responsive in turns; control was good, although elevator control was quite sensitive. Flying characteristics in rough air, previously reported as unsatisfactory for the first two N-9Ms, were satisfactory, due to new rudders and hydraulically powered elevons.

By October 1944, the authorized flight test program for the N-9MA had been completed. The aircraft had flown about 50 flights, and stability, con-

The third N-9M, designated N-9MA, is shown in final assembly, with the fourth aircraft, N-9MB, in the background. Arrayed along the trailing edge, from the wing tip toward the center line are the pitch trimmer with the split drag rudder included, the elevon, and landing flap. At the leading edge is a slot designed to improve flying qualities at high angles of attack.

The completed N-9MA awaits flight test. N-9M-1, N-9M-2, and N-9MA all had semicircular cooling air intakes at the leading edge of the wing. Paint schemes on the N-9MA and B were distinctive: the "A" was painted blue on top, yellow on bottom; the "B" was yellow on top, blue on bottom.

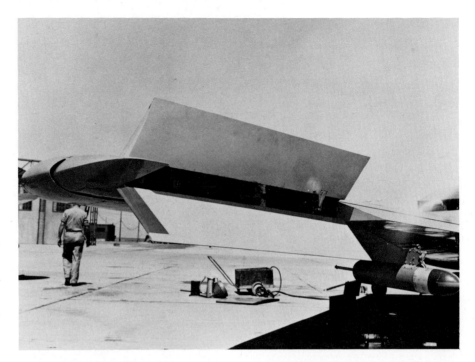

Wing tip details of the N-9MA at right show an open drag rudder, a split surface control mounted in another hinged control surface, the pitch trimmer. Each surface could be operated in conjunction with or independently of the other. The photograph below shows one of the exit flaps for engine cooling air and exhaust. (Courtesy G.H. Balzer)

"Don't look now but that thing is following us again." A fuselage and tail looking for a home is the subject of this cartoon reflecting the increasing public awareness of and fascination with Northrop's flying wing concepts of the 1940s.

Obviously a happy man, Jack Northrop has just finished his first ride in an N-9M in 1943. The cramped space behind John Myers was normally occupied by a fuel tank. Crew chief Orbie Blair shares the boss's enthusiasm. (Courtesy John Myers)

Harry Crosby relaxes on the wing of an N-9M while Alex Papana describes the sensations of his first flight in the aircraft in 1944. (Courtesy G.H. Balzer)

trol, and flying qualities were judged to be generally satisfactory. Several inadvertent half-turn spins had been experienced and recovery had been accomplished without difficulty. Northrop test pilot Alex Papana, who along with Harry Crosby had experienced some interesting rides in Northrop's experimental MX-334 glider, had even engaged in some extra-curricular aerobatics in the N-9MA, in one instance accomplishing four loops in quick succession.[5]

With the completion of the test program, the N-9MA was used by the Army to familiarize pilots with the craft. At about the same time, the fourth and last of the series, the N-9MB, was nearing completion. It would eventually be used to flight test the latest in configuration and improved systems that would be incorporated into the XB-35. As in N-9M-1, space for a passenger was created behind the pilot by removing a fuel tank.[6]

The N-9MB, with more powerful 300-hp Franklin engines, provided yeoman service in the flight test program, producing invaluable data that contributed directly to the engineering of the bomber program. The production of the B-35 had become bogged down by a shortage of engineers, design problems, conflicts with other production programs, and excessive requirements for production engineering. The cumulative effect was postponement of the first flight date. World War II ended, the program dragged on, and the N-9Ms continued to do their jobs.

Last in the series of four N-9Ms was the N-9MB, identifiable by its yellow top and oblong air inlets. The N-9MB had 300 hp, eight cylinder Franklin engines, a flight control "feel" system, autopilot, and a reversible power control system.

Northrop N-9M pilot Max Stanley was instrumental in checking out many Air Force pilots in the N-9MA shown here. Stanley went on to become the chief test pilot of the XB-35/YB-49 heavy bombers.

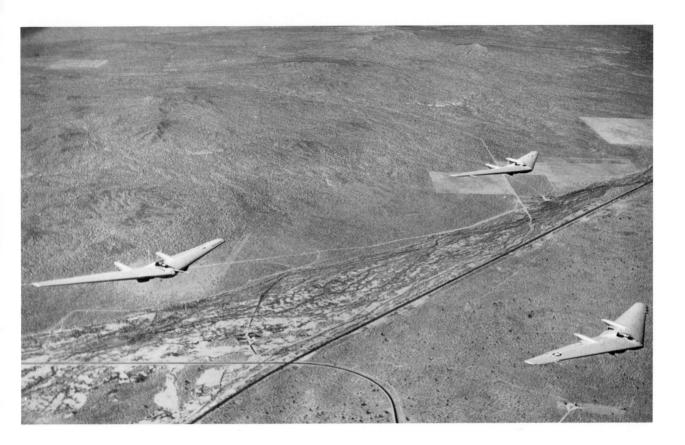

A rare sight indeed is this formation of three N-9Ms over the Mojave desert. The N-9MB is at left, N-9MA at right background, N-9M-2 at right foreground.

In May 1946, an Army test pilot assigned to Colonel Albert Boyd's Flight Test Section at Muroc summarized his observations and impressions of his one-flight evaluation of the N-9MB as follows:

> An hour's flight is hardly a fair basis for drawing decisive conclusions. However, the airplane flew surprisingly well, was more stable and handled far better than most would expect. It would take a few more hours practice to make good takeoffs and get the proper coordination on turns. But the technique could be mastered without too much difficulty. It serves its purpose well as a flying model.[7]

The pilot's name was Captain Glen W. Edwards. Almost two months later the first XB-35 made its initial flight, beginning a protracted flight test program during which Edwards would lose his life.

NOTES

1. Two additional N-9M flying models were ordered on September 10, 1942, to avoid delays in the event of an accident to No. 1 and to give the Air Materiel Command a model for study.

2. Plagued with engine problems on many of his test flights, John Myers finally went to engine designer Al Menasco to seek a solution. Menasco's advice: "Take my nameplate off the engines!" The Menascos used in the first three N-9Ms were second hand engines, spare parts were scarce, and the engines were not designed for horizontal installation, as in the N-9Ms. See J. Myers,

M. Stanley, and M. Stephens, interview with E.T. Wooldridge, Los Angeles, California, February 1982 (U.S., Northrop).

3. Max Constant, like Alex Papana, was European, and a veteran of the air show circuit. Born in Bordeaux, France, in 1899, Constant was active in the movie industry as writer and director before turning to a career in aviation. He participated in the Bendix Trophy races, placing fourth in the 1938 race flying Jackie Cochrane's Beechcraft. Known as an excellent instrument flight instructor, Constant worked in that capacity for a number of years at Burbank, California. He went to work for Northrop in 1943, only several weeks before his tragic accident.

4. According to Max Stanley, Northrop's leading test pilot on the Flying Wing bomber program, wind tunnel tests conducted prior to the N-9M accident indicated the airplane had normal stall and spin characteristics with a center-of-gravity forward of the midpoint of the wing; recovery from these maneuvers was normal. As the center-of-gravity moved aft, the stall and spin characteristics became increasingly unacceptable. These wind tunnel tests were confirmed repeatedly by actual flight tests.

5. Alex Papana's pay for performing certain N-9M flight tests seems trivial compared to some of the more inflated salaries of the 1980s. For "hazards including flights at low speeds, flights with unsymmetrical power settings, stall test and flights in rough air," Northrop paid Papana a bonus of $3500. See G.W. Monson, Treasurer, Northrop Aircraft, Inc., letter to AAF Resident Representative, August 16, 1944 (U.S., Northrop).

6. Jack Northrop became the first passenger on one of his flying wings when he rode in the N-9M jump seat. He also flew as a passenger on the second flight of the XB-35 bomber.

7. Glen W. Edwards, *Pilot's Observations on the N-9M Flying Wing*, p. 5 (U.S., Northrop).

Chapter 8

The Flying Wing Bombers: Triumph and Despair

The final chapter in the odyssey of Jack Northrop's quest for the true flying wing is a microcosm of all of the disappointments and glorious moments one could expect in the development of an aircraft as unconventional as the flying wing bomber. The piston-engined XB-35, and its jet-powered successor, the YB-49, were immensely pleasing to the eye, but to conservatives within the aeronautical community, they probably did not "look right", and therefore their ultimate success was in doubt.

The flying wing bombers enjoyed all the usual financial support and governmental interest normally associated with a wartime program. They also suffered through the chaotic period that came with war's end. The program endured, however, because of the enormous potential demonstrated by the unique aircraft. The enthusiasm for the program that was demonstrated by the Northrop "family" was shared to a great extent by many of the technical and management people of the Army Air Forces. Their foresight, assistance, and encouragement kept the development program going through the rough times.

Project MX-140, as the bomber program was called, was officially initiated by contract action on November 22, 1941, following previous discussions between Northrop and Air Force officials regarding performance requirements for a high altitude, long range, heavy bombardment airplane. The numbers that spelled out the airplane's vital statistics in formal Airplane Specifications NS-9A gave no hint of the sheer expansiveness of the airplane, and its spectacular performance. They also gave no hint of the problems that would attend its design, construction, and flight evaluation.

In size, the XB-35 would dwarf the B-17 Flying Fortress, with wing area and gross weight almost three times those of the legendary heavy bomber. The unconventional control system reflected years of study, wind tunnel tests, and flight test data gleaned from the N-1M and N-9M programs. The elevons and rudders were power operated. Thus, it was necessary to provide an artificial "feel" to the controls for these surfaces. This was accomplished by springs attached to the control wheels and rudder pedal mechanisms which

Jack Northrop greets General H.H. "Hap" Arnold, Chief of the Air Corps, during one of his visits to the Hawthorne plant. General Arnold's support was instrumental in sustaining the wartime development of the flying wings.

returned the controls to neutral and provided the "feel" necessary to prevent overcontrol of the rudder and aileron movement of the elevons. "Feel" to the operation of the control columns for elevator control was provided by ram air pressure in a bellows attached to the control columns.

Trim flaps, elevons, and landing flaps were arrayed in order from each wing tip inboard along the trailing edge of the wing. The electrically actuated trim flaps at the wing tips were used by the pilot in much the same manner as elevator or aileron tabs. Their primary purpose was to balance the large diving moments produced by the split trailing edge landing flaps, minimizing the upward deflection of the elevons and thus permitting them to be deflected over a greater range as elevators. The trim flaps could also be operate differentially to counteract unbalanced rolling moments.

Rudders consisted of split flaps that were incorporated as an integral part of the trim flaps at the trailing edges of the wing tips. Operated one at a time by the pilot's movement of the corresponding rudder pedal, the surfaces deflected above and below the trim flap. Simultaneous movement of the rudder pedals, which were not interconnected, opened both rudders for speed control.

Despite the unconventional arrangement and function of the control surface, the conventional control column with wheel and rudder pedals made the pilot feel right at home.

Contributing to increased longitudinal stability at high angles of attack were wing tip slots with automatically controlled cover doors. These doors were set to open at high lift coefficients, preventing wing tip stall and increasing stability. A switch actuated by the landing gear also opened the doors when the gear was down.

One of the primary concerns in the layout of the aircraft was the cockpit design. Despite unorthodox configuration, space was not a problem. The aircraft's cockpit featured convenient control and instrument arrangements and excellent visibility.

The pilot seated in the plexiglass bubble to the left of the aircraft centerline. The copilot was to the right of and below the pilot, behind a large window in the leading edge of the wing. An engineer's station was also in the forward part of the crew nacelle, as were stations for the radio operator, navigator, bombardier, and gunners. The mid-section of the crew nacelle had sleeping facilities for a relief crew of six people, a requirement for operational missions of 10,000 miles where crew fatigue would be a primary consideration. The after section contained the gunner's station. The seven-foot headroom in the crew's quarters was certainly adequate, and the accommodations were the first of such extent and complexity to have been incorporated into such a radical design.

A brief look at the overall arrangement would not be complete without at least some reference to the "main battery" of the XB-35—its eight bomb bays. Capable of carrying 10,000 pounds of conventional bombs (but not an atomic weapon), the bays were incorporated in the wings, arrayed four on each side of the crew nacelle.[1] Defensive armament consisted of twenty 0.50 caliber machine guns contained in seven remotely controlled turrets: four on the wing, two on the crew nacelle, and a tail stinger.

The power plants were also vital to the successful operation of this revolutionary weapons system. They consisted of four Pratt & Whitney Wasp Major engines, one pair each of R-4360-17 and R-4360-21 series equipped with single stage GE turbo-superchargers, each delivering 3000 hp. The "Achilles' heel" of the installation was the propulsion power train. Each engine was coupled to a remote gear box assembly by an extension drive shaft. Two sets of four-bladed, dual rotating, reversible pitch, full feathering, Hamilton Standard propellers were mounted on dual concentric shafts extending from each gear box. The engines were completely enclosed within the wing, an arrangement that imposed severe requirements on the aircraft's structure. Superchargers, intercoolers, oil coolers, and fans for ground-cooling and cooling at low speeds were located in the wing, as were cooling ducts and controls to diffuse the air around the engines and expel it through flaps near the trailing edge.

Translating 100 pages of statistics and technical terms into 100 tons of complex, futuristic airplane proved to be an almost insurmountable task. From contract approval in November 1941, to first flight of the XB-35 on June 25, 1946, there were interminable delays. At one time or another, changes in priorities, design and engineering difficulties, problems with ground testing engines, shortages of engineers, indecision by management,

Conventional instruments and control switches are arranged in a slightly unconventional manner in the XB-35 cockpit. Flight instruments are arrayed on the vertical panel between the pilot stations; radio equipment and prop controls are located on the pedestal separating the pilot stations. One set of throttle controls is suspended from the top of the cabin between the pilot and copilot, another is mounted in a quadrant at the engineers table further aft, along with the mixture controls. (SI Negative 75-01648)

constant shortages of government furnished equipment (GFE), and a myriad of other factors contributed to the lengthy production process. Of all the obstacles to orderly progress, the most frustrating involved the highly unsatisfactory working relationship between two major aircraft builders, Northrop and Martin.

Following an initial contract for one XB-35 airplane, approved November 22, 1941, Northrop received an order for an additional XB-35 as a backup in January 1942. Later that year, another 13 service test models were contracted for, to be designated YB-35. By June 1943, with a production contract for 200 B-35s on hand, and the first flight date still out of sight, it was apparent that Northrop production and engineering facilities, already heavily committed to production of P-61 Black Widow night fighters, were inadequate for

Ground support equipment and people are dwarfed by the immense XB-35 as it is rolled out of the hangar for engine and taxi tests in 1946. Arrayed along the leading edge of the wing are air inlets to supply cooling air to the engines.

This striking photograph, staged though it may be, dramatically shows the XB-35s' "Achilles' heel"—the eight, four-bladed, contra-rotating propellers. Constant troubles with government-furnished gear boxes and propeller governors severely restricted the systematic development of the XB-35 Flying Wing.

the job. If the program was to proceed, engineering and production assistance would have to come from some other source.

By the end of June 1943, the Glenn L. Martin Company of Baltimore, Maryland, at the AAF's request, had contracted to assist Northrop in engineering the XB-35 and YB-35 and also to manufacture 200 production B-35s. Delivery of the first production airplane was to be in June 1945. From a tactical and logistical standpoint, there was no further need for Martin's B-33 Super Marauder. The production contract was cancelled and the available engineering talent was diverted to the XB-35 project.

The engineering "partnership" that evolved between Northrop and Martin not only failed to produce a single B-35, but also engendered confusion, delays, and even ill will. Engineering work was carried out simultaneously at both companies on "X," "Y," and production airplanes, resulting in indecision, lack of coordination, and unresolved questions of priorities and responsibilities. Loss of engineers to the military draft aggravated an already untenable situation. As of March 1944, Martin had made no commitments to

Basic design similarities between N-9M and XB-35 are evident in this photograph of the XB-35, under tow prior to taxi tests at Northrop in May 1946. Split-flap rudders attached to the pitch trimmers, elevons and landing flaps are along the trailing edge; automatic wing slot is visible just aft of the leading edge on the left side.

materials and had not started tooling. The program was already 18 months behind schedule and relations between Northrop and Martin were considerably strained.

In May 1944, the AAF reviewed the entire program. It was the opinion of some officials that the attitude of Martin management was a significant factor in the lack of progress to date. Never enthusiastic about producing any airplane not of their own design, Martin continually put forth more reasons for not continuing their part of the production program. Martin management expressed little faith in the B-35 as a practical airplane.[2] The AAF decided to cancel Martin's production contract, with the understanding that Martin would continue to give Northrop engineering assistance on the "X" and "Y" models. Additional engineering assistance would be made available from the Otis Elevator Company. No production engineering was to be undertaken at that time. In effect, it was a conscious decision that the B-35 would be a post-war airplane.

December 1944, marked a significant turning point in the development of the Flying Wing bomber. By that time, both Germany and England were using turbojet-powered aircraft in combat. The Messerschmitt Me 262 first appeared on combat in July 1944, followed shortly by the first victory of the British Gloster Meteor over a German V-1 missile. In the United States, the Bell XP-59A Airacomet had flown in 1942, and by late 1944 the Lockheed P-80A Shooting Star was almost operational. It was becoming obvious that the world was on the threshold of the jet age and piston engined warplanes such as the B-35 would eventually become obsolete. On the other hand, a B-35 fitted with turbojet engines began to look extremely attractive.

Consequently, in December 1944, series of modification and conversion programs began that lasted until the final days of the Flying Wing bomber. Proposals for changes in the aircraft mission, combined with alternative power plant arrangements led to a bewildering variety of aircraft configurations and designations. After years of conversion and modification programs that ensued, only six were completed and flew, three of which had piston engines, and three with turbojets.

It was another year and a half after the modification proposals in December 1944, before an XB-35 would finally take to the air on its maiden flight. It was a frustrating period marked by engine development problems, delays due to lack of experience in construction of very large aircraft, late deliveries of major GFE items, and the acute conversion problems experienced by the defense contractors with the end of World War II.

The majestic XB-35 (42-13603) moved for the first time on its own wheels and under its own power on May 16, 1946. The occasion was a slow taxi test, and at the controls was the Northrop test pilot who would shepherd the Flying Wings through four turbulent years of flight tests, Max Stanley.[3] Accompanying Stanley as copilot was Fred Bretcher, who would be at his side during much of the flying program.

As the XB-35 began to move slowly down the 100-foot wide runway at Hawthorne, its 172-foot wing span seemed to dwarf even the building of the nearby Northrop plant from which it came. To Jack Northrop, standing at the flight ramp, the sound of four R-4360s running at the same time, even at taxi power setting, must have been overwhelming. As Max Stanley gave him a "thumbs up" at the conclusion of the satisfactory test, Jack Northrop surely must have been elated at this sign of progress and the prospect of a first flight in the not too distant future.

The day finally came. After dozens of high-speed taxi runs, during which speeds as high as 115 mph were attained, the aircraft seemed ready. June 25, 1946, was picked for first flight. Only a small crowd of sightseers and media people watched Max Stanley, Fred Bretcher, and Flight Engineer O.H. Douglas climb up into the flight deck, which by 10:00 A.M. was like an oven in the hot California sun. Absent were the thousands of designers, engineers, and shop workers who had labored for years over the engineering and construc-

In an historic moment Max Stanley lifts the world's largest flying wing off Northrop Field on its first flight on June 25, 1946. The uneventful flight terminated at Muroc Air Base.

The historic first flight of the Northrop XB-35 Flying Wing is over, to the obvious delight of pilot Max Stanley, flight engineer O.H. Douglas, and copilot Charles Fred Bretcher. (Courtesy American Hall of Aviation History Collection, Northrop University)

tion of the bomber. They had been restricted to their desks and work stations by company executives concerned over crowd control during the momentous occasion. Absent also was the man whose creative genius had spawned the giant wing, Jack Northrop, who, abiding by company policy, also remained at his desk, in an incredible display of self discipline.

"This is it!" With those words, Max Stanley advanced the throttles and, with 12,000 hp pushing the huge wing along, the XB-35 thundered down the narrow runway at Hawthorne. At 120 mph, Stanley slowly eased the control column back and at 10:32 A.M., the Flying Wing flew for the first time. Finally, after years of planning and experimenting, Jack Northrop had accomplished what Junkers, Soldenhoff, and other early pioneers had only dreamed of.

The first flight was essentially a ferry flight from Northrop Airport to Muroc Army Air Base. The idea was to get to Muroc with a minimum of trouble, but at the same time to learn about the flying characteristics of the airplane. Stanley tested the controls with the landing gear up and down several times. Highest airspeed attained was 200 mph, as the Flying Wing, with its P-61 Black Widow chase plane in company, cleared the mountains and began its descent to Muroc. As a precautionary measure, a no-flap approach was made, with a smooth touchdown at 112 mph. The 44-minute flight was uneventful, except for erratic operation of a propeller governor. Everyone associated with the project was jubilant, anxious to press on with the flight testing and prove the design once and for all.

But the minor problem with the propeller governor did not fade away. The XB-35 flew twice more in the next three months, accumulating only three hours of flight time by mid-September 1946. Problems with the Hamilton Standard propeller governors became chronic, with the propellers continually "hunting" around a constant speed setting and "creeping" in fixed pitch during air operations. Additionally, there was evidence that the huge counter-rotating propellers were operating under excessive stress, leading to a restriction of 80 hours operating time due to the danger of fatigue.

Another major problem with GFE arose. Troubles centered around the gear box assembly that coupled each engine to its propeller by means of a drive shaft from engine to gear box, and a dual concentric shaft from gear box to the counter-rotating propellers. Propellers and engine vibration caused frequent failures of the gear boxes. A flexible, vibration absorbing gear box mount was a vital necessity for successful flight testing.

At the beginning of 1947, the Flying Wing program consisted of one XB-35 flying, albeit occasionally, one XB-35 about to finish engineering inspection in March, two YB-49s (the jet engine configured B-35) and six YB-35s (built to XB-35 specifications) either complete or in the final stage of assembly. The remaining five YB-35s on the existing contract were to be equipped with more modern navigation and weapons systems, and thus were to be designated YB-35As.

The first XB-35 flew only intermittently during 1947, plagued by landing gear doors failing to retract and the continuing gear box malfunctions. The second XB-35 (42-38323) flew for the first time almost one year after the first,

Regardless of developmental problems, the Flying Wing in the air was the epitome of style and grace, exhibiting an extraordinary quality that caught the fancy and imagination of the public.

Northrop test pilots John Myers (left) and Max Stanley (right) discuss the merits of flying wings during a visit to the United States by John Cunningham, chief test pilot for the de Havilland Aircraft Company, Ltd. A legendary night fighter pilot during World War II, Cunningham assumed duties as chief test pilot after the tragic death of young Geoffrey de Havilland in the D.H. 108. Cunningham flew the initial flights of the D.H. 106 Comet, world's first jet airliner, the D.H. 110 Sea Vixen shipboard fighter, and D.H. 121 Trident transport. In 1948, he established a new world's altitude record of 59,446 feet in a D.H. 100 Vampire. (Courtesy American Hall of Aviation History Collection, Northrop University)

on June 26, 1947. It too, began to experience the same difficulties as the first aircraft. In desperation, the Air Materiel Command cancelled dual rotation propellers for the YB-35 and decided to use single rotation gear boxes and 15-foot diameter Hamilton Standard propellers, despite the resulting deterioration in performance. In April, both XB-35s were grounded for installation of the changes. Flight tests did not resume until February 1948.

The troublesome contra-rotating propellers eventually gave way to four new single-rotation propellers, shown here installed on the first XB-35. Despite the change, the piston-engined B-35 eventually became a victim of the jet age.

As a result of the 1944 study of the possibilities of converting the YB-35 to turbojet engines, two of these aircraft were modified to the YB-49 configuration. In the altered aircraft eight 4000-pound thrust TG-180 (J35) engines, designed by General Electric and built by Allison, were substituted for the four R-4360 reciprocating engines. Aside from the absence of propellers the most noticeable change was the addition of four vertical fins to the trailing edge of the wing. These mammoth fins, twice the height of a man, were added to provide the directional stability originally provided by the four propeller shaft housings and propellers. The dorsal fins were extended forward to a point near the leading edge of the wing to inhibit spanwise boundary-layer flow. The whole installation went entirely against Northrop's concept of a pure flying wing, but for a wing of that size, some protuberances were necessary.

155

By trading props for tailpipes and adding vertical fins, the B-35 acquired a new designation, B-49, and a new lease on life. Gross weight increased 30,000 pounds, maximum bomb load decreased from 44,800 to 32,000 pounds, and range decreased to about 4900 miles, despite the addition of fuel tanks.

156

Shown here is the right side bank of four J35 turbojet engines flanked by two fixed vertical fins. At the lower left is the right side landing flap in the extended position.

Local residents man the roof tops and line the fence at Northrop Field to watch the beautiful YB-49 depart on its maiden flight. For Max Stanley and his flight crew, the transition from props to jets was startling but caused no problems.

Highlight of the YB-49 test program was the long range test flight on April 26, 1948. The aircraft took off with a gross weight of 192,000 pounds, and flew a distance of 3528 miles at a true airspeed of 388 mph. A round robin course over the California and Arizona desert was flown. The only mishap was that a rough running engine had to be shut down two hours before landing at Muroc.

The eight-jet YB-49 (42-102367) was rolled out and unveiled to an admiring press at Hawthorne on Monday morning, September 29, 1947. The first taxi test was on October 20, with Max Stanley, Fred Bretcher, and O.H. Douglas at their accustomed crew stations.

The first flight on October 21, 1947, was from Hawthorne to Muroc; the 34 minutes in the air were uneventful. Orva Douglas summed up the reaction of the crew: "With its smooth (vibration free) flying, quiet operation, and phenomenal performance, the YB-49 is a dream."[4]

Flight testing of the YB-49 began in earnest, the aircraft flying almost as much time in the next two months as the two XB-35s had flown in 18 months. Nevertheless, problems with props and gear boxes were immediately replaced by failures of auxiliary power units that supplied current to the electrical system of the airplane, poor reliability of the J35 turbojet engines, and marginal stability that compromised the capability of the YB-49 to perform the bombing mission for which it was intended.

For most negative aspects of the YB-49 development program, however, spectacular demonstration of performance occasionally occurred which evoked superlatives. One such event was the highly successful long range test flight of the YB-49 on April 26, 1948. On that date, the aircraft remained aloft for 9.5 hours, of which 6.5 hours were flown at an altitude of 40,000 feet.

Cockpit of the YB-49 (42-102367) has a cleaner look to it compared to that of the XB-35. Two overhead throttles for eight jet engines replace the four piston engine throttles; the center pedestal is less cluttered with the absence of propeller and some radio controls. (SI Negative 81-01264)

An occasional passenger on routine test flights of the YB-49 was Jack Northrop (fourth from left), shown with pilot Max Stanley (left) and his flight crew.

This rare sequence of YB-49 model photographs, dated February 1950, was made during spin tests. The three views at the right show the radio-controlled model being released from a Sikorsky R-5A helicopter. In the sequence opposite, the model is shown in various phases of a fully developed spin.

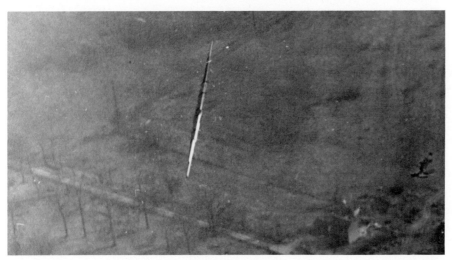

The five-man crew for the flight consisted of Max Stanley, Fred Bretcher, and Orva Douglas, augmented by Air Force Captain Jay Wethe and Northrop flight engineer Don Swift. The record breaking flight prompted high praise from General Hoyt S. Vandenberg, Chief of Staff of the U.S. Air Force, in a personal letter to Jack Northrop:

> Dear Mr. Northrop:
>
> Please accept the congratulations of the U.S. Air Force on the fine work you and your staff have done on the YB-49 aircraft. The accomplishments of the YB-49 on its recent test flights, and most particularly the time spent at high altitudes are most promising.
>
> Speaking for the Air Force as a whole, I wish to express appreciation for your tenacious pursuit of this development. We are looking to Northrop for continued progress in this critical period.
>
> Best of luck to you in all future developments of the Flying Wing, and personal best wishes.
>
> Sincerely yours,
>
> Hoyt S. Vandenberg
> Chief of Staff,
> United States Air Force[5]

It was an encouraging, well-deserved accolade for the Northrop team. Coming on the heels of the first flight of the second YB-49 (42-102368), flown on January 13, 1948, by Major R.L. Cardenas, it was followed in May by the first flight of the third and last of the B-35 series, the YB-35 (42-102366). All three B-35s were now equipped with the single rotation propellers and gear boxes.

Hard on these tangible signs of progress came disaster. On June 5, 1948, after accumulating almost 57 hours of flight time, the second YB-49 crashed and was destroyed. Killed in the crash were: Major D.N. Forbes, pilot; Captain Glen W. Edwards, copilot; Lieutenant E. Swindell, flight engineer; Mr. C. Leser, observer; and Mr. C. LaFountain, observer.[6]

The aircraft was on its twenty-fifth flight at the time of the accident. Recent flights had been devoted to the performance tests of the program, with Forbes as pilot and Edwards as copilot on all flights except #23, where Askounis acted as copilot in place of Edwards. Flight engineer for these flights was Lieutenant Swindell.

Date (1948)	Flight Number	Duration (hours: minutes)	Purpose
5-28	21	4:00	Takeoff; speed-power at 30,000 and 20,000 feet; descent at 0.06 Mach.
6-2	22	1:10	Familiarization
6-3	23	2:49	Takeoff; speed-power at 20,000 feet; landing.
6-4	24	3:53	Takeoff; climb at 7400 RPM; speed-power at 10,000 feet; airspeed calibration; landing.
6-5	25	1:11	Flight of accident

Throughout the Flying Wing development program, extensive wind tunnel tests were conducted to determine the flight characteristics of the full scale airplane. Right, engineers adjust controls on a scale flutter model of the XB-35 in the Wright Field wind tunnel in April 1946. Below is a tail-on view of a YB-49 rigged in the wind tunnel for stall tests.

The Northrop-Hendy XT-37 Turbodyne was considered for use in the EB-35B. Two of these powerful gas turbine engines, supplemented by six turbojets, would each drive two contra-rotating propellers by means of a drive shaft and reduction gears. Among the many advantages of the Turbodyne was its ability to use several different types of fuel, including gasoline, diesel oil, and kerosene. (SI Negative 79-01788)

The total flight experience in hours of the crew in YB-49 airplanes exclusive of the flight of the accident was as follows:

	Pilot	Copilot	Flt. Eng.	Observer
Forbes	11:58	19:19		
Edwards	13:42	10:02		
Swindell			50:14	
Leser				22:44
LaFountain				13:16

Major Forbes and his crew had taken off from Muroc in the early morning ostensibly for a performance test flight. Routine position reports over the Antelope Valley test range were received for about an hour. The aircraft was observed to crash in the desert about 20 minutes after the last report. The major portion of the airplane landed inverted, with no apparent horizontal velocity, and much of the airplane was destroyed in the explosion and fire that followed.

Parts of the airplane, including the outer wing panels and flap and elevator parts, were found in a narrow area extending two or three miles from the wreckage. During the investigation that followed, it was impossible to arrive at an incontestable conclusion regarding the cause of the accident. A major structural failure had obviously occurred in flight. Many specific causes were considered: exceeding flight restrictions, tumbling resulting from a stall, instability due to extreme aft center of gravity due to improper fuel usage, unintentional nose-up trim flap motion, hydraulic control system malfunction—the possibilities seemed endless. All were examined, many were discarded as impossible, some left open as possibilities.

In the final analysis, it appeared that the crash was caused by simultaneous failure of both outer wing panels from a positive loading condition. The failure could have been due to loads caused by excess normal acceleration, i.e., the airplane was overstressed during a high-G pullout. One of the most plausible explanations was that the overstress occurred during recovery from a stall or post-stall maneuver.

The setback in the program turned out to be temporary; the airplane's potential for a variety of roles was well recognized by the Air Force. A review of the Strategic Reconnaissance Program by the Air Force subsequently led to a formal contract in September 1948, for 30 reconnaissance versions of the B-49, designated the RB-49A. Even before the contract was signed, Northrop was instructed in June to arrange production of the airplane, except for an absolute minimum number, at the government-owned Fort Worth facility of Consolidated Vultee Aircraft Corporation (Convair). The Convair Fort Worth plant was engaged in B-36A production, to which only about 70 percent of the facility was devoted. With Northrop's production capacity of only three bombers per month at its Hawthorne facility, the shift would take advantage of Convair's unused production capacity.

The proposed subcontract was an unusual one for peacetime. It appeared to mark the emergence of the B-49 as a major factor in the strategic forces of the jet age. In reality, the days of the Flying Wing were numbered.

As B-49 testing continued and production plans took shape, the B-35 program continued to experience serious problems; doubts arose about the airplane's utility as an operational bomber, particularly in view of force level cutbacks and the inability of the Flying Wing to carry an atomic bomb. Vibration difficulties were being encountered with the single rotation propellers, engine cooling fans continued to fail from metal fatigue, and considerable maintenance problems were experienced with the intricate exhaust system of the R-4360 engines. Many configurations of the B-35 emerged, most involving some sort of conversion to turbojets. One proposal, which was well into the fabrication stage in late 1949, was the conversion of a YB-35 to a combination of turbojet and turboprop engines. Designated EB-35B, the airplane would have six turbojets: four in the wing, and two externally mounted below the wing, as well as two wing-mounted Northrop XT-37 Turbodyne engines.

The XT-37 Turbodyne was developed by the Northrop-Hendy Company, a jointly-owned subsidiary with the Joshua Hendy Iron Works. Research on the turbine that resulted in the Turbodyne dated back to 1939, when Vladimir Pavlecka,[7] then Northrop's chief of research, interested Jack Northrop in the potential of gas turbine power plants. Funded by a joint Army-Navy contract, the turbine development continued during the war years, and the first engine was completed in 1945. It was subsequently destroyed during tests, but a second machine continued in development. By 1950 its 50-hour endurance test was completed, delivering a record-breaking 7500 hp continuously. At the time, it was the most powerful aircraft power plant in the world, capable of delivering 10,000 hp with a suitable propeller. On the EB-35B, two Turbodynes were to drive large counter-rotating pusher propellers. With the cancellation of the EB-35B in 1949, prospects for flight tests of the engine ended. In 1950, at the direction of the Secretary of the Air Force, the patents, name, and technical data were released to the General Electric Company.

In November 1948, another step was taken toward the ultimate dissolution of the B-49 project. During informal discussions about recent bombing tests of the YB-49, Major Robert L. Cardenas, Air Force test pilot on the project, was quoted in official Air Force records as saying that the airplane was "extremely unstable and very difficult to fly on a bombing mission . . . because of the continual yawing and the pitching which was evident upon application of the rudders, undoubtedly due to the control arrangements or elevons peculiar to the YB-49." Until aerodynamic deficiencies could be corrected, it was the opinion of Colonel Albert Boyd, Chief, Flight Test Division at Muroc, and Major Cardenas, that the YB-49 was unsuitable for both bomber and reconnaissance work.[8]

Subsequently, Major Cardenas stated for the record that the airplane was marginally stable, rather than "extremely unstable." On November 16, 1948, an official Air Materiel Command report on the bombing evaluation, which was conducted under manual conditions, i.e., without autopilot, reiterated the inadequacies of the YB-49 under the test conditions, but referred to the "marginal directional stability of the aircraft in flight."[9] Installation of a satisfactory autopilot was considered a top priority.

On December 29, 1948, a Board of Senior Officers met to study the Air Force procurement program, and consider a proposed termination of the RB-49 program. The Board recommended cancellation of the 30 RB-49s.

On January 11, 1949, the Air Materiel Command directed Northrop to terminate work on all phases of the reconnaissance version except for completion and test of one YRB-49A, a six engine version equipped with special reconnaissance equipment. Conversion of certain YB-35s to jet engines continued. The progress of the conversion program as it stood in February 1949 can be seen in Table 1.

The decision in February 1949, to salvage, or scrap the two XB-35s (42-13603 and 42-38323) and the YB-35 (42-102366), which were the only piston-engined Flying Wings in flying status, spelled the end of that phase of the program. With only one remaining jet-powered YB-49 (42-102367) still flying, the future of the program looked bleak. In February, the YB-49 had a brief moment of triumph in an otherwise discouraging year.

Table 1
Designation Of Aircraft On Jet Conversion Program, February 1949[10]

USAF Serial No.	Contr. Serial/Desig	First Revision	Second Revision	Final Revision	Dispostion
42-13603	1484/XB-35	XB-35	ERB-35B		Salvage
42-38323	1485/XB-35	XB-35	EB-35		Salvage
42-102366	1486/YB-35	YB-35	RB-35B		Salvage
42-102367	1487/YB-35	YB-49	YB-49	YB-49	Continued flight test
42-102368	1488/YB-35	YB-49	YB-49	YB-49	Crashed
42-102369	1489/YB-35	YB-35	YRB-49A		Salvage
42-102370	1490/YB-35	YB-35	RB-35B	YB-35B	Shell
42-102371	1491/YB-35	YB-35	RB-35B	YB-35B	Shell
42-102372	1492/YB-35	YB-35	RB-35B	YB-35B	Shell
42-102373	1493/YB-35	YB-35	RB-35B	YB-35B	Shell
42-102374	1494/YB-35	YB-35A	RB-35B	YB-35B	Shell
42-102375	1495/YB-35	YB-35A	RB-35B	YB-35B	Shell
42-102376	1496/YB-35	YB-35A	RB-35B	YRB-49A	Reconn. prototype
42-102377	1497/YB-35	YB-35A	RB-35B	YB-35B	Shell
42-102378	1498/YB-35	YB-35A	Static	EB-35B	Turbodyne test bed

In airplanes with the designation "shell," all tactical equipment had been deleted from the airplane, which was then only suitable for flight test missions.

The YB-35B airplane, the YRB-49A, and the EB-35B airplanes were to be equipped with 6 J35A-19 jet engines in lieu of the 4 type R-4360 engines and associated equipment then installed.

The EB-35B airplanes were to have installed in addition to the six J35A-19 jet engines a type T-37 turbodyne with controls and a prop. Provisions would be incorporated in the airplane during the modification program for the addition of another T-37 engine at a later date. It was anticipated that if the single engine installation proved satisfactory, a second engine would be added during the flight test program so that actual performance of a flying wing airplane powered by turboprop engines could be obtained.

The YRB-49A would be equipped with an autopilot, APQ-24 radar set, and suitable camera installations. Also a flash bomb bay would be incorporated to carry six flash bombs. The bomb bay would be sufficiently large to take the new bombs then under consideration.

On February 9, 1949, the YB-49 flew non-stop from Muroc to Andrews Air Force Base, Washington, D.C., in 4 hours, 25 minutes, at an average speed of 511 mph. Major Cardenas was the pilot, with Captain W.W. Seller as copilot, and Max Stanley on board as pilot observer. The flight time compared favorably with the official transcontinental record of 4 hours, 13 minutes, 26 seconds, set by Colonel William H. Councill in a Lockheed P-80A on January 26, 1946. Councill had averaged 580 mph for the 2435-mile trip. The YB-49 flight came on the heels of a similar flight by its competitor, the Boeing XB-47, which the previous day had been flown by Major Russ Schleeh from Moses Lake Air Force Base in the state of Washington to Andrews in 3 hours, 46 minutes, at an average speed of 607 mph.

The flight on February 9 was the first public demonstration of the airplane's potential. At Andrews, it was exhibited to the public. President Truman was heard to observe, as he finished inspecting the giant Flying Wing: "This looks like one hell of an airplane. We ought to have some."[11] This offhand comment may have brought encouragement to Jack Northrop, but the effect would be short lived.

Both the versatility and the weak point of the YB-49 were dramatically demonstrated during the return flight to California, when it became necessary to cut four of the eight jet engines in flight because of oil starvation due to faulty maintenance at Wright Field. Major Bob Cardenas made an uneventful, unscheduled landing at Winslow Airport, Arizona with three engines operating on one side, and one on the other!

During the early part of 1949, Max Stanley conducted autopilot tests on the YB-49, and the Air Force made preparations to begin bombing tests with the E-7 autopilot in May 1949. Unfortunately, the official results of these tests are not available, but Max Stanley recalls the tests to evaluate the airplane as a bombing platform:

> Both Northrop and Air Force pilots participated in this program. The bombardier was an Air Force officer using the then highly secret Norden bombsight. After an evaluation by the Air Force of these tests, the aircraft was declared suitable for its mission.[12]

During April and June 1949, Major Russ Schleeh, who had replaced Major Cardenas on the Flying Wing project, flew the YB-49 11 times, evaluating the aircraft as a bombing platform both with and without the autopilot. According to Major Schleeh, the bombing results were very poor. In 1982, he recalled some of the problems.

> It was noted in the movies taken from a chase airplane that the 100-pound bombs dropped from the bomb bay almost without exception showed a pitching and oscillating movement, which at that time was attributed to the turbulence in the bomb bay. This no doubt caused some of the bombing inaccuracies we were experiencing. I cannot agree with the statement that the aircraft was declared suitable for its mission, as I would never have made such a statement for a number of reasons.[13]

Nonetheless, Air Force interest in the program dwindled as the year wore on, as did available funds. The eight-jet version would not be available until January 1950, and would have an inadequate operating radius; the six-jet model, the YRB-49A, planned for 1951, would be slower than the B-47; and the Turbodyne-equipped version would not be available until 1953, putting it in competition with the superior performing, all-jet B-52.

In the meantime, negotiations between Northrop and Convair officials over a proposed merger, originally proposed in July 1948 by the board chairman of Convair, Floyd B. Odlum, failed to produce an agreement satisfactory to either side.

In November 1949, the Air Force cancelled plans to convert the remaining YB-35s. All YB-35s were ordered scrapped, with the exception of one intended for use in the YRB-49A project. Despite Northrop efforts to save the program, no reprieve was granted. Scrapping of the B-35s began in January 1950; the lone flyable YB-49 was destroyed on March 15, 1950, in an accident caused by nose landing gear failure during simulated takeoff runs by Major Russ Schleeh.

On May 4, 1950, with the entire Flying Wing program in a shambles, the last of the majestic aircraft took to the air on its first flight. Even this last of

A transcontinental flight to Washington, D.C., in February 1949, was the occasion to show off the world's only jet-powered flying wing bomber. Major Robert Cardenas flew the YB-49 over the nation's capital (above), and President Harry Truman inspected the giant bomber at nearby Andrews Air Force Base (right).

Jack Northrop's Flying Wings must have been somewhat of a disappointment to him, as aesthetically pleasing and graceful as the airplane appeared to the casual observer. In addition to four vertical fins appended to all of the B-49 family for directional stability, the YRB-49A had two of its six Allison J35-A-19 engines suspended below the wing, to allow for greater internal fuel capacity. The idealistic goals of a completely aerodynamically clean airplane had given way to drastic modifications because of military requirements.

The YRB-49A was flown in an abbreviated series of flight tests at Edwards Air Force Base, then placed in storage at the Northrop facility at Ontario International Airport, California. It was officially authorized for reclamation in November 1953, and dropped from the Air Force inventory a year later.

Why did the Flying Wing fail to go into production? A popular explanation, with a ring of truth to it, is that the aircraft was 30 years ahead of its time. Even its most ardent supporters would not deny that it had problems. The B-35 series was doomed by overwhelming difficulties with propellers, gearboxes, and maintenance problems with the complicated exhaust system. Perhaps even more pertinent, it was overtaken by the jet age.

Eleven of the fifteen Flying Wings manufactured are in various stages of assembly and conversion to a turbojet configuration. All of these aircraft were eventually destroyed.

The last of the Flying Wings, the YRB-49A (42-102376) departs Hawthorne for its maiden flight on May 4, 1950. The crew nacelle was extensively modified to accommodate a faired radome installation and photographic equipment for its mission as a photo-reconnaissance bomber.

The B-49 was hampered by marginal directional stability that compromised its ability to perform bombing or reconnaissance missions. Pilots and engineers close to the program recognized that stability deficiencies would have been corrected with a proper autopilot and stability augmentation devices, given adequate time and support for the project.

The YRB-49A's performance would not have measured up to that of its competitors by the time a protracted development program had run its course. The airplane and the eight-engine versions were basically 400 mph airframes designed for piston engine performance. Replacing R-4360s with J35s did not automatically result in jet age performance.

For Jack Northrop, it was obviously a bitter disappointment to have devoted so many years of his professional life to a dream and to see it abruptly terminated. The most unfortunate aspect of the entire affair is that not one flyable aircraft was retained for a sustained research and development program to thoroughly explore all of the potential benefits and pitfalls of the flying wing design. The distinguished aviation and space pioneer Dr. Theodore von Kármán put one more slant on the subject, when he expressed the views of all those who have admired an airplane purely for its grace and beauty:

> I have always thought it a shame that Northrop's Wing failed. He believed that if something is beautiful it is right. Visionaries with his daring and imagination should succeed.[14]

NOTES

1. Northrop employed an old-but-new principle in designing the bomb bay doors. The principle of the roll-top desk inspired the newest type retracting bomb bay closure, which was an unbroken sheet of stainless steel wound on a drum mounted at the rear end of the bomb bay.

2. B.E. Meyers (Major General, USA), Memorandum from Deputy Assistant Chief of Air Staff (Materiel, Maintenance, and Distribution) to Chief of Air Staff. Subject: B-35 Project. May 6, 1944 (U.S., Northrop).

3. Max Stanley began flying in 1935 on the west coast, and eventually left the business world to pursue a career in aviation. He flew overseas ferry flights for Lockheed, Pan American, and United Air Lines before joining Northrop in 1943 to become an engineering test pilot. Stanley became an N-9M pilot, and was responsible for indoctrinating dozens of military pilots in the N-9M before he was selected to fly the XB-35 and the YB-49. Stanley possessed the right combination of piloting skill and temperament to guide the Flying Wing flight test program through some turbulent years.

4. O.H. Douglas, *Jet Flight Story Told by Douglas*, p. 1 (U.S., Northrop).

5. General Hoyt S. Vandenberg, USAF, letter to John K. Northrop, May 12, 1948 (U.S., Northrop).

6. Daniel Forbes had about 31 hours flight time in the YB-49. He was assigned to Muroc in 1948 to assist in the YB-49 flight test program. Forbes Air Force Base in Topeka, Kansas, was named for him in June 1949. Glen Edwards was an experienced combat and test pilot. Born in Medicine Hat, Alberta, Canada, Edwards grew up in Lincoln, California. Muroc was officially designated Edwards Air Force Base in his honor on January 25, 1950. Despite unofficial reports to the contrary, Major Daniel H. Forbes, Jr., not Captain Glen W. Edwards, was pilot and operator of the aircraft the day of the accident, according to official documents of the U.S. Air Force and Northrop Aircraft, Inc. that related to the accidents. See Investigation Committee, Northrop Report No. NM-13, dated June 1948, subject: Accident Investigation, YB-49 USAF 42-102368 (U.S.,

Northrop). Also Army Air Forces Report of Major Accident, Aircraft YB-49, 42-102368, dated June 5, 1948 (U.S., Northrop).

Major R.E. Schleeh observed the crash from the ground and rushed immediately to the scene. He rummaged through the wreckage but could not identify anything of consequence, including which pilot had been occupying the left hand, or pilot's, seat.

7. Pavlecka was one of the world's foremost proponents of giant airships. In 1922, he assisted in the design of the only operational metal-clad airship, the ZMC-2, built by the Aircraft Development Corp. of Detroit, Michigan. Pavlecka also contributed to the design of the DC-3 for Douglas Aircraft Co. Pavlecka saw Northrop as the best potential sponsor for support of his ideas on turbine research.

8. J.S. Holloner (Colonel, USAF). Chief, Aircraft Branch, Directorate of Research and Development (Office, Deputy Chief of Staff, Materiel) memorandum to D.L. Putt (Brigadier General, USAF). Subject: Bombing Tests of the YB-49. November 8, 1948 (U.S., Northrop).

9. W.C. Williams (Major, USAF). Engineering Division, Air Materiel Command Memorandum Report. Subject: Bombing Evaluation—Comparison Between Manually Controlled B-29 and YB-49 Aircraft. November 16, 1948 (U.S., Northrop).

10. Joseph T. McNarney (General, USAF). Commanding General, Air Materiel Command letter to Chief of Staff, U.S. Air Force. Subject: YB-35 Jet Conversion Program. February 17, 1949 (U.S., Northrop).

11. A. Myers, M. Stanley, and M. Stephens, interview with E.T. Wooldridge, February 1982 (U.S., Northrop).

12. Max R. Stanley, letter to E.T. Wooldridge, May 25, 1982 (U.S., Northrop).

13. R.E. Schleeh, letter to E.T. Wooldridge, November 24, 1982 (U.S., Northrop).

14. Theodore von Kármán, *The Wind and Beyond*, p. 176 (U.S., Northrop).

Chapter 9

The Fifties and Beyond: A Postscript

The scrapping of the Northrop B-35/B-49 bombers marked the end of a decade of unprecedented flying wing development. For the next 30 years, there was little if any public evidence of interest in applying the concept of the pure flying wing to military or commercial requirements. For all intents and purposes, the idea had died. The concept of the tailless aircraft remained alive, however, and even enjoyed a resurgence in the military and general aviation market. Eventually a tailless aircraft even became the first reusable spacecraft.

The most popular application of the tailless concept was the delta-winged configuration pioneered by Dr. Alexander Lippisch in Germany in the 1930s. The delta gave better low-speed handling than the swept wing designed for high speed operations, and was also efficient at supersonic speeds.

The United States, England, France, Sweden, and the Soviet Union adapted the delta to a wide variety of military requirements in the 1950s and 1960s. Although most of the aircraft were remarkably similar in appearance, they differed significantly in aerodynamics, propulsion, structure, and equipment. In the United States, Convair, with an assist from Dr. Lippisch, produced the first delta design to fly. This was followed by several operational supersonic fighters, a supersonic bomber, and the world's first supersonic seaplane.

Douglas Aircraft's Ed Heinemann, never an advocate of tailless aircraft, designed a tailless aircraft with a sweptback wing of extremely low aspect ratio in the early 1950s. The F4D-1 Skyray was the first supersonic shipboard fighter.

Another unusual carrier-based fighter of the 1950s was the Chance Vought F7U Cutlass, a strange-looking craft featuring sweptback wing, two vertical fins and rudders, and elevons. Resembling a praying mantis, the Cutlass proved to be somewhat less than spectacular.

Clearly one of the most amazing aircraft of the jet age is Lockheed's SR-71A Blackbird. This tailless design of the famous Clarence L. "Kelly" Johnson once flew from New York to London in less than two hours.

The Convair XF-92A was the first delta-winged aircraft to fly, on September 18, 1948. Powered by an Allison J33-A-29 turbojet with afterburner, the experimental aircraft was capable of high subsonic airspeeds. (Courtesy Consolidated Vultee Aircraft Corp.)

Another Convair tailless design of the 1950s, the B-58A Hustler was the first supersonic bomber put into production for the U.S. Air Force. An external pod was used to carry fuel and for nuclear weapon storage.

A derivative of the XF-92A, the Convair F-102A Delta Dagger entered U.S. Air Force service in 1955 as the first operational delta-winged fighter. Although preproduction versions lacked the expected supersonic performance, pinching the waist to provide a "coke bottle" effect resulted in Mach 1.25 capability.

The Convair XF2Y-1 Sea Dart was the world's first delta-winged seaplane, and a more powerful version, the YF2Y-1, became the first seaplane to exceed the speed of sound. Single and double retractable hydro-skis were evaluated during the flight tests conducted in the mid-1950s.

The Ryan X-13 was a tail-sitting Vertical Takeoff and Landing (VTOL) research aircraft that was controlled by varying jet thrust and deflecting the jet exhaust during takeoff, landing, and hovering flight. The first complete sequence of vertical takeoff, transition to horizontal cruising flight, and return to vertical landing was accomplished on April 11, 1957. (Courtesy Ryan Aeronautical Co.)

The Douglas F4D-1 Skyray was a tailless aircraft with a sweptback wing of extremely low aspect ratio. Designed as an all-weather interceptor for the U.S. Navy, the Skyray was the first supersonic shipboard fighter. (Courtesy Douglas Aircraft Co.)

The Lockheed SR-71A Blackbird aircraft evolved from the A-11 and YF-12A aircraft of the 1960s. Used for high-speed, high-altitude reconnaissance, the SR-71A once flew from New York to London in less than two hours at an average speed of almost three times the speed of sound. (Courtesy U.S. Air Force)

British fascination with the tailless airplane continued into the jet age. The Armstrong Whitworth A.W. 52 and de Havilland D.H. 108 of the immediate postwar years were followed by a number of delta designs. The Short Brothers' SC.1 was an attempt to investigate the VTOL/delta wing combination, while one decidedly different approach to the tailless concept was the Short S.B.4 Sherpa. The Sherpa featured a so-called "aero-isoclinic" wing, a relatively flexible structure with movable wing tips. Although the rotating tips were supposed to prove superior to conventional controls at transonic speeds, and would improve maneuverability at high altitudes, the idea apparently found no practical application.

The British carried out extensive research into the characteristics of delta wing aircraft with models such as the Boulton Paul P.111/120 and the Avro Type 707. From this latter series came an aircraft that had the most striking appearance of any produced in the 1950s, the Hawker Siddeley Vulcan. Designed originally as a strategic bomber, the adaptable Vulcan served into the 1980s in many missions and configurations.

Test pilot Peter Twiss became the first to set a world speed record over 1000 mph when he flew a Fairey Delta 2 research delta at an average speed of 1132 mph in 1956. The drooping nose of the Delta 2 reappeared 20 years later on the world's first supersonic airliner to enter regular passenger service, the Aerospatiale/British Aerospace Concorde.

The French demonstrated an early interest in postwar application of the delta wing concept. From early research efforts emerged the Mirage III, IV, and 5, delta wing members of the Dassault Breguet family of fighters and bombers. The Mirage brought considerable trade and prestige to France, with over 1200 of the Mirage IIIs sold by 1977 to countries around the world.

Designed to investigate the delta wing at transonic airspeeds, the Boulton Paul P.111 made its first flight in October 1950. The wing tips were detachable to permit tests with blunt or pointed tips; the pointed vertical fin also was detachable. The fairing at the base of the vertical fin on the left hand side of the airplane housed a parachute to reduce landing roll. (Courtesy Boulton Paul Aircraft Ltd.)

The Short Sherpa was built in 1953 to investigate the potential of the "aero-isoclinic" wing. Rotating wing tips took the place of ailerons and elevator, and were supposed to make the aircraft more maneuverable at high altitudes. (Courtesy Short Bros. & Harland Ltd.)

This Mirage IIIs of the Swiss Air Force is one of many variations of the French Dassault Breguet Mirage III series of tactical aircraft. In the 25 years after the maiden flight of the Mirage III prototype in November 1956, over 1300 of the Mirage III, and its variations, the Mirage 5 and 50, had been delivered to 21 countries. (Courtesy Swiss Air Force Museum)

Two Avro Vulcan bombers are shown with four of the five Avro Type 707 research deltas, one-third scale models of the Vulcan. The Type 707 series were used for low- and high-speed delta wing research in the early 1950s. The Vulcan bomber followed, entered service with the Royal Air Force in 1957, and was still in active service 25 years later.

Peter Twiss flew this Fairey Delta 2 research airplane to a new world's speed record of 1132 mph. The entire nose section, including cockpit, pivoted downward to improve the pilot's view during takeoff and landing, a feature later used in the Concorde supersonic transport.

Another in the line of Dassault Breguet tailless deltas, the Mirage 2000 was designed to be the primary combat aircraft of the French Air Force from the mid-1980s. Similar in design to the Mirage III/5, the Mirage 2000 featured automatic leading-edge flaps, "fly-by-wire" control system, and two-section elevons which form the entire trailing edge of each wing.

The Saab 35 Draken, similar in concept to the Saab 210, was a single-seat, all weather supersonic fighter. Like other Swedish-built tactical aircraft, the Saab 35F shown in this photograph had exceptional short field operating characteristics. (Courtesy Saab-Scania)

The Saab 210 Draken was built in 1951 to test the "double-delta" concept. The wing had a planform consisting of two triangles, with the inner section swept at 80 degrees, and the outer at 57 degrees. The center of gravity could be varied in flight by pumping liquid between trim tanks in the nose and tail. (Courtesy Saab-Scania)

Sweden carried the delta principle one step further. Beginning with the tiny Saab 210 Draken in 1951 the Swedes developed the distinctive "double-delta" wing configuration, a wing of extremely low aspect ratio with a planform made up of two triangles. From the Saab 210 evolved the famous Saab 35 Draken, a Mach 2, multi-role aircraft with good short takeoff and landing capabilities. Another double-delta variant, the Saab 37 Viggen, appeared in 1967, and was distinguished from its tailless predecessors by the presence of canard foreplane with trailing edge flaps.

Despite considerable development work with tailless aircraft and flying wings in the 1930s by such early Soviet designers as B.I. Cheranovskiy and Kalinin, there is little evidence of sustained, widespread interest in the U.S.S.R. in postwar years. The Soviet Air Force used the delta wing in some Sukhoi and Mikoyan/Gurevich tactical aircraft, but removed them from the tailless category with the addition of horizontal stabilizers. In the commercial field, however, the Soviet Union assured itself of a unique niche in aviation history with the world's first supersonic transport, the delta-winged Tupolev Tu-144. After its maiden flight on December 31, 1968, the Tu-144 underwent a prolonged development program, and finally entered scheduled passenger service in November 1977.

Military and commercial development of the delta wing concept resulted in a class of aircraft capable of spectacular, high speed performance that eventually became routine. At the other end of the performance spectrum, however, where flying for fun was more important than supersonic speeds, the delta and other tailless aircraft had a profound effect. In general aviation, preconceived notions about the flying qualities of tailless designs, flying wings, or canards had vanished from the scene by the late 1970s. Homebuilts, gliders, hang gliders, and "ultralights" existed in different tailless configurations that reflected the infinite variety of tastes and performance goals of their designers. Early pioneers such as Weiss, Etrich, Dunne, and the Hortens would have recognized many of their ideas and concepts in those personal aircraft of the jet age.

Charles Fauvel, the noted French designer of tailless gliders and powered aircraft, continued to demonstrate his excellence in the field. His AV.3 sailplane of 1951, and the improved AV.361, were sold to well over 100 soaring enthusiasts in almost 20 countries. Plans for the AV.361, and the later AV.45 and AV.222 powered gliders, became available for amateur construction. An AV.45 was even configured with a 150-pound thrust turbojet and successfully flight tested in 1967.

The urge to build and fly your own aircraft was not restricted to a small section of the aeronautical community; by 1981 there were some 9000 ultralights flying in 15 or more countries worldwide, 6000 in the United States alone. In 1966, the prestigious aeronautical annual *Jane's All the World's Aircraft* even added a separate section for homebuilt aircraft to facilitate reference and selection of a particular design by potential builders and pilots. In the 1980s, tailless ultralights carried such nicknames as Minibat, Super Wing, and Easy Riser; they flew alongside a name from the past, the Pterodactyl.

The Soviet Tupolev Tu-144 occupies a secure niche in aviation history as the first supersonic transport to fly, on December 31, 1968. The Tu-144 in this photograph is in the landing configuration, with drooped nose to give the pilot better visibility, and extended noseplanes for better control at low speeds.

Twenty years in development as a joint project by France and Great Britain, the Aerospatiale/British Aerospace Concorde was the world's first supersonic airliner to enter regular commercial service. The graceful, tailless delta halved the flying time on many international routes. (Courtesy British Aerospace)

Constructed of wood and foam from plans or a complete kit, the Mitchell U-2 featured a bubble canopy, retractable tricycle landing gear, and outer wing panels that folded for transportation and storage. Designed to accept engines in the range of 10–22 hp, the U-2 carried 7 quarts of fuel, good for a two hour flight at a cruising speed of 75 mph. (Courtesy Don Mitchell)

The ultimate in tailless aircraft, the Space Shuttle Orbiter "Columbia" makes a successful touchdown after its second space mission. The wing is a double-delta planform, with 81 degree sweepback on the inner wing, and 45 degrees on the outer. Control in pitch and roll is provided by two-segment elevons on each trailing edge. (Courtesy NASA)

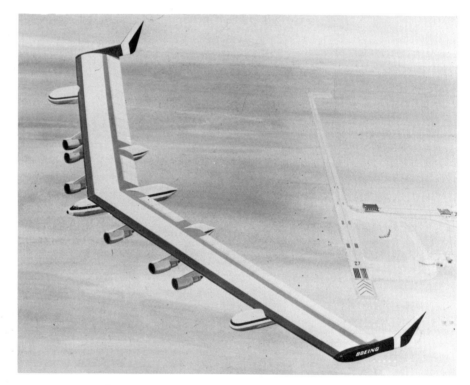

This Boeing conceptual drawing is one of many advanced designs being considered by leading aerospace companies as cargo carriers in the 21st century. A typical "span-loader" would carry a half-million pounds of cargo inside a thick wing with 250-foot span some 5000 miles at subsonic speeds. Some variations envision wingspans of 500 feet, and a takeoff weight of almost 5 million pounds, powered by 12 turbofans of 52,000-pounds thrust. (Courtesy NASA)

Among the more widely accepted designs of the times were the Mitchell B-10 and U-2 ultralight flying wings. Don Mitchell's designs featured unique "handling stabilators" which provided both lateral and pitch control. Shaped like upside-down airfoils, the control surfaces were attached below the trailing edge of the wing. There they acted as separate aerodynamic surfaces, rather than as hinged portions of the wing itself, providing exceptional stability and control.

What does the future hold for the flying wing or tailless aircraft? The beginning of regularly scheduled runs of the National Aeronautics and Space Administration's (NASA) Space Shuttle to and from Earth orbit in 1981 marked yet another example of the remarkable adaptability of Alexander Lippisch's tailless delta to a wide range of performance requirements.

In 1982, there was speculation by the news media that the new "Stealth" bomber, an aircraft designed to be impervious to radar detection, would bear a marked resemblance to the B-49 which preceded it by 40 years.[1] But 30 years after the British introduced jet propulsion to commercial aviation in the late 1940s, there is little evidence other than occasional conceptual studies, that leading aerospace companies in the United States and Europe see a practical application of Jack Northrop's pure flying wing concept.

On a positive note, however, the following letter was received by Jack Northrop in April 1979:

Dear Mr. Northrop:

Your recent meeting with members of our aeronautical research staff was a memorable occasion for NASA. In a field as dynamic as aviation we sometimes lose track of important historical lessons, and your discussion of the B-35/B-49 background and flight experience was most valuable to us.

As you know, our studies of technology needs for potential future large cargo/logistics aircraft have led us to investigations of span-loaded configurations during which we have, in effect, rediscovered the flying wing. Obviously, we recognized the pioneering Northrop work in that area as an essential source of information, and in the course of our investigations we reexamined considerable NACA B-35/B-49 wind-tunnel data. Our analyses confirmed your much earlier conviction as to the load-carrying and efficiency advantages of this design approach, and studies performed for us by the major manufacturers of large airplanes have further corroborated these findings.

We do not yet know when the commercial market or military requirements will create demands for new long-range cargo carriers. We are continuing our related research and technology efforts, and have as yet found no reason to disagree with you as to the potential benefits of the tailless span-loader approach for such applications.

Again, let me express our appreciation—for your many valuable contributions to aeronautics in general, as well as your frank and informative discussion of the flying wing experience in particular.

Very truly yours,

Robert A. Frosch
Administrator[2]

John Northrop died on February 18, 1981, at the age of 85.

NOTES

1. To determine the Flying Wing's probability of detection by search radar, Max Stanley flew the YB-49 on a number of prearranged flights against coastal sites south of San Francisco. The aircraft was never detected except when it was directly above the radar site.

2. Robert A. Frosch, letter to John K. Northrop, April 3, 1979 (U.S., Northrop).

Restoring the Northrop N-1M

BACKGROUND

On June 6, 1946, the Northrop N-1M was placed in temporary storage at Freeman Field, Indiana. On July 12, 1946, the aircraft was delivered to the Museum Storage Depot at Park Ridge, Illinois, where it became part of the collection of historic military aircraft which General H. H. Arnold had established after World War II. Custody of the collection was assumed by the National Air Museum of the Smithsonian Institution on May 1, 1949. By that time the collection amounted to 115 aircraft and some 160,000 assorted components of inestimable historic value.

Packed in two boxes, the N-1M was moved to the National Air Museum's Preservation, Restoration, and Storage Facility (now Paul E. Garber Facility) at Silver Hill, Maryland, in the early 1950s. The aircraft remained boxed and stored until May 1979, at which time the restoration project began.

MATERIAL CONDITION

As the various components of the N-1M were removed from the storage boxes in 1979, it was immediately apparent that restoration of the N-1M would be an exercise in woodworking for the next few years. Made predominately of mahogany and spruce, the N-1M had suffered the effects of almost 30 years of storage. High temperatures and moisture had caused severe deterioration of the mahogany skin of the two outer wing sections. Large pieces of skin had fallen off and the interior wooden structure had undergone considerable rot and delamination.

On the other hand, the intact center section of the wing was in relatively good shape. Wooden skin was in place and restorable, as were interior bulkheads. Some corrosion was evident in metal components such as landing gear, engine cooling shrouds and ducting, and metal tubing.

The N-1M is shown in these three photographs as it appeared after almost 30 years in storage. The left-hand wing section (foreground on the wooden skid) has lost large pieces of mahogany plywood skin (above). The center section appears worse for wear (right), but was in much better shape than the outer wing sections. Just to the left and right of the "Flying Wing" marking are the outlines of two windows that were covered up early in the test program. Two more windows, which were to improve pilot visibility, were located directly below the top two. The trailing edge trim flaps (below) have been cranked to the "up" position. (SI Negatives 79-7226-19, 79-7226-22, 79-6183-27)

RESTORATION PROCEDURES

The N-1M did not lend itself to the usual approach taken in so many of the Silver Hill restorations. The basic design of the aircraft, and the deterioration of the wooden structure were not conducive to a systematic "strip down to bare bones, restore, and reassemble" procedures. Each wing tip and elevon was removed, and restored separately. Each of the outer wing sections were mounted vertically on supports to facilitate access. Landing gear, trim flaps, landing flaps, and engines were also removed to be dealt with separately.

The restoration team was led by Reid Ferguson, who called on 24 years of experience in airplane restoration to cope with a "one of a kind" machine.

During most of the restoration, Ferguson would be assisted by John Cusack. Later Garry Cline would join the team to work on the right hand wing section, and during the final few months, Karl Heinzel performed the cockpit restoration and Richard Horigan helped out with the center section of the wing.

There was a noticeable lack of uniformity in construction techniques throughout the wing, and the untold number of minor alterations and major reconfigurations throughout the serice life of the N-1M complicated the task of restoration enormously. The overall philosophy of restoration was "over-build," then cut down to the desired shape, replacing only the wood that was totally decayed or missing.

WING TIPS AND OUTER WING SECTIONS

Almost every rib, spar cap, truss, and stringer required repair, from regluing delaminated spruce or mahogany to replacing a considerable portion of a structural member. Every effort was made to retain as much of the original structure as possible, resulting in an inordinate number of manhours spent "cutting and pasting."

An observation of the restoration crew reflected the unique role played by the N-1M. To a man they agreed that a different crew had built the right-hand wing section than the left-hand section. Different techniques, different dimensions, and different types of wood were evident when wing sections were compared. Garry Cline thought the wing appeared to have been ad-libbed rather than engineered. Most of the differences were probably due to reconstruction of the right-hand wing after damage by vibration when Moye Stephens lost a propeller tip at Muroc.

The wing was tapered in both thickness and width; thus the ribs varied in size from wing root to wing tip, although the cross-sectional shape of each rib was the same throughout. Ribs were built up of laminations of spruce glued together and reinforced by mahogany.

Another indication of the modifications performed on the N-1M was the presence of several aluminum tubes secured in the wing sections that appeared to serve no practical function. They appeared to have been part of the control cable routing system for a configuration that was tested and dis-

The left-hand wing tip is shown before restoration. The tip had decayed to the point where it literally fell apart when the skin was removed. (SI Negative 80-4113-35)

After many hours of painstaking work by Reid Ferguson, the tip is finished and ready for reskinning. Surprisingly little of the original wood had to be replaced. (SI Negative 81-8165-9)

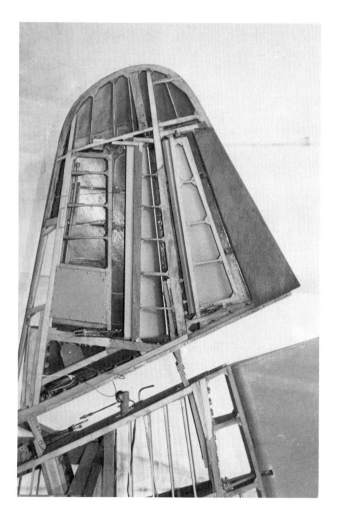

John Cusack checks the angle between spar and rib during restoration of the left hand outer wing section. (SI Negative 80-5640-7)

190

carded at some time. The tubes, like others in the wing, were removed, chemically cleaned, treated with corrosion control materials, and reinstalled.

The wing tips posed no more of a problem than the rest of the wing sections, but two interesting points were raised during the restoration. There was no evidence of the split trailing edge rudders with which the N-1M was originally built. The tips had been so heavily modified to accommodate existing spoiler-type rudders that all traces of the previous configuration had vanished.

The tips seemed heavy for the type of mounting used to attach the tips to the outer wing. Two large steel fittings were used to anchor each wing tip to its respective outer wing section. One fitting was bolted through a few blocks of wood to the auxiliary spar web; the other fitting was attached in similar fashion to blocks of wood built up to four inch thickness just forward of the main spar. Two metal fittings were secured in like manner inside the wing tip. The tip fittings were then mated to the wing fittings by three bolts at each juncture, leaving about six inches clearance between tip and wing section. Extra holes were bored in the fittings where they joined to permit adjustment of the wing tip droop for flight test purposes.

Reid Ferguson had the exacting task of reskinning the outer wing sections and tips of the N-1M. Using cardboard patterns, Ferguson cut sections of mahogany plywood to match. Eleven or twelve sections were required to cover one side of each wing, with thickness varying from 5/32 inches at the butt rib to 1/8 inch at the wing tip. Edges of the plywood sections were scarfed, i.e., cut at an angle to permit overlapping and a smooth fit. Those sections that needed contouring, such as the leading edge, were softened by soaking in water, then bent to the proper shape. The skin was glued on using plastic resin, with brass nails also being used to hold some of the sections in place.

Restoration of the elevons revealed still another chapter in the continuing story of the N-1M configuration changes. The elevons are fabric covered control surfaces attached to the trailing edge of the wing. As John Cusack tore down each surface for restoration, he discovered that each surface had in effect two leading edges, one behind the other. Apparently for balance purposes, lead weights had been attached to the original leading edge, with pieces of balsa wood used as fillers to provide a properly contoured leading edge. New fabric was applied and a new elevon had been created.

WING CENTER SECTION

In the absence of a conventional fuselage the wing center section of the N-1M seemed to qualify for that appellation for a number of reasons. It had been conveniently separated from the outer wing sections at the attachment points which were used to adjust angle of sweepback. It had been packed separately from the two outer wing sections, had suffered less deterioration over the years, and was thus considerably easier to restore than the other components.

The left-hand wing section is ready for reskinning by Reid Ferguson. Photograph at right is the upper surface; below is the lower surface. (SI Negatives 81-8165-18, 81-8165-7)

The job of reskinning the outer wing sections was an extremely demanding one performed in outstanding fashion by team leader Reid Ferguson. Working from cardboard patterns, Ferguson fashioned matching mahogany plywood sections, which were glued on with plastic resin.

Garry Cline (right) is surrounded by the tools of his trade as he painstakingly rebuilds the right-hand wing section (below).

In this view, the right-hand wing section has been rotated 180 degrees and elevon and wing tip are attached. The linkage to the right-hand rudder, and the slot through which it rotated into the wind stream, are evident on the skinned wing tip at right.

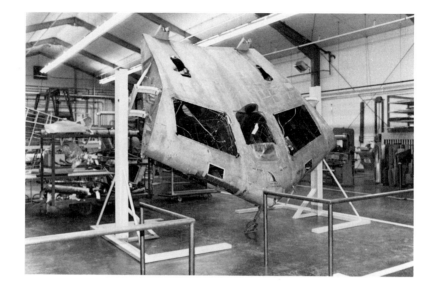

Stripped of engines and outer wing sections, the N-1M center section was mounted on a specially designed framework to permit ready access to the cockpit, wheel wells, engine bays, and interior structure.

John Cusack views with evident delight a temporary respite from woodworking as he strips down one of the Franklin engines for overhaul. Aside from an impending bearing failure in the left-hand engine, the two Franklin engines were in reasonably good shape.

Looking slightly the worse for wear, the N-1M cockpit had a rustic, home-made look about it. The control wheel and column and engine controls on the right-hand bulkhead seemed out of place in a cockpit of fighter-like proportions.

To the restoration crew, therefore, it had an identity all its own and it remained the "fuselage."

The plywood skin remained basically intact. Some fabric patches required replacing, but the exterior restoration was essentially one of paint removal, cleaning, priming, and repainting. As much of the interior hardware as possible was removed and given routine chemical treatment and zinc chromated. John Cusack and Richard Horigan, working together on the center section, stripped the interior bulkheads of old varnish, washed them with a mixture of acetone and cleaning fluid, and revarnished them.

Another example of a "quick fix" was found during restoration of the trailing edge trim flaps. The upper surface of each wooden flap had been covered with a metal sheet which, in effect, increased the thickness and lengthened the chord of each flap. In general, though, there seemed to be fewer surprises in the center section than in the outer sections where most of the configuration changes had occurred.

ENGINES

Certainly one of the most time-consuming and frustrating jobs of the restoration project was that of removing the two Franklin engines (Model 6AC264F2, serial numbers 300101 and 300102). A complicated cooling air system made the engines practically inaccessible for anything but minor maintenance.

Removal of an engine required removing, in turn, the shroud around the engine which routed cooling air, magnetoes, oil coolers, other accessories, and the drive shaft. Finally the aft end of the engine (actually the front of the engine in the pusher configuration) could be tilted up and out through the access hole in the top of the wing. When the process was complete and restoration began, the unique construction and configuration of the little flying wing once again became topics of conversation.

Aircraft systems to support flight operations of the N-1M were minimal. There were no engine starters, compressed air system, or generators. Electrical power was supplied by battery; a Burgess 1941 dry cell battery was found installed in the N-1M during restoration. A CO_2 bottle was installed to be used in the event of engine fire. The bottle was purposely activated during restoration after the engines had been removed. The system worked perfectly, enveloping a considerable portion of the aircraft and nearby observers in a cloud of CO_2 vapor. A hydraulic system, operated by a hand pump in the cockpit, was used for actuation of the landing gear and flaps.

Each engine was disassembled, cleaned, chemically treated, lacquered where appropriate, and reassembled. Two unusual situations were noticed by John Cusack during the procedure. Due to a failure of the thrust bearing located fore and aft of the No. 2 main crankshaft bearing support for the left hand engine, the bearing had started to melt and cracks had started to appear in the support webbing for the bearing. The engine would probably have not operated much longer without a failure of some consequence. Also of interest were the cables leading from the cockpit to the carburetor air temperature controls of each engine. The cables were disconnected at the cockpit and the engine, and the alternate air valves were wired in the open, or "cold," position.

COCKPIT

The cockpit of the N-1M was filthy, with some corrosion evident in the control column, rudder pedals, and assorted metal fixtures, cables, controls and fittings present. None presented any serious problems to Karl Heinzel who was selected both for his skill and his size as the right person for this task. The N-1M cockpit was particularly confining; there was no bucket seat, merely a depression in the wood flooring for the pilot's parachute. A control wheel and column dominated what little space remained between pilot and instrument panel and obscured from the pilot's view the cluster of nine flight and engine instruments.

The cockpit had a transitory, unfinished look about it. Comparison with 1941 era photographs shows some instruments, probably those specially installed during various phases of the flight test program, had been removed. Conspicuous by its absence was the carburetor air temperature control located on the right side of the cockpit. The original control consisted of a throttle quadrant with two throttles to control the carburetor heat for each engine. The quadrant had been removed and the cables taped to the bulkhead.

Karl Heinzel completely stripped the cockpit of instruments and hardware. The wood panels were cleaned with acetone and revarnished. Instruments were disassembled, cleaned, sprayed with a preservative, and reassembled. Assorted metal work was chemically cleaned and cadmium plated, covered with water white or chromate, or painted, whatever was appropriate.

196

FINISH

Choosing the finish and markings for the N-1M was relatively easy. The aircraft had always been painted a distinctive Air Force glossy lemon yellow 505 (later called light yellow) throughout its service life. This is equivalent to Federal Standard 595a 13655. There were two sets of markings, however. During most of its flight test the N-1M carried civil markings, registration number NX-28311, on the upper right and lower left wing surfaces, and on the tail wheel fairing. Later, at some undetermined time, civil markings were removed and military markings consisted of a white star over an insignia blue field were added to the upper left and lower right wing surfaces, as well as the tail wheel fairing. The Northrop logo, with the words "Flying Wing" underneath, was also added to the center section immediately in front of the cockpit. Since the N-1M was restored to its last operational configuration, the decision was made to retain the national markings and Northrop logo.

Prior to final assembly, the wing sections were thoroughly sanded and covered with primer surfacer. This process was repeated until the surfaces were smooth, at which time a sufficient number of coats of yellow enamel were applied to produce the desired finish. The aircraft was assembled and the distinctive Northrop logo applied to the nose section as a finishing touch.

Finally, on March 4,1983, after 11,500 manhours of effort, restoration of America's first true flying wing was completed. Soon, it would join the Alpha, Gamma, Vega, and other examples of the Northrop genius on display.

The N-1M restoration team (left to right): Harvey Napier, Karl Heinzel, Richard Horigan, John Cusack, Garry Cline, and the leader of the highly talented team, Reid Ferguson.

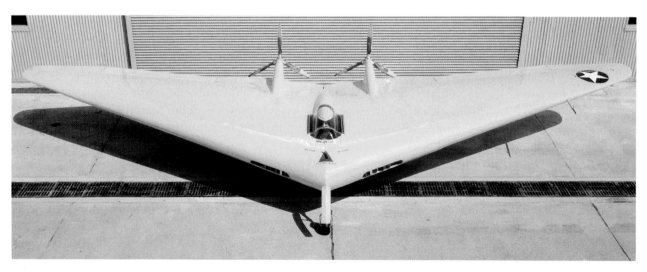

The attention to detail and high standards of workmanship that are the trademarks of NASM's restoration crew are quite evident in this series of photographs of America's first true flying wing after its complete restoration.

Airplane Specifications of the XB-35, YB-35, and YB-35A

This document prescribes the detailed dimensions, area, control movements, weights, capacity, and armament for the construction of the prototype and service test versions of the B-35 Flying Wing bomber.

MFG - NUMBER - NAME   NORTHROP XB-35, YB-35 & YB-35A

TYPE   Heavy Bomber (Flying Wing) N-9

DIMENSIONS:

Span   172' (2064")

Length   53.08' (637")

Height   20.28' (240.3")   85.5" Thick at R. C.

Aspect Ratio   7: 4 Taper Ratio 4:1

Incidence   0° R.C.   -4° T.C. Dihedral 0°53' LE.

Sweep   26° 57' 48" LE   10° 15' 22" TE

M. A. C.   315" (210" AFT STA 0) (C.G. @ 35.4% MAC)

Airfoil Section   R.C. NACA 65,3-019; T.C. NACA 65,3-018 R.C. 37.5' (450");

T.C. 9.33' (112")

Track   41.2' (497")

Wheelbase   23.5' (281.6")

                                 Goodrich Tire

Wheel Size   MG (4) 65" Dia Goodyear Wheel   Tire Pressure 70PSI

N. G. (1) 56" Dia Goodyear Wheel Tire Pressure 75PSI

AREAS:

Wing (total)   4000 Sq. Ft.

Aileron   See Elevon

Stabilizer (total) N. A.

Elevator   (Elevon) 182.3 Sq. Ft. each (132.4 Sq. Ft. each aft of hinge)

Fin (total)   None

AREAS (Cont.):

    Rudder   Trim Flap Box 36. 4 Sq. Ft. each & Trim Flap 89. 0 Sq. Ft. each

                     Rudder-Upr & Lwr 52. 6 Sq. Ft. each

    Flap (total)   200. 4 Sq. Ft. each

    Dive Brake   N. A.

CONTROL MOVEMENT:

    Aileron   Trim Flaps 30° UP, 7. 5° Down

    Rudder   0° - 60° Open (Split Drag Rudders)

    Elevator   35° UP, 25° Down

    Flap   50° Down

    Dive Brake   N. A.

WEIGHTS & LOADINGS:

    Empty   95, 339# Normal (95711# Per Spec NS-9 Supp. Z)

    Gross   168, 150# Normal Gross (206, 000# Design Gross)

    Overload   225, 296# Max Fuel; 225, 244# Max Bombs

    Wing loading   38. 8 #/Sq. Ft. (Design)

    Power loading   12. 9 #/HP (Design)

    Disposable load   12, 811# Normal; 129, 958# Max Fuel; 129, 906# Max Bomb

CAPACITY:

    Crew   9 Normal, 6 Relief

    Passengers   N. A.

    Cargo   N. A.

    Fuel   8000 Gal. Normal; 10, 000 Gal. Max. Bombs; 18, 000 Gal. Max Fuel

    Oil   340 Gal. (Normal); 600 Gal. (Max); 10 Gal. Supercharger

POWER PLANT:

Type _____ (4) Pratt & Whitney R4360-17&-21 Wasp Major (2 Ea.)

No. of Cylinders _____ 28

H. P. - Bore - Stroke _____ 3000HP ea. - 5.75 - 6"

Volumetric Capacity _____ 4363 Cu. In.

Compression Ratio _____ 6:7

Propeller _____ Hamilton Std. 8 Blade Coaxial 183" FWD Dia. 181" AFT Dia.

No. of Burners _____ N. A.

Static Thrust _____ N. A.

Fuel Consumption _____

ARMAMENT: _____ (20) .50 Calibre M.G. - 1000 Rounds/Gun; 4 lighting stations,

Max Bomb Load 32 - 1600# Bombs (52,193.#)

Normal Bomb Land - 10,600# (20000 Rounds - 6000#)

(20-.50 Guns - 1482#)

REMARKS: _____ Load Factor 4.5 (Ult - Gust), Area Aft of trim flap

hinge -76.0 sq. ft., slot door area - upr 20.7 ea.,

lwr 11.1

each INB'D extension shaft 27.7', OUTB'D 13.4' 6" Aver. Dia.,

5000 Gal. Fuel integral - 3000 Gal. Bomb Bay - Additional

10000 Gal. in 8 Mareng & 5 Bomb Bay Tanks.

Flying Wing Bomber Record

FLYING WING BOMBER RECORD

MODEL	FUNCTION	ENGINE	NUMBER ORIGINALLY ORDERED	NUMBER STARTED OR COMPLETED*	NUMBER FLOWN	FIRST FLIGHT DATE	REMARKS
XB-35	BOMBER	4-PISTON (BURIED)	2	2	2	6-25-46 6-26-47	
YB-35	BOMBER	4-PISTON (BURIED)	13	6	1	5-15-48	5 YB-35's BECAME B-35A
B-35A	BOMBER	4-PISTON (BURIED)	205	5	—	—	GLENN L. MARTIN 200 A/C
YB-49	BOMBER	8-JET (BURIED)	2	2	2	10-21-47 1-13-48	CONVERTED FROM YB-35
RB-49A	RECON-NAISSANCE	8-JET (6 BURIED/ 2POD)	30	—	—	—	CONSOLIDATED-VULTEE 29 A/C
RB-35B	RECON-NAISSANCE	6-JET (4 BURIED/ 2 POD)	10	10	—	—	CONVERTED FROM YB-35
EB-35B	TURBODYNE TEST BED	6-JET/ 2-TURBODYNE (6 BURIED/ 2 POD)	1	1	—	—	CONVERTED FROM YB-35A
YB-35B	TEST	6-JET (4 BURIED/ 2 POD)	6	1	—	—	CONVERTED FROM YB-35
YRB-49A	RECON-NAISSANCE	6-JET (4 BURIED/ 2 POD)	1	1	1	5-04-50	CONVERTED FROM YB-35
			270	28*	6		

*15 BASIC AIRFRAMES MANUFACTURED TOTAL

Source: Fred Anderson, *Northrop: An Aeronautical History,* p. 110.

Table of Early Tailless Aircraft

A summary of the characteristics of some of the tailless aircraft designs flown in Europe in the 1920s and 1930s follows. The various types of tailless aircraft are illustrated on page 204 of the Appendix.

Table II

Designation	Lippisch, model 1921-22	Lippisch "Experiment 64, 1925"	Lippisch "Storch" 1928	Lippisch "Fl.Dreieck" 1930-31	Kirchner "Futurum" 1930	Soldenhoff-Langgut 1929	Longgut Commercial Airplane 1929	Haydn "Haydn" 1925-26	Nihm "Zaunkönig" 1927	Schul-Marczinsky "Stadt Magdeburg" 1930-31	Wenk "Feldberg" 1921	Wenk "Baden-Baden-Stolz" 1922	Kupper "Uhu" 1929	Kupper "Muster5" 1930	Winter "Charlotte I" 1922	Winter "Charlotte II" 1923	Tscheranowski "Parabola" 1924	Tscheranowski "Parabola VII" 1930-31	Hill "Pterodactylus IA" 1925-26	Hill "Pterodactylus IIB" 1930	Latimer-Needham "Halton-Meteor" 1928
Type[1]	whM	chM	shM	cmM	shM	wlM	cA	chM	shM	shM	swhM	chM	chM	chM	shM	shM	cA	cmM	shM	shM	cmM
Engine	—	—	7/9 PS DKW	28/32 PS "Cherub"	—	28/32 PS "Cherub"	3×490PS "Liberty"	—	—	—	—	—	—	—	—	—	—	100 PS "Lucifer"	90/40 PS "Cherub"	75 PS "Genet"	2×32 PS "Cherub"
Length m		2,20	3,80	4,20		4,79	23,40	4,20	3,66	3,10	3,50	3,50			2,00	4,50	4,10	3,75	4,70		3,73
Height m		1,10	2,00			1,68	5,50	1,80	1,80	1,20		1,20			1,16	1,50	1,25			2,80	
Span m	11,00	10,00	12,37	13,00	8,60	10,00	50,00	6,00	8,97	14,00	16,00	14,50	17,00	13,00	15,20	14,50	10,00	12,14	13,70		13,86
Wing area m²	12,00	12,00	18,50	25,00	12,40	17,00	500	16,00	12,56	26,00	17,00	16,00	24,00	10,60	20,00	19,50	20,00	80,00	20,70		16,72
Chord in middle m		1,50	1,87	3,00		2,00	12,00		1,80	1,20		1,45			1,50		1,50	3,75	2,80		1,98
Chord at tip m		1,30	1,17	0,85		1,80	8,00		1,00			1,45				2,80	0	0	1,52		0,58
Aspect ratio	10,08	8,34	8,26	6,76	5,95	5,88	5,00		6,40	7,52	15,05	13,16	12,05	15,95	11,55	10,78	5,00	4,91	9,07		10,70
Sweepback		~3°	~16°			37°	24,5°		10°									24°			
Dihedral			~2°			6,5°											8°	7°			2,5°
Profile[2]			J	RRG		G,E	G,E		sG	M.12			E	E				G	RAF	RAF	E
Aileron area m²		1,30	1,86	2,76		1,77	27,73		1,90						2,80		5,00		5,10		2,78
Elevator area[3] m²			2,76				82,00		1,14						2,80	2,60					
Rudder area m²			1,60						0,71						0,66	1,00	0,80			1,20	1,47
Weight of fuselage kg		16,0		160	14,0	184						32,0		22,0	39,0	38,0					
Weight of wing kg		42,0		}160	26,0	96						58,0		}36,4	44,0	47,5	42,0	}300	165		
Weight of control surfaces kg												10,0			21,0	14,5	8,0				
Weight of structure kg	44,0	58,0	170	320	40	280	5600	80,0	45,0	210	48,0	100,0	122	58,4	104	133	50,0	612	208		160
Total weight kg	114	128	250	520	110	480	16800	140	125	280	118	170	192	128,4	174	205	120	850	300		260
Wing loading kg/m²	9,5	10,7	13,5	20,8	8,9	28,2	33,6	8,8	10,0	10,8	6,6	10,6	8,0	12,1	8,7	10,4	6,0	28,3	14,5		15,6
Power loading kg/hp			27,8	13,3		19,2	13,3											8,5	7,5		4,06

Remarks:

- Lippisch model 1921-22: With cooperation of Espenlaub. Dunne wings
- Lippisch "Experiment 64, 1925": Dunne wings, pusher propeller. DKW engine
- Lippisch "Storch" 1928: With pusher propeller
- Lippisch "Fl.Dreieck" 1930-31: With pusher propeller
- Soldenhoff-Langgut 1929: With pusher propeller, load factor 6
- Longgut Commercial Airplane 1929: Design not carried out; 3 tractor propellers
- Haydn "Haydn" 1925-26: Copied from model 6 of Lippisch; tail surfaces added later
- Nihm "Zaunkönig" 1927: NACA profile M12 in center portion of wing
- Wenk "Feldberg" 1921: Thin profiles
- Kupper "Uhu" 1929: Also tried unsuccessfully as a powered airplane
- Tscheranowski "Parabola VII" 1930-31: Göttingen profiles 386 and 486
- Hill "Pterodactylus IA" 1925-26: With pusher propeller; profiles (cg. split; d/t=0,077 (d=285mm)
- Hill "Pterodactylus IIB" 1930: With tractor propeller; pre-file RAF airscrew 4,16° decrease in angle of attack. Automatic HP slotted wing; rudder-control wheel in bow; rotatable wing type as elevators and ailerons.
- Latimer-Needham "Halton-Meteor" 1928: With pusher propeller

1) M = monoplane; h = high wing; m = medial wing; l = low wing; A = all-wing; w = wire braced; s = strut-braced; c = cantilever.

2) M = Munk; G = Göttingen; J = Joukowsky; RRG = Rhön-Rossitten Gesellschaft; E = special profile; s = symmetrical profile.

N.A.C.A. Technical Memorandum No. 666

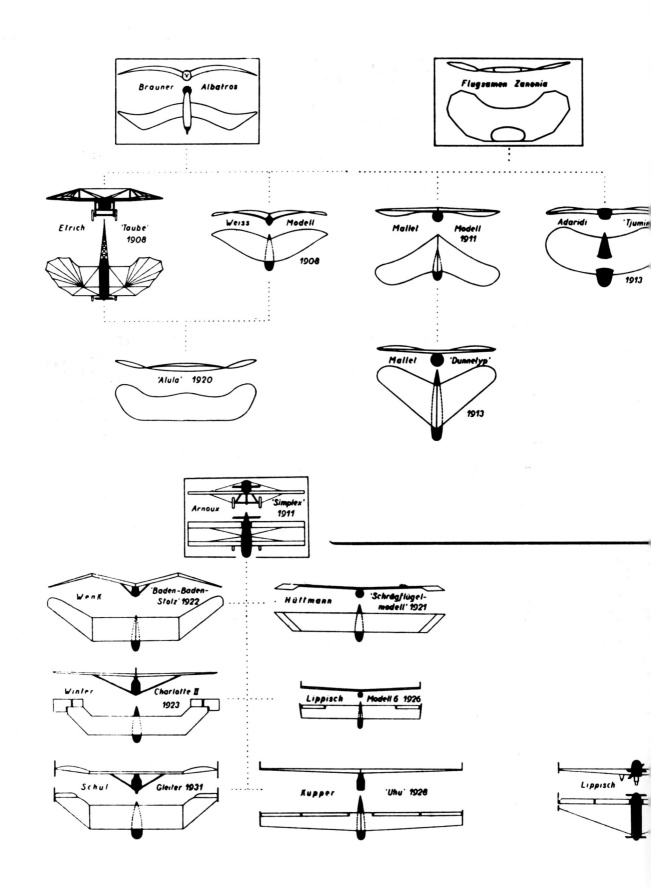

Brauner Albatros

Flugsamen Zanonia

Etrich 'Taube' 1908

Weiss Modell 1908

Mallet Modell 1911

Adaridi 'Tjumin' 1913

'Alula' 1920

Mallet 'Dunnetyp' 1913

Arnoux 'Simplex' 1911

Wenk 'Baden-Baden-Stolz' 1922

Hüttmann 'Schrägflügel-modell' 1921

Winter Charlotte II 1923

Lippisch Modell 6 1926

Schul Gleiter 1931

Kupper 'Uhu' 1928

Lippisch

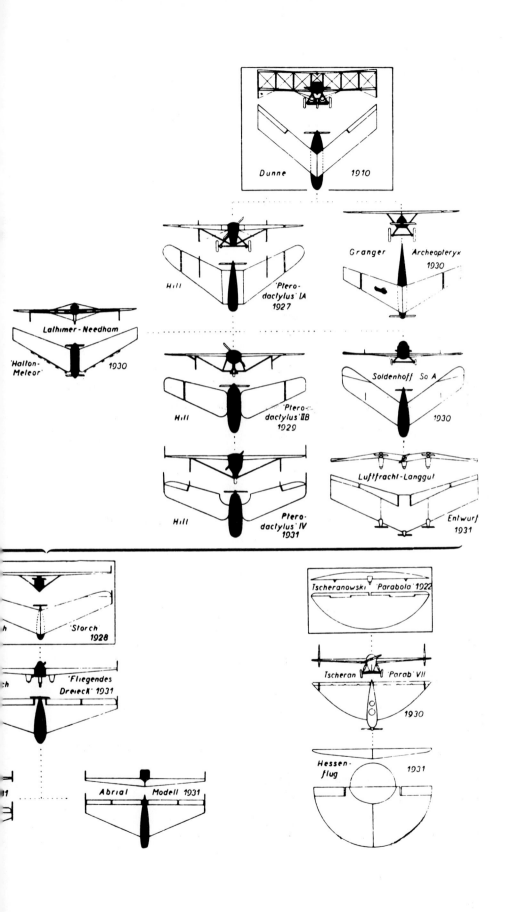

Dunne   1910

Hill   'Ptero-dactylus' IA   1927

Granger   Archeopteryx   1930

Lathimer - Needham

'Halton-Meteor'   1930

Hill   'Ptero-dactylus' IIB   1929

Soldenhoff So A   1930

Hill   'Ptero-dactylus' IV   1931

Luftfracht - Langgut   Entwurf   1931

'Storch'   1928

'Fliegendes Dreieck' 1931

Abrial   Modell 1931

Tscheranowski   'Parabola' 1922

Tscheran   'Parab' VII   1930

Hessen-flug   1931

Glossary of Aeronautical Terms

Aileron—A hinged or movable portion of an airplane wing, the primary function of which is to produce roll about the longitudinal axis.

Angle of attack—The angle between the chord line of an airfoil and its direction of motion relative to the air (relative wind).

Angle of incidence—The acute angle between a chord line of an airfoil and the longitudinal axis of an aircraft.

Aspect ratio of a wing—The ratio of wingspan squared to wing area.

Boundary layer—The very thin layer of air, immediately adjacent to the surface of an airfoil, that is retarded by surface friction.

Boundary layer control—The modification of the boundary layer thickness and flow by the use of slots or some other mechanical means to obtain greater control over lift and drag forces.

Camber—The rise in the curve of an airfoil section from its chord line. "Upper camber" refers to the upper surface of an airfoil and "lower camber" to the lower surface.

Canard—A type of airplane having the horizontal stabilizer in front of the main supporting wing.

Center of gravity—The point of application of the resultant of all the weight forces in a body for any position of the body.

Center of pressure—The point along an airfoil chord or body axis through which the resultant aerodynamic force acts.

Chord line—A straight line connecting the leading and trailing edges of an airfoil.

Chord—The length of an airfoil from its leading to trailing edge.

Controllability—The quality of an aircraft that determines the ease of operating its controls and the effectiveness of the controls in producing change in its attitude in flight.

Decalage—A difference in the angles of incidence of the wings of a biplane.

Dihedral—An upward inclination of the wings from the root to the tip, showing a V shape from a front or rear view.

Directional stability—An airplane is said to be directionally stable if, after

206

being thrown off its flight course, it tends to immediately return to its original direction of flight.

Drag—The retarding force exerted on an aircraft as it moves through the air.

Dutch roll—A lateral oscillation with both rolling and yawing components.

Elevator—A movable auxiliary airfoil, the function of which is to impress a pitching moment on the aircraft. The elevator is usually hinged to the stabilizer.

Elevon—A control surface on the trailing edge of the wing that serves as elevator and aileron on a tailless airplane.

Empennage—The airplane tail assembly, consisting of the vertical fin and rudder, and the horizontal stabilizer and elevator.

Fixed wing slot—A slot that is built into or permanently fixed in an open position in the wing structure.

Flap—A hinged or pivoted section, usually forming the rear portion of an airfoil, used to vary the effective camber.

Flying wing—An airplane in which the wing structure is the major portion of the structure. The conventional fuselage and tail section are eliminated.

High-lift devices—Mechanical methods employed to increase the lift on a wing section. The increase in lift is utilized to secure a steeper glide path and slower landing speed and sometimes used to enable the plane to take off with a greater load. The most common forms are wing flaps and wing slots.

Horizontal stabilizer—The fixed horizontal surface of the tail unit to which the elevators are attached.

Laminar flow—A particular type of streamline flow. The term is usually applied to the flow of a viscous liquid near solid boundaries, when the flow is not turbulent.

Lateral stability—Stablility with reference to disturbances about the longitudinal axis of an aircraft in flight; i.e., disturbances involving rolling or side slipping. The characteristic or ability of an airplane to remain laterally level or return to the level flight attitude when once disturbed.

Longitudinal stability—Stability with reference to disturbances about the lateral axis of an aircraft, i.e., disturbances involving pitching.

Maneuverability—The quality in an aircraft that determines the rate at which its attitude and direction of flight can be changed.

Monocoque construction—A type of fuselage or nacelle construction in which the skin or shell carries a large part of the bending and shear stresses.

Rudder—A hinged or movable auxiliary airfoil on an aircraft, usually attached to the rear of the vertical fin, the function of which is to impress a yawing moment on the aircraft.

Slat—A movable auxiliary airfoil, attached to the leading edge of a wing, which when closed, falls within the original contour of the main wing, and when open, forms a slot.

Slot—A nozzle-shaped opening through a wing whose primary object is to improve the flow conditions at high angles of attack. It is usually near the leading edge and formed by a main and an auxiliary airfoil, or slat.

Span—The maximum distance, measured parallel to the lateral axis, from tip to tip of an airplane wing inclusive of ailerons, or of a stabilizer inclusive of elevators.

Spoiler—A small, narrow, hinged, strip-like flap arranged to be projected above the upper forward surface of a wing, usually ahead of the ailerons. Its purpose is to disturb the smooth air flow, increase the drag, and reduce the lift.

Stabilizer—Any airfoil whose primary function is to increase the stability of an aircraft. It usually refers to the fixed horizontal tail surface of an airplane, as distinguished from the fixed vertical surface. It is usually located at the rear of an aircraft, and is approximately parallel to the planes of the longitudinal and lateral axes. Also called "tail plane."

Stable airfoils—Airfoils which are so designed that the center of pressure travel is very small, and which require a small amount of corrective forces from a tail surface in order that the airplane may be in aerodynamic balance.

Stall—The condition of an airfoil or airplane in which it is operating at an angle of attack greater than the angle of attack of maximum lift. It is caused by air flow separation on the upper surface of the airfoil. Lift decreases drastically, drag increases suddenly, and airspeed and control effectiveness drop sharply.

Sweepback—The backward slant of the leading edge of an airfoil.

Tailless airplane—An airplane without a vertical tail surface, or horizontal tail surface, or without any tail section at all.

Taper—The gradual decrease in depth and/or width of a member along its length.

Variable camber—Variable camber refers to the ways and means to mechanically vary the camber or wing curve in flight.

Variable incidence—Used in reference to a wing or stabilizer that is so designed that its angle of incidence may be varied in flight.

Vertical fin—A fixed vertical auxiliary airfoil surface, the function of which is to give directional stability to the aircraft, i.e., its purpose is to reduce the yawing tendencies about the vertical axis.

Wash in and washout—A permanent warp of the wing tips of an airplane. Wash in is an increase of the angle of incidence toward the tip, and washout is a decrease. Washout is usually incorporated into both wing tips for the purpose of delaying tip stall.

Wing—An airfoil whose principal function is providing lift.

Wing root—The inner ends of wings or their intersection with the fuselage or center section. In the case of a tapered wing, which is continuous from tip to tip, it may be the center of the wing.

A Selected Bibliography
of Tailless Aircraft

General

Barnaby, Ralph Standton. *Gliders and Gliding.* New York: Ronald Press Co., 1930.

Bicher, Robert F.B. (First Lieutenant). *Trends of Development in Flying Wing and Tailless Aircraft.* Report No. F-TR-101-DN. Wright Field, Dayton, Ohio. February 27, 1946.

Burns, B.R.A. "Tailplanes: Tailless and Canard Design." *Air International,* 1980, 18(3):126–129.

Collinge, George B. "Lift and Thrust." *Sport Aviation,* 1981, 30(4):52–58.

Development of Tailless and All-Wing Gliders and Aeroplanes. NACA Technical Memorandum No. 666. Washington, D.C., 1932.

"Discussion on Stability." *Aeronautical Journal,* 1913, 17(68):235–244.

Dufause De Lajarte, A. *Chief Charactaristics and Advantages of Tailless Airplanes.* NACA Technical Memorandum No. 794. Washington, D.C., May 1936.

Fin Design For All-Wing Airplanes. Report No. AM-22. Hawthorne, Calif.: Northrop Aircraft, Inc., November 1945.

Gibbs-Smith, Charles H. *Aviation.* London: Her Majesty's Stationery Office, 1970.

——————. *Aviation: An Historical Survey from Its Origins to the End of World War II.* London: Her Majesty's Stationcry Office, 1970.

——————. *The Invention of the Aeroplane 1799–1909.* London: Faber and Faber, 1965.

Goodlin, Chalmers H. "Airframe Design—Are We in a Rut?" *Aviation Age,* 1950, 14(4):22–23.

Green, William. *War Planes of the Second World War. Volume 4: Fighters.* Garden City, New York: Doubleday and Company, 1967.

"Jet Propelled Flying Wing." *Science Newsletter,* October 1941, p. 243.

Kappus, Peter G. *The Tailless Construction of the Turbo-Jet Fighter Compared to the Standard Model*. Report F-TS-555-RE, Headquarters Air Materiel Command, Wright Field, Ohio, 22 May 1946.

Klemin, Alexander. The Tailless Airplane. *Scientific American*, August 1926, No. 135:143–145.

Krauth, Harold. "The Flying Wing: Blunder or Blessing?" *Soaring*, 1971, 35(11):18–24.

Latimer-Needham, Cecil H. *Sailplanes: Their Design, Construction and Pilotage*. London: Chapman and Hall, 1932.

Lippisch, A. *The Development, Design and Construction of Gliders and Sailplanes*. NACA Report No. 637, Washington, D.C., September 1931.

——————. *Effect of Aerodynamic Design on Glider Performance*. NACA Technical Memorandum No. 762. Washington, D.C., September 1931.

——————. *Recent Tests of Tailless Airplanes*. NACA Report No. 564, Washington, D.C., May 1930.

Marlowski, Michael A. *Ultralight Aircraft: The Basic Handbook of Ultralight Aviation*. Hummelston, Pa: Ultralight Publications, 1981.

Miller, Ronald, and David Sawers. *The Technical Development of Modern Aviation*. London: Routledge and Kegan Paul, 1968.

Neely, Fredrick R. "Wing Talk." *Collier's*, May 11, 1946.

Norton, F.H. *Practical Stability and Controllability of Airplanes*. NACA Report No. 120. Washington, D.C.: Government Printing Office, 1921.

Phipps, Walter H. "The Question of Natural Stability in Aeroplanes." *Aircraft*, 1913, 4(7):156–167.

Sanders, Robert. *Aerodynamic Tests of a Low Aspect Ratio Tapered Wing with an Auxiliary Airfoil for use on Tailless Airplanes*. NACA Report No. 477, Washington, D.C.: U.S. Government Printing Office, November 1933.

"The Tailless Aeroplane." *Engineer*. April 1926, 141: 498, 501.

Taylor, John W.R., editor. *Jane's Pocket Book of Major Combat Aircraft*. New York: Collier Books, 1974.

——————. *Jane's Pocket Book of Research and Experimental Aircraft*. New York: Collier Books, 1977.

——————. *Jane's All the World's Aircraft, 1909–1981*. New York: McGraw Hill Book Co.

Turner, C.C. *The Old Flying Days*. London: Sampson Low, Marston and Co.

Von Romer, B. *Prospective Development of Giant Airplanes*. NACA Technical Memorandum No. 463. Washington, D.C., 1928.

Weick, Fred, E., and Robert Sanders. *Aerodynamic Tests of a Low Aspect Ratio Tapered Wing With Various Flaps for Use On Tailless Airplanes*. NACA Technical Note No. 463, Washington, D.C., June 1933.

Weiss, J. Bernard. *Gliding and Soaring Flight: A Survey of Man's Endeavor to Fly by Natural Methods*. London: Sampson Low, Marston and Co., 1923.

Weyl, A.R. "Tailless Aircraft and Flying Wings." *Aircraft Engineering*, December 1944, 16(190):340–352, 360; January 1945, 17(191):8–13; February, 1945, 18(192):41–46.

United States Tailless Aircraft

John K. Northrop Designs

Ackerman, J.S. *Air Force Model YRB-49A Photo Recon Airplane.* Report No. A-l45. Hawthorne, Calif.: Northrop Aircraft, Inc., August 1960.

The Aerodynamic Characteristics of the Northrop All-Wing Airplane. Report No. Am-9. Hawthorne, Calif.: Northrop Aircraft, Inc., February 22, 1940.

Aerodynamic Data for Structural Design. Report No. A-36. Hawthorne, Calif.: Northrop Aircraft, Inc., July l942.

Aerodynamics, Wind Tunnel on a Split Trailing Edge Type Rudder. Report No. A-lT-2. Hawthorne, Calif.: Northrop Aircraft, Inc., April 10, 1941.

"Air Force Boosts B-49 Orders." *Aviation Week,* 1948, 49(5):11–12.

"Air Force Confirms YB-49 Record." *Aviation Week,* November 8, 1948, 49(19):14.

"Air Force Offers Streamlined Buying Plan." *Aviation Week,* 1948, 49(10):15.

"An 'All-Wing' Monoplane." *Flight,* 1930, 22(15):411–412.

Anderson, Fred. *Northrop: An Aeronautical History.* Los Angeles: Northrop Corp., 1976.

Army Air Forces. Report of Major Accident, Aircraft YB-49, 42-102368. June 5, 1948.

"Army Proclaims Northrop Plane First Successful Flying Wing." *American Aviation Daily,* 1941, 17(49):227–229.

Balzer, Gerald. "The Aircraft of Jack Northrop." *Journal of the American Aviation Historical Society,* 1981, 26(1):80–87.

Bangs, Scholer. "Design Details of the Northrop XB-35." *Aviation,* April 1947, 46:37–41.

"Big Wing." *Western Flying,* 1946, 26(5):22–24.

"Boost for Flying Wing." *Time,* July 6, 1942, 40:65.

Brachiss, Louis. "Evolution of the Northrop XB-35." *Air Force,* 1946, 29(6):29–52.

Brannon, W. *Performance Summary: B-49.* Report No. A-156. Hawthorne, Calif.: Northrop Aircraft, Inc., August 1949.

Cardenas, Robert L. (Brigadier General, USAF, Ret.). The B-35/B-49 Flying Wings. Edited transcript of interview conducted at Edwards Air Force Base, Calif. Interviewer unknown, n.d. [NASM Archives].

Case History of the XB-35 Airplane Project. Wright Field, Ohio: Historical Office, Air Materiel Command,1950.

Case IIistory of the YB-35, YB-49 Airplanes (Supplement to Case History of the XB-35 Airplane). Wright Field, Ohio: Historical Office, Air Materiel Command, 1950.

Characteristics of Northrop YB-35 Airplane. Report No. A-99. Hawthorne, Calif.: Northrop Aircraft, Inc., May 14, 1948.

Characteristics of Northrop YB-35A Airplane. Report No. A-100. Hawthorne, Calif.: Northrop Aircraft, Inc., May 14, 1948.

Cline, Al. "Northrop Flying Wing Tops 500 mph Average on Cross Country

Hop." News release, Hawthorne, Calif.: Northrop Aircraft, Inc., 1949.

Colbert, Stanley L. "Airline Wing?" *Aviation Week*, 1948, 49(20):18.

Contract No. 40-7432: Invitation, Bid, and Acceptance for Models and Engineering Data on Tailless Airplane. Wright Field, Ohio: Materiel Division, Army Air Corps, April 18, 1940.

De Denzo, Herbert. *Free Flight Model Data.* Report No. A-16. Hawthorne, Calif.: Northrop Aircraft, Inc., September 4, 1940.

Determination of the Stability and Control Characteristics of a Tailless All-Wing Airplane Model with Sweepback in the Langley Free Flight Tunnel. Report No. L5A13 Wartime Report, February 1945, from Wartime Reports, V3, 1944–1946 [NASM Archives].

Direct Cost Operating Analysis. Report No. Am-25A. Hawthorne, Calif.: Northrop Aircraft, Inc., January 11, 1946.

Donahue, J.A. "Jack Northrop: Airplane Designer for the Golden Age of Flight: An outline of his projects." January 15, 1979. Unpublished [NASM Archives].

Douglas, O.H. "Jet Flight Story Told by Douglas." *Northrop News,* Hawthorne, Calif.: Northrop Aircraft, Inc., 1947, 7(15):1–2.

Dunlap, David E. "The Giant Flying Wing." *Aero Digest*, 1932, 20(2): 35, 92.

Dunn, C.J. "Northrop B-35 Landing Gear." *Aero Digest*, 1948, 56(5): 59–60, 116–118.

Edwards, Glen W. *Pilot's Observations on the N-9M Flying Wing.* Army Air Forces Air Technical Service Command Memorandum Report, May 3, 1946.

Estimated Flying Qualities. Report No. AM-26. Hawthorne, Calif.: Northrop Aircraft, Inc., April 1946.

"First Military Rocket Plane Northrop Built." *Northrop News,* Hawthorne, Calif.: Northrop Aircraft, Inc., February 12, 1947, 5:1–2.

"The Flying Wing Bomber." *Northrop News,* Hawthorne, Calif.: Northrop Aircraft, Inc., May 1, 1946.

"Flying Wing Bomber." *Time*, May 6, 1946, 42:86–90.

"Flying Wing Bomber Nears Completion." *Time*, March 29, 1947, 51:194.

"Flying Wing in New Form." *Science News Letter*, October 1942, 42:248.

"Flying Wing Goes Jet: Northrop YB-49." *Popular Science*, April 1947, 150:89.

"Flying Wing Has Novel Cockpit Layout." *Aviation Week*, 1947, 47(15):33.

"Flying Wing Jet Bomber Completed." *Aviation Week*, 1947, 47(15):14.

"Flying Wing Pictures Shown." *Northrop News,* Hawthorne, Calif.: Northrop Aircraft, Inc., February 23, 1942.

Frosch, Robert A. (NASA Administrator). Letter to John K. Northrop, April 3, 1979 [NASM Archives].

Green, William. *Rocket Fighter.* New York: Ballantine Books, 1971.

Gunston, Bill. "The All-Wing Northrops." *Aeroplane Monthly*, 1974, 2(1):442–449.

Hall, Harry W. "'Flying Wing' Important Advance in Aerodynamics—Proves Airworthy." *San Francisco Chronicle*, February 9, 1930.

Hallion, Richard P. "X-4; The Bantam Explorer." *Air Enthusiast Quarterly,* 1976, 3:18–25.

Handbook Flight Operating Instructions USAF Model YB-35 Airplane. Hawthorne, Calif.: Northrop Aircraft, Inc., 1948.

Handbook Flight Operating Instructions USAF Series YRB-49A Aircraft. USAF, 1950.

Holloner, J.S. (Colonel, USAF). Chief, Aircraft Branch, Directorate of Research and Development (Office, Deputy Chief of Staff, Materiel) memorandum to D.L. Putt (Brigadier General, USAF). Subject: Bombing Tests of the YB-49. November 8, 1948.

Hotz, Robert. "Industry Leaders Tell of Merger Plans Details." *Aviation Week,* 1949, 51(9):14.

————. "Why the B-36 was Made the USAF Top Bomber." *Aviation Week,* 1949, 51(7):14.

"Inside the Flying Wing." *Popular Mechanics,* April 1947, 87:124.

Investigation Committee. *Accident Investigation: YB-49 USAF.* Report No. NM-13, Hawthorne, Calif.: Northrop Aircraft, Inc., June 1948.

"Jet-driven Northrop Flying Wing Set to Fly in Midsummer." *Northrop News,* Hawthorne, Calif.: Northrop Aircraft, Inc., February 1947, 5:1–7.

"Jet Wing Takes Off—YB-49." *Life,* November 3, 1947, 23:39–40.

"John K. Northrop: Aviation Pioneer-Designer of Wings." *Nuance,* 1981, 2(1):4–10.

Kohn, Leo J. *The Flying Wings of Northrop.* Milwaukee, Wis.: Aviation Publications, 1974.

Krieger, S.A. *Characteristics of Northrop B-49 Airplane.* Report No. A-12, Hawthorne, Calif.: Northrop Aircraft, Inc., May 1948.

————. *Flight Test Summary: N-9M-B.* Report No. AM-27. Hawthorne, Calif.: Northrop Aircraft, Inc., April 1946.

————. *Performance Calculations: N-9M.* Report No. A-37. Hawthorne, Calif.: Northrop Aircraft, Inc., February 1942.

"Labor Report." *Aviation Week,* 1948, 49(2):18.

Lateral Stability of Tailless Airplane. Report No. A-36, Hawthorne, Calif.: Northrop Aircraft, Inc., December 1, 1941.

Leland, D.G. "Building the XB-35." *Western Flying,* 1946, 26(12):20.

Leunam, Margaret. "Evolution of the Flying Wing." *American Helicopter,* 1946, 3(7):18.

"Looking Into the XB-35." *Popular Science,* May 1947, 150:116–118.

Luce, Stewart. *Jack Northrop's Life and Aircraft Designs.* March 1979, publisher unknown [NASM Archives].

Maloney, Edward T. *Northrop Flying Wings.* Corona del Mar, Calif.: World War II Publications, 1980.

McLarren, Robert. "Low Drag Accented in All-Wing." *Aviation Week,* 1948, 49(25): 21–28

McNarney, Joseph T. (General, USAF). Commanding General, Air Materiel Command, letter to Chief of Staff, U.S. Air Force. Subject: YB-35 Jet Conversion Program. February 17, 1949.

Meyers, B.E. (Major General, USA). Memorandum from Deputy Assistant Chief of Air Staff (Materiel, Maintenance, and Distribution) to Chief of Air Staff. Subject: B-35 Project. May 6, 1944.

Monson, G.W. Letter to A.A.F. Resident Representative, Northrop Aircraft, Inc., August 16, 1944.

"MX-324-Step to Manned Rocket Flight." *Astronautics and Aeronautics*, 1964, 2(10):55.

"MX-324; XP-79-B." *Journal of American Aviation History Society*, 1981, 26(1):86.

Myers, John, Max Stanley, and Moye Stephens. Taped interview with E.T. Wooldridge, Los Angeles, California, February 1982 [NASM Archives].

"Northrop Activities: Details of the XB-35 Flying Wing." *Flight*, 1946, 49(1950):469–470.

"Northrop's Flying Wing." *Aero Digest*, 1941, 39(5):116, 118, 121.

"Northrop Flying Wing." *Fortune*, October 1947, 36:112–115.

"Northrop Flying Wing." *U.S. Air Services*, 1941, 26(11): 15–16.

"Northrop's Flying Wing." *Western Flying*, 1941, 21(11): 40–42.

Northrop, John K. "The All-Wing Type Airplane." *Aviation*, 1930, 28(13): 645–648.

——————. "The Development of All-Wing Aircraft." Address before the Royal Aeronautical Society, London, May 29, 1947 [NASM Archives].

——————. "Development of All Wing Aircraft." *Shell Aviation News*, December 1947, No. 114:pp. 12–19.

——————. "The Flying Wing." *Western Flying*, 1930, 7(3):46–49.

——————. Interview with E.W. Robischon, Santa Barbara, California, July 23, 1968.

——————. Letter to Major General H.H. Arnold, July 12, 1940.

——————. Letter to J.C. Mingling, November 3, 1941.

——————. "The Northrop 'All-Wing.'" *Aviation Week*, December 1941, p. 82.

——————. "The Northrop 'All Wing' N-1M." *Aviation*, November 1941, p. 3.

——————. *Northrop Patent on Flying Wing*. No. 2, 406, 506. U.S. Patent Office. August 23, 1946.

——————. "The Northrop Wing." *The Norcrafter*, December 1941, pp. 16–19.

——————. "The Northrop XB-35 Flying Wing Superbomber." *Aviation*, 1946, 45(8):55–61.

"Northrop Model 1 Mockup." *Air Enthusiast*, 1972, 21(4):220.

"The Northrop Story." *Model Airplane News*, 1944, 31(4):9.

"Northrop Wing Makes Front Page News." *The Norcrafter*, October-November 1941, pp. 6–7.

"Northrop XB-35 Flying Wing Set for Flight Tests." *Aviation*, 1946, 45(5): 92–93.

"On the Wing: Flying Wing." *Newsweek*, May 6, 1946, 27:71.

"100 Ton Flying Wing Outflies B-29." *Popular Science*, May 1946, 148:178–180.

Payne, Lee. "The Great Jet Engine Race and How We Lost." *Air Force*, January 1982, 65(1):58–64.

Performance Summary: XB-35 Airplane. Report No. A-56a. Hawthorne, Calif.: Northrop Aircraft, Inc., December 20, 1943.

Phelan, Arthur J. *The Northrop Turbodyne XT37-1: A Chronology of the Conception, Design and Development of Possibly America's Earliest Aircraft Gas Turbine Power Plant*. Hawthorne, Calif.: Northrop Aircraft, Inc., July 23, 1970.

Pilot's Handbook for the XB-35 Heavy Bombardment Airplane, Serial Number AAF 42-13603 (Northrop Number 1484). Hawthorne, Calif.: Northrop Aircraft, Inc., 1950.

Raetz, G.S. *Analysis of Long Range Test Flights of April 26, 1948*. Report No. AM-62. Hawthorne, Calif.: Northrop Aircraft, Inc., May 1948.

Sadoff, Melvin, and A. Scott Crossfield. *A Flight Evaluation of the Stability and Control of the X-4 Swept-wing Semitailless Airplane*. NACA Research Memorandum, August 30, 1954.

Schleeh, R.E. Letter to E.T. Wooldridge, November 24, 1982 [NASM Archives].

Schwartz, A.M. "The Genesis of the Northrop XB-35." *Interavia*, 1947 2(4):27–31.

Sears, W.R. "Flying Wing Airplanes: The XB-35/YB-49 Program." Paper presented at the Air Force Museum, Dayton, Ohio, March 19, 1980 [NASM Archives].

—————. "XB-35 Drag." Northrop Aircraft Inter-Departmental Memorandum, December 29, 1942 [NASM Archives].

Silsbee, Nathaniel F. "Northrop Flying Wing." *Skyways*, 1946, 5(6): 42–43, 80–81.

Stanley, Max. "The Flying Wing." Paper delivered at the XXIV Symposium Proceedings of the Society of Experimental Test Pilots, Beverly Hills, California, September 24–27, 1980 [NASM Archives].

—————. "I Flew 'The Wing.'" *Flying*, 1946 39(3):34–35, 66–68.

—————. Letter to E.T. Wooldridge, May 25, 1982 [NASM Archives].

Stephens, Moye W. *Northrop N-1M Test Program*. Typed unpublished report, n.d. [NASM Archives].

—————. "After The Flying Carpet." *The AOPA Pilot*. 1964, 7(7):40–47.

—————. Letter to E.T. Wooldridge, May 17, 1982 [NASM Archives].

Stevens, Victor I., Jr., and Gerald M. McCormack. *Power-off Tests of the Northrop N9M-2 Tailless Airplane in the 40 by 80 Foot Wind Tunnel*. Report No. A4L14. Moffett Field, Calif.: National Advisory Committee for Aeronautics, December 1944.

"Tailless Fighting Plane." *Popular Science*, May 1940, 136:73.

Taylor, F.C. *Performance Data*. Report No. A-63A. Hawthorne, Calif.: Northrop Aircraft, Inc., 1948, pp. 1–6.

Thorton, O.B. (Captain, USAF). *Final Report of Development, Procurement, and Acceptance of the XP-56 Airplane.* Technical Report No. 5114. Wright-Patterson AFB, Dayton, Ohio, July 30, 1948.

Thurston, Richard A. "John K. Northrop Oral History Transcripts." Interview with John K. Northrop, April 27, 1972 [Library, University of California at Santa Barbara].

"Two-Motored Flying Wing." *Popular Mechanics,* January 1942, 77:25.

"U.S.A.: Northrop Tailless Aeroplane." *Interavia,* November 18, 1941, No. 791: 9–10.

"USAF Cancels Wing." *Aviation Week,* 1949, 51(19):l6.

"U.S. Shows off Northrop Flying Wing." *Life,* July 8, 1946, pp. 23–25.

Vandenberg, Hoyt S. (General, USAF). Letter to John K. Northrop, May 12, 1948.

Vecsey, George, and George Dade. *Getting off the Ground.* New York: E.P. Dutton, 1979.

von Kármán, Theodore. *The Wind and Beyond.* Boston: Little, Brown and Co., 1967.

Walton, Russell. "Jack Northrop and His Wonderful Wing." *Flying,* February 1948, 42(2): 19–21, 56–58.

Whitcomb, David W. *Stability and Control Characteristics of the MX-334 Glider.* Army Air Force Technical Report, February 6, 1945.

Wilkins, George H. (Captain). *Flying the Arctic.* New York: Grosset and Dunlap, 1928.

Williams, W.C. (Major, USAF). Engineering Division, Air Materiel Command Memorandum Report. Subject: Bombing Evaluation—Comparison Between Manually Controlled B-29 and YB-49 Aircraft. November 16, 1948.

"The Wing." *Flight,* March 1947, 51(1995):241.

"Wing Without a Tail." *Popular Mechanics,* May 1940, 73:645.

XB-35 Performance with Northrop 1500 Turbodyne Gas Turbine Units. Report No. AM-15. Hawthorne, Calif.: Northrop Aircraft, Inc., June 1, 1944.

Non-Northrop Designs

Able, C.R. (Major). *Final Report on Development, Procurement, Performance and Acceptance of the XP-55 Airplane.* AAF Technical Report No. 5306. Dayton, Ohio: Army Air Forces Materiel Command, October 22, 1945.

"American Arrowhead 'Safety Plane' Designed by the Late Glenn Curtiss." *Airways,* February 1931, 7:624.

"An 'All-Wing' Monoplane." *Flight,* 1930, 22(15):411–412.

"Batwing Ready for Tests." *Western Flying,* 1938, 18:28.

"The Boland Tail-Less Biplane." *Aeronautics,* November 19, 1911, pp. 156–159.

Bowers, Peter M. *Curtiss Aircraft 1907–1947.* London: Putnam, 1979.

Boyne, Walter. "Rocheville: Imagineer Emeritus." *Aviation Quarterly,* 1974, 1(2):92–111.

"Burgess Aeroplanes." [ca. 1915]. Printed by Cox-Berlau Press, New York.

Burnelli, V.J. "Exponent of Wing-shaped Fuselage." *Aviation and Yachting,* 1946, 14(7):5.

——————. Testimony before the U.S. House of Representatives Appropriations Committee, April, 1948.

"Burnelli vs. Northrop." *Aviation Week,* 1948, 48(26):7.

"Fast Air Freighter Will Enter Races." *New York Times,* August 19, 1932.

"Flying Wings Coming." *Popular Mechanics,* March 1942, 77:14–17.

"Flying Wings of the Future." *Popular Mechanics,* February 1938, 69:232–235.

"Flying Wing Plane Built by Veteran Pilot, Now Dead, Has 7800-Mile Range." *New York Times,* August 27, 1933.

Fredericks, Hamilton. "Pancake Light Plane." *Flying,* 1947, 41(1):33–34, 62.

"Giant 'Flying Wing' Tested for Orient-U.S. Nonstop Flight." *Chicago Herald-Examiner,* April 24, 1930.

Goddard, Robert H. *The Papers of Robert H. Goddard, Volume I: 1898–1924.* New York: McGraw-Hill Book Co. 1970, pp. 553–557.

Gould, Bartlett. "The Burgess Story." *American Aviation Historical Society Journal,* 1965, 10(2):79–87; 10(4):241–249; 1966, 11(4):270–277; 1967, 12(4):273–280; 1968, 13(1):37–42.

Graham, Frederick. "Will Tomorrow's Planes Look Like This?" *The Saturday Evening Post,* January 29, 1944, pp. 36–39.

Hall, Harry W. "'Flying Wing' Important Advance in Aerodynamics—Proves Airworthy." *San Francisco Chronicle,* February 9, 1930.

Hoffman, Raoul J. "A Novel All-Wing Airplane." *Popular Aviation,* 1935, 16(3): 163, 196.

Levy, Howard, and Richard Riding. "Burnelli's Lifting Fuselages." *Aeroplane Monthly,* March 1980, 8(3):144–148; April 1980, 8(4):172–176.

McLarren, Robert. "XFG-l." *Model Airplane News,* 1946, 34(4): 14–15, 93–95.

"May Be Flown In Pacific Attempt." *Aviation,* 1930, 28(19):956.

"Merrill Aircraft Demonstration: Flight at Glenn Curtiss Airport." Merrill Aircraft Company Press Release, Long Island, New York, February 11, 1931.

Merrill, Albert. "The Movable-Wing Biplane." *Western Flying,* 1928, 4(10): 49–64.

——————. "A Technical Description of the Merrill Type Monoplane." New York, December 6, 1932 [NASM Archives].

——————. "The C.I.T. 9 Preliminary Report." Undated [NASM Archives].

"New Type Plane Found Faulty." *Herald Tribune,* October 13, 1932.

"Oakland Pilot Hops East For Record." *Washington Times,* October 12, 1932.

Official Performance Data on the CT Seaplane. Report of Bureau of Aeronautics, Navy Department, March 24, 1922.

Perl, Harry N. "Military Gliders of World War II." *Soaring,* 1952, 16(1): 12–15.

217

Preliminary Report of Operational and Tactical Suitability Test of the XCG-16 Glider. Report of the Army Air Forces Board, Orlando, Florida, November 2, 1944 [NASM Archives].

Pritchard, R.J. "Small Plane Develops." *Western Flying,* 1935, 15(5):10.

Schoeni, Arthur L. "Vought XF5U-1 Flying Flapjack." *Historical Aviation Album,* 1970, p. 8.

Stone, Ralph W., Jr., and Lee T. Daughtridge, Jr. *The Influence of Dimensional Modification Upon the Spin and Recovery Characteristics of a Tailless Airplane Model Having its Wings Swept Forward 15° (Cornelius XFG-1).* Report No. SL8HlF, NACA Research Memorandum for Air Materiel Command, U.S. Air Force, Washington, D.C., September 1948.

Swanborough, Gordon, and Peter M. Bowers. *United States Military Aircraft Since 1908.* London: Putnam, 1971.

—————. *United States Navy Aircraft Since 1911.* Second edition, Annapolis, Md.: Naval Institute Press, 1976.

"Tailless Airplane is Hailed As Foolproof." *Popular Mechanics,* September 1926, 46:366.

"Tailless Private Aeroplane: Waterman Aeroplane." *Scientific American,* January 1936, 154:32.

True, Ernest L. "Wings of Waldo Dean Waterman." *American Aviation Historical Society,* 1966, 11(4):240–243.

Warren, Cecil R. "The Arrowhead Safety Plane." *Southern Aviation,* 1930, 2(4): 13–14, 16.

"Waterman Arrowbile." *Historical Aviation Album,* 1966, 3:132–138.

"Waterplane Sport in America." *Flight,* 1915, 7(39):715–716.

Weaver, Truman C. *Sixty-Two Rare Racing Airplanes from the Golden Years of Aviation.* New York: Arenar Publishing, n.d.

Werner, Steve. "How Mitchell Makes His Flying Wing Work." *Homebuilt Aircraft,* 1980, 6(10):22–25.

Non-United States Tailless Aircraft

Canada

"Canadian Flying Wing." *Aeroplane Monthly,* August 1976, 4(8):403–405.

Denmark

Foltmann, John (Captain). "A Visionary Proved Right." *Danish Foreign Office Journal,* May 1956, 19:11–14.

France

"Ader: A Pioneer." *Flight,* 1909, 1(1):10–11.

"L'Avion sans queue." *L'Aérophile,* 1922, 30/31(7/8): 98, 24.

Bascaylet DeMonge Commercial Tri-Motored Monoplane Type 7.2. G-2 Report No. 5110 by Aeronautical Development and Research, November 24, 1923 [NASM Archives].

Dyle and Bacalan Aircraft.   Report to National Advisory Committee for Aeronautics, April 25, 1928 [NASM Archives].

The Dyle and Bacalan DB70 Commercial Airplane (French): An All-Metal High-Wing Monoplane.   Aircraft Circular No. 113, National Advisory Committee for Aeronautics, March 1930.

Dumas, Alex.   "Le 'Stablavion' R. Arnoux." *L'Aérophile*, January 15, 1913, 21(2):35–37.

Fauvel, Charles.   "L'Avion à 'aile pure' Fauvel." *L'Aérophile*, 1933, 41(10): 310–312.

————.   "L''Aile volante.'" *L'Aérophile*, 1935, 43(4):115–118.

Foxworth, Thomas G.   *The Speed Seekers.* New York: Doubleday & Co., 1975.

Gibbs-Smith, Charles H.   *Clément Ader: His Flight Claims and his Place in History.* London: Her Majesty's Stationery Office, 1968.

Gordon, Arthur, Marvin W. McFarland, and Alvin M. Josephy, editors.   *The American Heritage History of Flight.* New York: Simon & Schuster, 1962.

Gray, Archibald E.   *New Type Bombing Plane.* Military Intelligence Division, Report No. 34310. Bordeaux, France. November 1931.

King, H.F.   "Swing-Wing Variable Incidence, Air-Cushion Hydrofoil." *Flight*, 1965, 88(2958):68–70.

Magoun, Alexander F., and Eric Hodgins.   *A History of Aircraft.* New York: Whittlesey House, 1931.

"A New French Night Bomber."   *Flight*, 1932, 24(9):170.

"Le planeur sans queue de Fauvel."   *L'Aérophile*, 1934, 42(1):12.

Richardson, Holden A.   "Prophecy in Retrospect." *Southern Flight*, 1943, 19(2):28–29, 39–40, 44, 49.

"Tailless Aircraft."   Report No. 6923-W, Military Attaché, Paris. March 16, 1923.

"Tailless Airplane."   Report No. 6926-W, Military Attaché, Paris. February 23, 1923.

Germany

"Aircraft Factory—Horten Peninsula."   Report No. 53225, Military Intelligence Division W.D.G.S. London, January 16, 1943.

Bicher, Robert F.B.   *Trends of Development in Flying Wing and Tailless Aircraft.* Technical Report No. F-TR-101-DN. Headquarters, Air Materiel Command, Wright Field, Ohio. February 27, 1946 [NASM Archives].

Bist, M.A. (Lieutenant Commander, USNR).   *Messerschmitt Advanced Fighter Designs.* Report No. 5-246, Combined Intelligence Objectives Subcommittee. July 1945.

Cowin, Hugh W.   "Blohm und Voss Projects of World War II." *Air Pictorial*, 1963, 25(12):404–406.

DeMasfrand, Albert.   "Expériences d'aviation de Messrs. Etrich et Wells." *L'Aérophile*, March 1908, pp. 77–82.

Description of the Project P 01-114 Under Construction.   Report No. 540. Wright Field, Dayton, Ohio, April 1946 [NASM Archives].

deVries, John A. (Colonel). *Taube, Dove of War*. Temple City, Calif.: Historical Aviation Album, 1978.

Dowd, R.E. "Tailless Airplanes." *Aero Digest*, 1932, 20(2):84–85.

"Edmund Rumpler, Airplane Expert." *New York Times*, September 10, 1940, Section C3, p. 23.

Ethell, Jeffrey L. "Rocket Fighter." *Wings*, 1977, 7(2): 10–19, 56–57, 65–67.
——————. *Airpower*, 1977, 7(3): 38–49, 64–65.

Etrich, Igo (Doktor Ingeneur h.c.). *Die Taube, Memoiren des Flugpioniers*. Vienna: Verlag Waldheim-Eberle, n.d.

"The Etrich Monoplane." *Flight*, 1911, 3(45):973–976.

"The Evolution of the Etrich 'Taube.'" *Scientific American*, May 1, 1915, pp. 284–286.

"The First Tailless Fighter." *The Aeroplane*, August 15, 1934, p. 197.

Georgii, Walter (Doktor). *Ten Years Gliding and Soaring in Germany*. Paper delivered to Royal Aeronautical Society, London, February 19, 1930. In *Smithsonian Report for 1930*, Washington, D.C.: U.S. Government Printing Office, 1931.

"German Aircraft New and Projected Types." Reprint of British Air Ministry A.I.2$_{(g)}$ Report No. 2383. Wright Field, Dayton, Ohio, August 1946.

German High Speed Airplanes and Design Development. Combined Intelligence Objectives Sub-Committee, G-2 Division, SHAEF, August 1945.

Green, William. "The Komet." *Royal Air Force Flying Review*, 1963, 18(8): 27–30, 44, 47.

Haddow, G.W., and Peter M. Grosz. *The German Giants*. London: Putnam, 1962.

Hallion, Richard P. "Lippisch, Gluhareff, and Jones: The Emergence of the Delta Planform and the Origins of the Sweptwing in the United States." *Aerospace Historian*, 1979, 26(1):1–10.

Heinze, Edwin P.A. *The Dreieck I Tailless Airplane (German)*. Report No. 159. NACA, Washington, D.C., March 1932 [NASM Archives].
——————. "The New German 'Tailless.'" *Flight*, 1931, 23(41):1008–1009.

Hohbach [?], and [?] Eichner. *Night Fighter and Destroyer Fitted with Two Hes-011 Power Plants P1079 (Heinkel Report)*. Report No. F-TS-675-RE. Wright Field, Dayton, Ohio, October 1946 [NASM Archives].

Horten Aircraft. A.D.I. Report No. 296/1945 [NASM Archives].

Horten Aircraft: Development of the "Flying Wing" Type. A.D.I. Report No. 341/1945 [NASM Archives].

"The Horten IV: An Amazing German Tailless All-Wing Glider." *Flight*, 1943, 44(1806):139–140.

"Horten IV Flying Wing." *TAM News*, Spring 1980, pp. 1–2.

Horten III Tailless Glider. Foreign Equipment Descriptive Brief No. 45–19. Freeman Field, Seymour, Indiana, November 28, 1945.

Horten 229 Bat Wing Ship Construction. Technical Intelligence Report No. 1–4. Headquarters, U.S. Strategic Forces in Europe, May 12, 1945.

Horten, Reimar, and Walter Horten. "Plastic, All-Wing Horten Aircraft."

Flugsport, 1943, 35(16): 249–251. Translated by H.I. Lewenz [NASM Archives].

Horten, Reimar, and Peter R. Selinger. *Nurflügel: Die Geschichte der Horten-Flugzeuge, 1933–1960.* Graz, Germany: H. Weishaupt Verlag, 1983.

Interrogation of Herr Eckhardt Kaufmann Concerning HO 229 Aircraft. Technical Intelligence Report No. 1–3. U.S. Strategic Air Forces in Europe, May 19, 1945.

The Junkers "G38" Commercial Airplane: A Giant High-Wing Monoplane. Aircraft Circular No. 116. National Advisory Committee for Aeronautics, May 1930.

Junkers, Hugo. "Metal Aeroplane Construction." *Journal of the Royal Aeronautical Society.* 1923, 27(153):406–449.

"Keeping Pace with Aviation—The Latest Inventions." *Popular Science Monthly,* February 1930, 116:40.

LeBlanc, N. *German Flying Wings Designed by the Horten Brothers.* Report No. SU-1110, Headquarters, Air Materiel Command, Wright Field, Ohio, January 10, 1946.

Lippisch, Alexander M. "About the Evolution of Tailless Aircraft." *Publications of the German Academy for Aeronautical Research,* Edition 1064/43, No. 27.

————. "Delta Winged Aircraft in the 1930s." *Air World,* 1981, 33(2): 12–15.

————. *The Delta Wing: History and Development.* Translated by Gertrude L. Lippisch. Ames, Iowa: Iowa State University Press, 1981.

————. "The Seed That Became a Tree." *Soaring,* 1953, 17(2): 3, 10–15.

————. "The Tailless Aeroplane." *Flight,* 1932, 24(50):1168.

————. "Tailless Tailpiece." *Air Enthusiast,* 1972, 3(3):136–138.

"Lippisch Tailless Series." *Aeroplane.* 1932, 42(24):1078.

Maloney, Edward T., and Uwe Feist. *Messerschmidt 163 Komet.* Fallbrook: Aero Publishers, 1968.

Messerschmitt Advanced Fighter Designs. Report No. 125-145 for U.S. Naval Technical Mission in Europe, New York, July 1945.

"Messerschmitt-Projekte Me P 1111 und Me P 1112." *Aerokurier,* June 1963, p. 212.

Mock, Richard M. "The Junkers G-38." *Aviation,* 1930, 28(3):113–117.

Nauber, [?]. "Comparisons of the 8-229 and the GO P-60 All-Wing Airplanes." Wright Field, Ohio: Headquarters Air Technical Service Command, April 1946.

Opitz, Rudolph. "Developing a Rocket Fighter." *Royal Air Force Flying Review,* 1965, 21(1):27–29.

Pollog, Carl Hanns (Doktor). "Tailless Plane Test Flown at Tempelhofer Airport." *Air Transportation,* 1929, 10(7):22.

Poturzyn, Fischer B. *Junkers and World Aviation.* Translated from German edition by Edward Morley. Munich: Richard Pflaum Verlag, 1935.

Preliminary Design Information on Heinkel Airplanes. Report No. 342–45,

U.S. Naval Technical Mission in Europe. New York, September 1945.

"Rocketing Without a Tail." *The Aeroplane,* 1930, 38(19):856.

Root, L.E. *Messerschmitt Aircraft Design.* Report No. 37, U.S. Naval Technical Mission in Europe, New York, August 1945.

Schmid, [?]. *Tentative Description of Construction of Flying Wing 229.* Report No. 526, Wright Field, Dayton, Ohio, April 1946.

"Schwanzloses Flugzeug Lippisch 'Delta 1.'" *Flugsport,* 1931, 23(26):557–560.

Scott, Jan. Letter to Donald Lopez, May 31, 1981.

"Segelflug und Motorflug." *Flugsport,* 1931, 23(12):240–242.

Shoemaker, J.M. *Messerschmitt Aircraft Design Development.* Combined Intelligence Objectives Sub-Committee Report No. 5–64. No date.

Single Place Fighter with Lorin-Jet. Translation of Heinkel Report for Headquarters Air Materiel Command, July 22, 1946 [NASM Archives].

Single Place Fighter with Turbo-Jet Hes-11 (P-1078). Translation of Heinkel Report for Headquarters Air Materiel Command, September 1946. [NASM Archives].

Smith, J.R., and Anthony Kay. *German Aircraft of the Second World War.* London: Putnam, 1972.

Spate, Wolfgang, and Richard P. Bateson. *Messerschmitt Me 163 Komet.* Windsor: Profile Publications, 1971.

Stamer, Fritz. "The Flying School at the Wasserkuppe." Paper delivered to Royal Aeronautical Society, London, February 19, 1930.

"Tailless Light Planes." *Scientific American,* January 1930, 142:71.

Theories about Tailless Airplanes. Report No. 516, Wright Field, Dayton, Ohio, March 30, 1946.

Winter, Frank H. "1928–1929 Forerunners of the Shuttle: The 'Von Opel Flights.'" *Spaceflight,* February 1979, 121:75–83.

Japan

Francillon, René. *Japanese Aircraft of the Pacific War.* London: Putnam 1979.

Kimura, Hidemasa. "Clear Skies and Turbulence." *Aireview,* 1966, No. 1, p. 91. [Translation by Jack Magara at NASM Archives.]

——————. *Kayaba Tailless Gliders.* Test Reports, pp. 1–4, 1945 [NASM Archives].

Switzerland

Evangelisti, Giorgio. *Machine Bizzare Nella Storia dell Aviazione.* Florence, Italy: Editoriale Olimpia SpA., 1973, pp. 97–106. [Translation at NASM Archives.]

"Foolproof Aeroplane: Soldenhoff's Design." *Aeronautics,* 1930, 6(1):97.

"Schwanzloses Flugzeug Soldenhoff." *Flugsport,* 1931, 23(25): 536–539.

"The Soldenhoff Tailless Plane: A Swiss Light Plane Two-Seater." *Flight,* 1930, 22(52):1478.

Turkey

"The Turkish Air League: Training and Constructional Activities of Tailless Glider Among Original Designs." *Flight*, 1949, 55(2100):350–351.

United Kingdom

"Airborne Wing." *Flight*, 1947, 52(2035):724–725.

"Another International Record by de Havilland." *The de Havilland Enterprise*, Hatfield, England, April 12, 1948.

"The A.W. Flying Wing." *Flight*, May 9, 1946, 49(1950):463–468.

Babington-Smith, Constance. *Testing Time-The Story of British Test Pilots and Their Aircraft*. New York: Harper and Brothers, 1961.

Barnes, C.H. *Handley Page Aircraft Since 1907*. London: Putnam, 1976.

Barnes, Chris. "Tailless Experimental." *Aeroplane Monthly*, 1980, 8(1):4–9.

"British Flying Wings Prepare Way for J-P Airliners." *Aviation*, 1946, 45(8):63–64.

"British Jet Wing Project Progresses." *Aviation News*, 1947, 7(1):8–9.

Brown, Eric. *Wings on My Sleeve*. Shrewsbury, England: Airlife Publishing Ltd., 1978.

"Captain Dunne's Biplane at Eastchurch." *Aero*, 1910, 47(2):301.

"Captain Hill's Lecture on the Tailless Airplane." *Aviation*, 1926, 20(22):831–835.

De Havilland 108 "Swallow" Data and Comments on Cause of Recent Crash. Report No. R-4242-46, U.S. Military Attaché, Great Britain. October 15, 1946.

Delanay, M.A. "La Théorie de l'appareil Dunne." *La Technique Aéronautique*, February 15, 1914, 9:97–104.

Derry, John D. "High-Speed Flying." *Journal of the Royal Aeronautical Society*, October 1951, 55:626–641.

"The D.H. 108 Experimental Aircraft." *The de Havilland Enterprise*. Hatfield, England, May 31, 1946.

D'Oray, Ladislas. "France Acquires Dunne Autostable Biplane." *Aero and Hydro*. 1913, 6(26):485.

"The Dunne 'Auto-Safety' Monoplane." *Flight*, 1911, 3(3):280–286.

"The Dunne Biplane." *Flight*, 1913, 5(46):1241–1244.

Dunne, J.W. "The Theory of the Dunne Aeroplane." *Aeronautical Journal*, 1913, 17(66):83–102.

"The Dunne Machine in Flight." *Flight*, 1912, 6(25):563.

"The Dunne Monoplane." *Flight*, 1911, 3(25):542–545.

"The Dunne Monoplane." *Aero*, April, July 1911, 5:12, 107–110.

"The Dunne Stable Aeroplane." *Flight*, 1912, 6(3):56.

"Les essais de l'aéroplane Dunne." *L'Aérophile*, 1913, 21(17):397–398.

"Faster Than Sound." *The de Havilland Enterprise*. Hatfield, England, September 14, 1948.

Felix, Julien. "The Remarkable Dunne Aeroplane." *Flying*, 1913, 2(9):10.

"The Fighting 'Pterodactyl.'" *Flight*. 1934, 26(1342):914–916.

"First Flight of the A.W.52." *Flight*, 1947, 52(2030):567.

"General Aircraft Research Gliders." *Flight*, 1948, 53(2036):14.

Gibbs-Smith, Charles H. *Aviation*. London: Her Majesty's Stationery Office, 1970.

"Hill's Tailless Aeroplane." *Journal of the Royal Aeronautical Society*, September 1926, pp. 519–544.

Hubbard, Thomas O'Brien. "The Dunne Automatic Stability System." *Aeronautics*, March 1911, pp. 81–83.

Jackson, A.J. *De Havilland Aircraft Since 1909*. London: Putnam, 1978.

Krönfield, Robert. "From Tailless Glider to Jet Aeroplane." *Interavia*, 1948, 3(1): 48–49.

Lewis, Peter. *The British Fighter Since 1912*. Fourth edition, London: Putnam, 1979.

"Lieutenant Dunne's Atholl Aeroplane 'No. 5.'" *Flight*, 1910, 2(15):278.

"Mach 1 Plus." *Flight*, 1948, 54(2073):334.

"Le Monoplan experimental sans queue Westland-Hill Pterodactyl." *L'Aéronautique*, 1930, 12(138):422–423.

Poulsen, S.C. "Laminar-Flow Wing Construction." *Aircraft Production*, 1947, 9(101):88–96.

Poulson, C.M. "The Fighting Westland 'Pterodactyl.'" *Aircraft*, November 1934, pp. 33–35.

"The Pterodactyl Aeroplane." *Engineering*, July 1931, p. 152.

"The Pterodactyl." *Airways and Airports*, 1934, 11(4):140.

"Pterodactyl." *Flight*, 1931, 23(51):1232–1233.

"Pterodactyl to Sherpa." *Flight*, 1953, 64(2339):680.

"Professor G.T.R. Hill." *Flight*, 1956, 69(2450):5.

Sayers, W.H. (Captain). "Tail-less Aeroplanes, Ancient and Modern." *The Aeroplane*, 1926, 30(17):446–458.

Sellers, M.B. "The Dunne Aeroplane." *Aeronautics*, 1913, 13(3):87–89.

"Tailless Achievement." *The Aeroplane Spotter*, 1947, 8(184):66–68.

"Tail-Less Triumph." *Flight*, 1948, 53(2051):404.

"Tailless Twins." *Flight*, 1949, 55(2101):369.

Tapper, Oliver. "Armstrong Whitworth's Flying Wing Experiments." *Aeroplane Monthly*, 1974, 2(12):998–1004.

—————. *Armstrong Whitworth Aircraft Since 1913*. London: Putnam, 1973.

"Test Pilot Profile No. 3, John Derry." *Aeroplane Monthly*, 1981, 9(6):338–342.

Thetford, Owen G. *Aircraft of the Royal Air Force Since 1918*. New York: Funk and Wagnalls, 1968.

"Towed Tailless." *Flight*, 1946, 50(1970):327–330.

"Twin-Jet A. W. 52." *Flight*, 1946, 50(1982):673–679.

Walker, P.B. *Early Aviation at Farnborough: The History of the Royal Aircraft Establishment. Volume II: The First Airplanes*. London: MacDonald and Co., 1974.

"Westland-Hill 'Pterodactyl.'" *The Aeroplane*, 1934, 47(7):197.

USSR

Anoshchenko, N.D., editor. *History of Aviation and Cosmonautics.* Vol. 1, NASA Report TTF-11, 427. Washington, D.C.: National Aeronautics and Space Administration, November 1967.

Nemecek, Vaclav. "Soviet Stratospheric Aircraft, 1935–45." *Air Pictorial,* 1966, 28(4):133–135.

Nowarra, Heinz J., and G.R. Duval. *Russian Civil and Military Aircraft, 1884–1969.* London: Fountain Press, 1971.

Silman, A.I. *Tailless Gliders of the Ninth All-Union Meet.* Report presented to the Central Aero-hydro-dynamic Institute, 1934 [NASM Archives].

Index

(Italicized page numbers refer to illustrations)